Workin' It

Leon E. Pettiway

Workin' It

Women Living Through Drugs and Crime

Temple University Press

Philadelphia

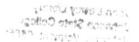

Temple University Press, Philadelphia 19122

Copyright © 1997 by Temple University.

All rights reserved

Published 1997

Printed in the United States of America

Text design by Erin New

∞ The paper used in this publication meets the requirements of American National Standard for Information Sciences—Permanence of Paper for Printed Library Materials, ANSI Z39.48-1984

Library of Congress Cataloging-in-Publication Data

Pettiway, Leon E., 1946–
    Workin' it : women living through drugs and crime / Leon E. Pettiway.
        p. cm.
    Includes bibliographical references.
    ISBN 1-56639-579-8 (cloth : alk. paper). —
ISBN 1-56639-580-1 (pbk. : alk. paper)
    1. Prostitutes—United States—Biography. 2. Prostitution—
United States—Case studies. 3. Prostitutes—United States—Social
conditions. 4. Drug abuse—Social aspects—United States.
I. Title.
HQ144.P4   1998
306.74'0973—dc21   97-21497

In memory of my mother

BLONNIE J. PETTIWAY

DECEMBER 17, 1910–JULY 20, 1994

By her strength, sacrifice, and courage,

she was an example and gave me more than life.

Contents

Acknowledgments

The accounts presented here originated in a research project funded by the National Institute on Drug Abuse (NIDA) of the Department of Human Services under Grant number RO1 DA 05672 while I was a faculty member in the Department of Sociology and Criminal Justice at the University of Delaware. I would like to extend my appreciation to Mario De La Rosa, my project officer at NIDA, for his technical assistance, moral support, and professionalism.

At the University of Delaware I would like to offer my appreciation to Mary Richards, dean of the College of Arts and Sciences, and Frank Scarpitti, then chair of the Department of Sociology and Criminal Justice. They provided me with the resources necessary to complete the research project.

When I joined the faculty of the Department of Criminal Justice at Indiana University in Bloomington in 1994, Dean Morton Lowengrub of the College of Arts and Sciences provided research incentive funds that enabled me to transcribe the remaining taped interviews. I would also like to extend my appreciation to Stephanie Kane, Kip Schlegel, Katherine Beckett, Judith Allen, and Robert Orsi at Indiana University for their support and critique. In addition, Margaret Andersen (University of Delaware), Marilyn Frye (Michigan State University), and other reviewers around the country challenged my voice. I thank them immensely. I am grateful to my partner, Rick Greiner, for the simple acts of kindness he extended throughout this project.

My field staff and I spent eighteen months in 1990–91 collecting data from 431 individuals, including both drug- and non-drug-using criminals. Life history interviews were conducted with forty-eight individuals, some of whom were a part of the larger sample. My deepest thanks go to my staff members. The field staff consisted of Althea Heggs, Karen D'Arcy, Kevin McCann, Thurston Collier, and Bernard Bryant. Though they were not responsible for conducting the interviews in this book, they conducted thousands of quantitative interviews and suggested and recruited some of the individuals who are presented here. At the Project Office at the University of Delaware, I would like to thank Tracey Dixon, Kimberly Bell, Linda Granger, Teresa Robeson, Linda Keen, and Eloise Barczak for transcribing many of these life history interviews, ranging from five to ten hours in length.

I extend heartfelt thanks to the staff of Temple University Press. In particular, I would like to thank David Bartlett, director of the Press, for his enthusiasm for this project, and Doris Braendel, my editor, for her professionalism and good cheer.

During the time I conducted this research, my priest, Father Tim Lyons, was my spiritual counselor and assisted me in ways I could never express. Over the years he and other members of the St. Vincent's Catholic community have given my life new meaning. I thank him and other members of that community and all my friends back East who supported me during this project.

Bloomington, Indiana

"Oppressed people resist by identifying themselves as subjects, by defining their reality, shaping their new identity, naming their history, telling their story."—bell hooks, Talking Back

Introduction

Lifting Their Voices

Living in an abandoned house, Laquita carves out a space where she can survive. Once-plastered ceilings reveal rafters and holes in the roof that let in flying things and falling rain. Windows have lost their panes and no longer hinder the wind and the cold. Strips of wallpaper dangle from walls and ceilings. When winter comes, Laquita and her partner bundle in blankets to stay warm. In the evening, they illuminate the darkness with candles and flashlights. At the end of their day's activities, when darkness finally fills the room, the lights of street lamps and passing cars reveal scavenging rats and roaches that bolt for cover and hide among the litter.

Like Laquita, the other four women—Margaret, Charlie, Tracy, and Virginia—are defined to some extent by the spaces where they live. Charlie and Margaret live with their male partners in rented apartments. Tracy shares an apartment with a fellow addict in the same housing project where Virginia lives with her mother. Whether in abandoned houses, public housing projects, or rented rooms, the women assert their dignity in the face of often excruciating difficulties. Mothers attempt to protect their daughters, but all too many become victims of violence and disease. Women mourn their dead. From these places and marked by the seasons of the year, these women worry about which utility they can afford to keep. In familiar and awkward places they experience the synchronous and syncopated rhythms of love making, which have placed some of them on hospital beds to wait for the crowning of their offspring's head. Childbirth is something their men rarely witness, either because they did not have the stomach to watch a miracle or because they viewed it as the domain of "womyn," womyn's burden and womyn's pain. More than they would like, their children become the wards of the state or of grandmothers who have limited means, limited resources. These are poor women, living in a city where urban resources can no longer keep pace with the demands of a growing "underclass." Too many people have abandoned the city for the space, the quiet, and the perceived safety of the suburbs. Too many people have abandoned the poor and what they represent. But the poor continue to create their own livelihoods and their own worlds.

This book serves as a reminder of what we stand to lose in human capital if our policies and structures continue to corral the "unwanted" in the barrios and ghettoes of this country. It also seeks to challenge. Its voice is rooted in the understanding that "scientific" concepts are marked by the human experiences of their creators. Gender, race, class, culture, and age color our ways of knowing and interpreting the social world around us. This book and its stories are not meant to meet the methodological norms embodied in the hypothesis testing of traditional empiricism. Rather, this is a book concerned with the contexts, the color, the nuance of living, the shadowy worlds between right and wrong, fiction and fact, compassion and condemnation. It recognizes that women—especially poor women—have been excluded from the process of defining culture, and it recognizes that it is against a backdrop created by men, who have largely defined disciplinary relevance, that women have been conceived as the "other" (Behar and Gordan, 1995; Harding, 1986).

Margaret, Charlie, Virginia, Tracy, and Laquita are not the neatly constructed middle-class caricatures on which so much of the public's perception of "womanhood" is grounded. These are poor urban women living through and in spite of mothers, fathers, husbands, male and female intimate partners, and children. Their gender becomes a social construction, accomplished through their social interactions, that produces success or

failure, joy or tragedy, hope or sorrow. These are drug-using women attempting to capture the memory of the first time heroin was pushed into
their veins to produce that nod or the first time clouds of smoke accu-
mulated in a crack pipe to provide the blast that sent them to their knees.
They live in spite of drugs. These are women hustlers using their bodies as
resources and using their minds as assets to ensure their survival. They are
skilled in the arts of evaluation and manipulation. They are not noble sav-
ages or transcendent urban poor heroines; their lives bear no resemblance
to the categories of pathos and comedy experienced by those who have not
been defined as "deviant" or "other."

During the interviews, I was continually reminded of the differences that
biology brings and the extent to which the patriarchal masculine ideal constrains, denies, and oppresses both men and women. Although black men
have experienced racial oppression and although they are not homoge-
neous, we are subject to the preconceptions forced on us by the phallocentric masculine ideal articulated and supported by the dominant culture. In
deciding to write this book, I was mindful of my past and where I stand.
Born in a place where black workers toiled in cotton and tobacco fields,
worked as maids, took in laundry, and worked at the most menial of jobs
with great dignity and self-sacrifice for their children. Born at a time and in
a place where I learned of oppression and learned to accept the double-
edged legacy of the psychology of oppression. I believe my legacy as a great-
grandson of slaves and as a son of segregation gives me a voice, just as these
women's struggles shape the color of their voices. However, when confronted with the lives of women who experience oppression engendered by
class, racism, sexism, and homophobia, I see clearly that, though I have experienced both racism and homophobia, I am nonetheless a recipient of
male privilege.

From these women's personal stories we are called to remember the stories of other oppressed peoples. We are called to remember the holocausts
of Jews, Native Americans, and others who mourn their disenfranchised
dead killed in gas chambers, on the great plains and on mountainsides, on
the streets, and on the turbulent seas. We are called to mourn those lying in
unmarked graves. We must listen with greater compassion to the lives of

oppressed peoples, and we must give greater appreciation to the ways they withstand the various assaults to their humanity.

This is deliberately a noninterpretive work. Nevertheless, my voice is implicitly present: after all, I framed the questions, focused the interviews, and shaped the narratives[1] they created. But I want to refrain from speaking with the authority of a researcher and a university professor about the meaning of these women's lives. Certainly, what is presented here is the product of a reflexive process and portrays only part of the participants' existential reality. We sat alone in one of the small offices that housed what was known on the streets as the "Urban Lifestyles Project," just one woman, a tape recorder, and me.[2] They lifted their voices to tell me about the wisdom and follies, the courage and fears, the hopes and dreams, and the tragedies and successes of their lives. I heard how women construct identity even as they are trapped by the interlocking strands of poverty, abuse, drug use, racism, and sexism. Again and again they spoke of their desire for others to hear them and to understand the lives they face.

These women are a diverse group who vary in age, race, experience, and temperament. Though they are only five of the forty-eight people I interviewed, they best represent the unique and ordinary expressions of the twelve drug-using and criminally involved women I interviewed. From the very beginning, the physical and verbal abuse Charlie suffers is readily apparent. Margaret's seemingly matter-of-fact acceptance of her life characterizes the lives of many of the women interviewed. Understanding Tracy's environment shows us how individual choices are structured by external forces. Virginia speaks for those women who assume responsibility for the personal choices they make, and Laquita's pointed language communicates her determination to live according to her construction. She provides countless examples of how women resist the pressures and restrictions of a culturally hostile world.

Charlie was thirty-six at the time of the interviews; Margaret and Tracy were both thirty-three; Virginia was twenty-six; Laquita was twenty-three. All of them except Charlie are African-American; Charlie is white and Puerto Rican. All five are serious drug users: Margaret uses cocaine intravenously; Charlie uses heroin; Tracy is a former heroin user who has recently turned to crack-cocaine; Virginia and Laquita also smoke crack.

These are women whose households are not organized around hegemonic gender roles (see Richie, 1996), and few aspire to the ideological norms associated with a "normal" family structure and its gendered arrangements. Virginia, like Laquita, is a lesbian. Margaret, Charlie, and Tracy, though basically heterosexual, also provide accounts of sexual intimacy with other women. Tracy lives with a roommate, with whom she has shared not only drug use and hustling activities but also childcare responsibilities.

Margaret, Charlie, and Tracy support their drug habits by participating in the sex industry. Charlie works in one of Jefferson's main sex-working districts and vividly communicates street life and the perils of the sex industry. Margaret, for the most part, relies on her friends and associates as clients to support her cocaine use. Tracy also stays within her circle of acquaintances; she is too terrified of the streets to solicit clients there, relying instead on the ample supply of men in her public housing complex.

Like my earlier book, *Honey, Honey, Miss Thang: Being Black, Gay, and on the Street* (1996), this book seeks to provide a glimpse into a world that most Americans seldom witness. The sting of biological determinism and pathology is perhaps nowhere stronger than in criminology's evaluation of women.[3] In *Honey, Honey, Miss Thang* I pointed out that the positivist tradition in criminology assumes that it is possible to arrive at verifiable knowledge or truths about the nature of events using some system of scientific objectivity. But this view of knowledge poses a tremendous epistemological problem. The Kantian assumption that offenders are interchangeable and that they assimilate knowledge in the same manner—that the unique and particular experiences of subjects are unimportant—leads some positivists to reject the notion that women (or any other group of individuals) have any inherent uniqueness. In its adherence to grand and totalizing theory and rejection of significant individual variations, there is some question whether orthodox criminology can possibly explain criminal behavior or unravel the "crime problem," which seems as multifarious as the people involved in it.[4]

For the most part, criminology is unreflective. While conscious that researchers should not bring their prejudices to the research table, many criminologists, in their search for neutrality, fail to consider their own identity in their investigative enterprises. Perhaps this is the aftershock of attempting to impose the strictures and methods of the physical sciences on criminology in our effort to make it more "scientific." Therefore, armed with the proper scientific rigor that ensures replication, some criminologists so distance themselves from their hearts and souls, and from the context and fabric of their subjects, that they assume they are the objective observers of "criminals" and the conduit through which others understand the activities of "deviants."

The truth is that social scientists are always involved in the text of language, and concepts are not only referential but also relational. As such, language does more to enable ideas than to name them (Derrida, 1981). To anyone attuned to the distinctions associated with language and conceptualization, it was shocking to hear a leading male scholar stand before a crowd of fellow criminologists and assert that research on women and crime was inconsequential. Since men commit the vast majority of crimes, he reasoned, investigations centering on women are a waste of time and energy. Although there have been some improvements in the quality and quantity of studies devoted to female criminality, criminological research continues to suffer seriously from this kind of phallocentric criminological discourse.[5] Adler (1975) and Simon (1975) suggest that, as women became "liberated" from the social and economic constraints of their traditional and historic roles, they became more like men in their patterns of offending. According to this formulation, women could be as violent, greedy, and crime-prone as men.[6]

When one excludes research that attempts to fit male theories to women's crime participation,[7] the research on women becomes paltry[8] and a critique of male criminality goes largely unexplored. Moreover, when researchers have focused on female criminality, whether it is the manner in which business is conducted on the stroll (Freund, Leonard, and Lee, 1989; Perkins and Bennett, 1985) or in crack houses (Inciardi, Lockwood, and Pottieger, 1993), some of these accounts center on the explicit and "sordid" sexual acts performed in these settings. Although these accounts may quench our voyeuristic appetites, they may also represent yet another form of exploitation and oppression. We learn little of the individual humanity of the women being studied, since their stories are filtered through the theoretical lenses of disciplinary discourse.

Even more than their white sisters, black women have been disregarded by both black and feminist criminologists (see Rice, 1990). Few criminologists have sufficiently acknowledged the legacy of struggle associated with sexism and racism endured by African-American women. Thus, the voices of Margaret, Virginia, Tracy, and Laquita reveal accounts of sensibilities made vulnerable to the denigration and violence visited on them by their race membership and their class. (It is interesting that Charlie, the one non-black women in this collection, chooses to identify as a woman of color specifically to escape what she perceives as the oppression she experiences in claiming her white heritage.)

These women express what everyone knows but few can articulate with the proper measure of power and conviction it deserves: Race and racism invade every aspect of American life. Nowhere is that fact more salient than in those communities marginalized by structural oppression. Like the social scientists who study them, these women recognize that the barrios and "hoods" of America have been severely affected by drugs, but they see this influx as a weapon of genocide. Margaret reasons: "That's a nice way to get rid of us, 'cause it is doing that. I mean, they think that the next war gonna be with guns and stuff. It might not be 'cause the drugs is about the best killer I've seen. And it's definitely doing that in one form or another."

Besides recognizing the racism imposed on her from outside, Tracy voices the internalized racism that many African-Americans would never admit, the subjugation that sometimes makes us turn against our own. Our own self-hatred and our own belief in the limited abilities and opportunities of African-Americans are perhaps the cruelest and most enduring legacies of white hegemony and oppression. Tracy says:

> If I saw a black doctor, right—you know something, this is fucking strange—
> if I saw a black doctor or something, I figure, I wouldn't want him. I would prefer
> a white doctor to work on me. Now, I swear! I don't think they're qualified enough
> to be in that position. I don't know. That they don't belong in that type of profes-
> sion. . . . I figure white people put one hundred percent into everything they do,

and you ain't put no hundred percent. So something gonna go wrong. You ain't supposed to be up here. Not a doctor. Not nobody working on life and death. You just not qualified enough.

But, see, I don't know if it's because of the way I was brought up that had something to do with it. I know better. That this black man is damn near more qualified, probably worked even harder, did have to work harder to achieve what they got, had to, you know, than that white person there. But my heart know this, but my mind will say, "I don't trust him. Still snuck and cheated on his test to get passed, you know." That's the way I think. But I know better. I know in my heart. I know. Goddamn! It's about time I see a black face. But don't work on my ass.

The depth of the race hatred is seen and played out profoundly when Charlie discovers that her mother has lied to her about her ethnic origin and that she is the very person she was taught to loathe:

I looked at her and I'd just opened the car door and I got out and he said, "I'm your father." I said, "Oh, no! What are you? A spic? A nigger? What?" You know. I looked at her and she said, "Charlene, let me . . . " I said, "Oh, I hate you." I said, "Why didn't you ever tell me? All these years the kids have been spitting at me." I said, "You lived in a white neighborhood, and let me . . . " I said, "I hate you!" I just ran.

Women drug users have been viewed in terms of their reproductive capabilities and the effect of their drug use on the development of the fetus (Glynn, Pearson, and Sayers, 1983; Murphy and Rosenbaum, 1995). It is known that women metabolize alcohol and drugs differently from men (Straus, 1984),[9] and it is assumed that women drug users have greater psychological disturbances than male drug users. Drug-using women like those presented here have been viewed as self-destructive, insecure, and socially immature individuals who manifest other symptoms of an inadequate personality (Colten, 1979). For these women, different "styles of pathology" (Horwitz and White, 1987) are said to emerge: female "deviant" styles are characterized by internalized distress, and male "deviant" styles are more outwardly directed and antisocial. Thus, the women in this book have been stigmatized in countless ways, because women who use drugs are viewed as having deviated from a woman's expected gender role.[10]

In much of our history and culture, violence and other assertive measures of expression have been seen as the more effective responses to oppression and domination. For some, being in control means usurping the icons of power. But when a women is poor, drug-using, and criminally involved, and is by her gender and by her race constructed as a powerless individual, how does she maintain a sense of self and dignity that shields her against the oppressive assaults of a hostile culture and environment? I believe the extent to which she resists her agents of disapproval mitigates or intensifies the psychological consequences of her social situation. I believe the degree to which she has the ability to be a strong evaluator and to be reflective of her social situation, which is conditioned by race, class, and gender oppression, affects the extent to which she resists her agents of disapproval. In some instances, these women actively resist, but in many other instances, they resist passively or not at all. When they fail to resist, they succumb to the pressures of culture and reproduce those facets of it that have been responsible for their own victimization.

These are accounts of women who manage to resist and to survive with self-definition and self-valuation in a world even more turbulent than that of their "mainstream" sisters. Through their experiences, we see not only their inner feelings but also their reactions and responses to the outer world. They speak of a web of experiences created out of race and ethnicity, sexual orientation, drug use, poverty, and urbanization. They think in ways that men may never fully understand and that their female counterparts of higher status may never have to consider.

Although they are primarily poor women who commit crimes, they are also self-determined and self-defined. It is in these ways that they resist, and it is their self-determination and self-definition that become the keys to their empowerment. Afro-American feminists argue that for Afro-American women, life does not necessarily coincide with the focal concern of white women, the primacy of patriarchal domination (hooks, 1981). Although family life might be a haven against the experience of racism for some black women (Walby, 1990), it is seldom a haven for these women. It is often in this family context that they resist the most.

For these women, social class becomes one of several institutional and cultural arenas where race and gender identities are constructed, and their stories confirm the belief that African-American women simply respond differently than their white counterparts to conditions of poverty and racism (Hill and Crawford, 1990; Collins, 1986).[11] Their class, in some respects, constrains the ways they can resist.

If we are to understand the behavior of these women, we must attempt to understand the relationship between the social structures of which they are a part and the human agencies they construct. Their agency is marked by their ability to be strong evaluators, to see their desires in a dimension that takes them to the center of their existence (Taylor 1996). Their identity is tied to certain evaluations of themselves, and their self-interpretations emerge from their individual experiences. Rather than being superficial hustlers who live on the surface, seeking only to fulfill their desires and to enjoy the glamour of life, these women reflect on their experiences and on the meaning of their lives.

Their descriptions of their motivations and their attempts to frame what is important are not simple or arbitrary. They are, as Charles Taylor concludes, "more or less adequate, more or less truthful, more self-clairvoyant or self-deluding interpretations" (1996:38). Rather than merely speaking of these women's motives as errors of judgment and moral failures, we might want to emphasize the illusion or delusion of their descriptions as well as the ways they overcome oppressive forces or succumb to these forces. By recognizing that our failure to understand their lives is based on the limits of our experiences, we may begin to gain some insight into their motivations and into what is important and valuable in their lives. We might be able to see that resistance is sometimes subtle and even passive.

We begin with the recognition that these women have a personhood. It is rooted in their life experiences and distinguished by their sense of self and their construction of the future and the past. They have a moral center. They are holders of values and choices as well as adapters and evaluators of life's plans, regardless of how damaged these capacities may be in practice.

Certainly the identity of Margaret, Laquita, and Tracy as sex workers challenges the sexist notion of female sexual passivity. Their actions are autonomous and do not necessarily arise out of sexual satisfaction and fulfillment. Their primary concern is not to please their clients. Rather, sex is part of the economic reality of their lives. Acquiring money is directly tied to their bodies; pleasure is perhaps more directly tied to the money and drugs they receive. Therefore, sexual performance only partially defines aspects of their identity and their relationship to others (see hooks, 1989). This characterization denies their recognition of their body as a resource and as a means actively to resist the economic strictures they face.

For some of these women, sex with men is like what Miss Celie describes in the *Color Purple:* "What is it like? He git up on you, heist your nightgown round your waist, plunge in. Most times I pretend I ain't there. He never know the difference. Never ast me how I feel, nothing. Just do his business, get off, go to sleep" (Walker, 1982:81). Although only Virginia and Laquita are fully realized lesbians, Margaret, Charlie, and Tracy recall the tenderness of their intimate relationships with other women and communicate the pleasure they received from those relationships. Where Freud saw the vagina as a valued "place of shelter for the penis" (1923:312), these women, for the most part, endow the penis with no such status. The male body is described as hard and men's actions as rough and uncomfortable. Margaret explains it best by saying:

If he was sucking on my breast, he would be biting and it would be hurting, you know. And his hair was rough and I would get bruises on my face from him rubbing it, you know. I mean, he wasn't trying to be rough. It was just the way he was. So mostly when we had sex, I would have sex totally for him. The pleasure I got out of it was pleasing him. He never brought me to orgasm. . . .

So give me the woman! It just feels better! Everything about it is better. Ain't nothing going up in you, making you uncomfortable. All right? It's just your body and her body and it feels better.

The fact that all these women have had sexual relationships with other women, regardless of their sexual identification as lesbians, suggests that their attitudes toward sexuality go beyond being able to envision some recognizable lesbian body (Creed, 1995) or some other ascribed definition of sexuality. Their definition of their body resists the rigidity of conventional sexual expression. The flexibility with which these women express same-sex intimacy appears to be very different from the situation for most men, gay or straight. Certainly, for a man, participation in a same-sex intimate relationship can destroy his whole social identity and can stigmatize him as "entirely" deviant and perverted. In some communities, boys quickly learn that the only thing worst than a no good man is a sissy (Staples, 1973).

The nature of female socialization and the depth of female relationships may make it possible for women to view sexuality in far more fluid terms than men. Certainly, avowed lesbians such as Virginia and Laquita describe their sexuality in the most matter-of-fact manner. But what about Margaret, Charlie, and Tracy? Some people may argue that these women have all experienced same-sex relationships because of their subcultural membership and the norms and values associated with such membership rather than their gender membership. Such thinking suggests that their subculture does not stigmatize homosexual desire or that subcultural members are so "deviant" that they are immune to the disapproval of family and friends. Readers must form their own opinions. But it seems to me that Margaret, Charlie, and Tracy understand their bodies and are sufficiently self-realized to express their sexuality in a direction that many of the rest of us will never achieve.

Male domination, subordination, and oppression frame many of their descriptions of men. For the most part, men who have played significant roles in their lives have been brutal and insensitive. Men abrogate their financial and emotional commitments to women and children, men bond with other men at the expense of women, men do not respect women, men are possessive and controlling, men exploit women, and men are driven by the rise and fall of their penises. They are misogynists, the perpetuators of "the problem that has no name" (Frye, 1983). Margaret, recalling having her jaw broken, says:

> He said I was being too nice. I never did understand that. . . . He was at this hotel with this girl and I went around there and all I did was ask him what time

he was coming home. That was bad. To him I came 'round there to catch him doing this, but that wasn't why I came there. How was I 'posed to know he was there with her, you know? But in his mind, I came there for that purpose, to find something, you know, that he was doing wrong. Hit me with his fist and broke my jaw. He's not a big guy but he's strong.

And Tracy speaks with the sadness and horror that is shared by many rape victims: "God! Jesus Christ! Some things, I swear, I will try to forget 'cause it's painful. I swear, I try to forget. Oh, Jesus! I think I was thirteen or fourteen when I got raped. I didn't tell anyone. I was home. It was three guys. They was in my house."

All have had their share of violence at the hands of men or have witnessed the physical and sexual violence waged against their mothers and their older sisters by male partners. In the latter instances, they merely reproduce the behaviors experienced in the social worlds and the family forms of which they were a part. As a child, Tracy saw herself as her mother's protector, and she lived in terror of the awful fights that seemed to be connected directly to her mother's independence and self-definition. As an adult, it is Tracy's independence of spirit that triggers her husband's rage and leads to her abuse. Thus, independence and self-definition are no longer powerful forms of resistance but the catalysts for abuse and domination.

These women are aware of the social differences between men and women. Tracy and Virginia understood that however much they might base their respect (or lack of respect) for their mothers' partners on the actions of the men themselves, their brothers felt differently. In the world of men, gender prevails (see hooks, 1981), and their male siblings bonded with their father figures regardless of the violence those men perpetrated against female family members. Virginia saw her mother's tolerance for physical abuse as pathological: "I thought she was the stupidest bitch in the world to be going through that. . . . Ain't that much love in the world." Margaret similarly reflects on what violence does to the human spirit when she remembers the abuse she suffered at the hands of her husband: "Well, when I was married, fighting was killing me. That's why it didn't last very long, 'cause it was killing me. Not my physical body but my inner self. It was killing me." But she began to resist these attacks actively and says, "Yeah, in the beginning, I had that dumb thought in my mind that, you know, if the man slaps you, you just take it. I don't feel that way anymore." Now, in her current relationship, Margaret attempts to protect herself from physical abuse by saying, "If he try to hurt me, I'm gonna try kill him." She also realizes, however, "If I wanted him, I probably would take more [violence] than I take now." Allowing the abuse to continue is certainly one strategy used by countless women, and in that sense they surrender to their abusers. Even when Margaret physically fights her attacker and withholds sexual intimacy for a brief period, she fails to resist in the most significant way, extricating herself from an abusive relationship that she claims has no significance.

The black family has been cited as having a deteriorating structure (Moynihan 1965). The mother has been a central figure. She has been depicted as an ineffective leader of the household but has also been described as the archetypal "ball-buster" who rules her roost with precision. In contrast is the vision of the black woman as madonna, the sacrificial lamb bestowing unconditional love on her children (Staples 1973; Christian 1985). At different times she has also been portrayed as mammy, matriarch, and welfare queen (Collins, 1990). These labels are perhaps the extremes, but they mark the diversity of motherhood and the reality that parenting images differ by race, historical period, and class. An understanding and assessment of these images may lead to a greater appreciation of the unspoken self-definition of these women and the intricate expressions of their ability to resist oppression.

Women are also often seen as oppressors in these accounts. Mothering is frequently described as an exploitative burden that many women are not prepared to bear. Throughout these stories we encounter mothers whose attempts to protect their children are perverted by a lack of necessary skills and support mechanisms, often brought about by gender, race, and class oppression. For many of these women, the boundaries and opportunities for mothering are fluid and changing. They may from time to time assist other mothers in their childcare responsibilities, as Margaret babysits for one of her lover's children, or exchange help with other mothers, as Tracy and Laurie do. They themselves are sometimes the product of families in which caregiving was done by friends or extended family members. Virginia's godmother, as a member of her extended family, took Virginia into her home as a child when her mother was inattentive. In fact, the mothers in this book—Charlie, Tracy, and Laquita—are no longer the primary caregivers for their children. Their mothers, as grandparents, or the state has assumed that responsibility. Informal networks and extended families do not appear to be central in their narratives, however, and in that sense these accounts are not typical of the community-based child care ethic so representative of members of the African-American diaspora (Shimkin et al., 1978).

Collins (1990) maintains that community-based childcare helps individuals resist oppression because it rejects one of the fundamental assumptions of the capitalist order, that children are property. The style of parenting embraced by these women's mothers, however, suggests, that the mothers clearly saw their children as pieces of property. It was common for mothers to admonish neighbors and friends, sometimes violently, if they attempted to punish and discipline their children. Tracy recalls:

> If someone in the neighborhood had disciplined me because I had done something I wasn't supposed to do, she would have cussed them out. Don't fuck with her children! And we were allowed to kick off. Yes. "Get your fucking hands off me. Don't be touching . . . don't be saying shit to me." We was allowed to say what we wanted to say to adults, and she would back us up. Goddamn right. I would cuss them out, and she would cuss them out too. Damn right. They would get a double bubble.

This failure to extend the reins of discipline to individuals outside the immediate family probably stems from the mothers' desire to ensure that their children survived the dangers of the hostile world of the inner city. Mothers realize that women with a strong sense of self-definition could face tremendous hardship.

These accounts suggest that mothers tried to ensure their children's physical and social survival by being strong disciplinarians and overtly protective. Mothers attempted to shield their daughters from sexual exploitation by monitoring their dress and behavior and by imposing restrictions on when and under what conditions they were allowed to see young men. Laquita characterizes her mother as being obsessed with issues related to Laquita's body and recalls that her mother's vigilance increased in intensity once she entered puberty: "[My mother] started to change about then. It was like she had a dog on a leash. I mean, she would sniff me out anywhere I was. Come find me."

The issue of who is going to control a young woman's sexuality becomes a test of wills between mother and daughter. Laquita continues:

> So it seems that when I got my period, the discipline got stronger. I started getting more beatings and stuff, but I was becoming more defiant. Yeah, I was. Because she was like "I don't want you with this person, I don't want you with that person, I don't want you with the guys." And I was like "Fuck this," you know. "You're not going to knock off my fucking fun. I'm gonna hang out with who I want to be with and I can talk to who I want to talk to and I wanna go where I wanna go."

These factors generate considerable tension between mothers and daughters. Though daughters may claim that their mothers loved them and did the best they could, they also maintain that their mothers were "bitchy"—that they provoked fights, were strict and uncommunicative, were physically and verbally abusive, and sacrificed their children for relationships with abusive men. These mothers may have been genuinely concerned about their daughters, particularly in the area of pregnancy prevention, but their solutions centered on restricting access rather than providing their daughters with the support and education they deserved. Race and class hindered their access to information and styles of communication that might have made them more successful in reaching their daughters. The result is that genuine concern for their daughters was turned against itself. These households typify the many ways in which gender, race, and class oppression terrorize the lives of women. Within the context of a hostile environment, women grapple with issues and solutions learned in their youth, which they in turn transmit to their daughters, who are similarly victimized.

Under these conditions and as an act of defiance, girls stop listening to their mothers in favor of following their own desires as colored by the lure of the streets and their peers. Laquita says: "I didn't listen and do what she asked me to do. She used to beat me. To make me do what she wanted me to do. I've always been a little hard-head, stubborn bitch." Similarly, Margaret defied her mother in order to see her boyfriend:

> I didn't always listen when I [was] growing up. Not always. I've never stopped doing everything she told me really. Just some things. Like I would sneak and go to a party if she was at church. If I said I was sick or whatever, I would sneak and go to a party. Got caught and got beat most of the time. And then she told me I couldn't see boys until I got out of school. I just flat out went against that.[12]

In Tracy's case, there was simply very little supervision:

> I was on my own. I had the option whether to go to school or not go to school. So I didn't go to school. If I came home from school with bad grades my mother wouldn't do nothing. Business as usual. If I was misbehaving in school she wouldn't do nothing either. I tell you, it was like we was sisters. She didn't give a . . . I did what I wanna do. She did what she wanna do. Wasn't no sit down and talk.

In some of these families, mothers worked; in all of them, they wanted their daughters to receive good educations. All five women spent at least some time as children in Catholic schools. A few of the mothers also attempted to supervise their children's school behavior or have older siblings do so. And even in the case of those mothers who do not appear to have taken an active or visible role monitoring their children's performance, the fact that they committed their meager resources to their children's education shows the extent to which they wanted to provide better lives for their daughters.

Nevertheless, this desire was not enough to protect them. A few of the young women left home to escape what they saw as mental or physical cruelty. For others, the seduction of the fast life, inducements from friends, and environments ridden with drugs and crime were in large measure responsible for their entry into the world of drugs and crime (see Katz, 1988; Miller, 1986; Richie, 1996). Margaret admired the way her sister dressed and envied her dates with attractive young men. Tracy wanted to be like her mother, a woman who had fun, who went to the bars to drink, and who wore glamorous clothes. Virginia started stealing in order to purchase clothing so she could be "fly": "I just wanted the money. It started out money for the things I wanted. The other stealing was for the 'caine. So it started with, yeah, like if my girlfriends come to school with all this new fly stuff on. Man! I wanted it too. You know what I mean? I've always likeded nice things too, you know."

Invariably, turning points or pathways in the life course of these women brought them to the place where we meet them (see Shaw, 1930; Sutherland and Conwell, 1937; Katz, 1988; Pettiway, 1996). All five women illustrate the interlocking set of trajectories and transitions of life that exist as time-order patterns of behavior (Elder, 1985) and that form turning points in their lives (Sampson and Laub, 1993). Reading these accounts, one can easily see what some have referred to as "low self-control" (see Gottfredson and Hirschi, 1990). The paradigms of neglect, conflict, deviant behaviors and attitudes, as well as disruption, as key dimensions of family functioning and juvenile misconduct, are also readily apparent (Loeber and Stouthamer-Loeber, 1986). We see parents who do not monitor, discipline, or seem to care about their children (see Patterson, 1980; Gottfredson and Hirschi, 1986, 1990; Hagan, 1989), just as we see parents who stigmatize their children, practice neglect and abuse, and indulge in draconian punishment regimes. But these are also parents who care and children who have strong attachments to their parents.[13]

Although the markers of strong social control may be conspicuously lacking in these accounts, their absence only partially tells the story. Ultimately, these are stories of women surviving under horrible circumstances. By focusing solely on inadequate social control characteristics, we fail to recognize how such women build self-defined lives and, indeed, from their standpoint, how they build lives of value. Given the nature of the criminological discourse, it not surprising that some have asserted that the hallmark of a "criminal life style" is the rejection of restrictions and duties (Gottfredson and Hirschi, 1990).

Turning points in the life course, however, also condition and broaden the human experience. These women's persona is more complex than the canons of criminology would acknowledge. As I said in an earlier book that portrays the lives of gay, male sex workers:

> One can find dignity, compassion, strength, resilience, and love in unexpected places and in unexpected lives. They demonstrate that lived experiences are complex and move between and include times of triumph and defeat, humiliation and pride. They reveal what we always knew—that life is filled with ambivalence and ambiguity. It is never neatly situated along the axes of hope or despair, pleasure or pain, dignity or defeat, good or bad. (Pettiway, 1996: xii)

These accounts also challenge some of the basic canons of criminological discourse. Social control has been defined as "the capacity of a social group to regulate itself according to desired principles and values, and hence to make norms and rules effective" (Sampson and Laub, 1993:18), and women who use drugs and commit crimes to support their habits are ordinarily seen as falling outside social control boundaries. But these stories suggest that there may be order and purpose, and, indeed, working social control mechanisms, in the world of those defined as "deviant." These women practice self-evaluation and choice and have a deep understanding of individual accountability and responsibility. What is missing from the criminological discourse is an understanding of what it truly means to become marginalized, and whether marginalized individuals search for respect and a sense of accomplishment in the most accessible places (see, for example, Bourgois, 1996).

These accounts provide the domestic and cultural frames that help shift the ways women construct their identity (see Miller, 1986; Richie, 1996). For the women in this book, the functioning and structural conditions of their families and environments as children made it impossible for them to imagine or desire anything materially different in the future. Their choices are "structured choices." Their behaviors do not simply result from a rejection of restrictions and an avoidance of a sense of duty. They are not merely individuals who have "given up," "dropped out," or "copped out." These accounts provide some understanding of the relationship between female agency and structurally induced marginality, which limits the agency of these women at unique turning points in their lives.

Their entry into the drug subculture marks a significant turning point in their life course. And as adults, their drug use continues to deprive them of the emotional and material opportunities to approach the future optimistically. Drug use appears to be an almost natural consequence, given the nature of the structural conditions of the environments in which these women were raised. As Tracy remarks, "Everybody was doing it. My environment was doing it. My older sister did it. Her friends did it. So I was always around them. Always around drugs." Though Tracy intends to say no to drugs in the future, she communicates the power of crack-cocaine when she says, "I had twenty-eight days clean. I was going crazy. I told them, 'Please.' They say, 'Girl, fight it.' 'I don't know how.'" She faces the misery of her existence and hopes that her two children will have lives that are better than her own. She is tormented by the unknown impact crack-cocaine will have on the fetus that she carries, but she makes no effort to seek psychological or medical assistance. She seems powerless to change.

Margaret, Charlie, Virginia, Tracy, and Laquita differ in how they entered the drug subculture. Unlike the other women, Margaret was an adult when she began to use drugs. Propelled into the drug subculture by the departure of her husband and her association with new friends, she began using "monster" (methamphetamine) when a friend suggested putting some in her coffee to help keep her warm because she could not afford to pay her heating bill. Eventually, drug use became a way of life. In the matter-of-fact and resigned manner that characterizes many of these women's remarks, she says, "I'm a drug addict and I don't wanna be one but I'm one. So I'm just being that."

Unlike Margaret, Tracy began using drugs when she was twelve. Faced with the option of doing whatever she wished, confronted with an environment where drug use was normative, and terrified and burdened by the horror of rape, she began to experiment with drugs and ran errands for her neighbors to earn drug money. Like all the women, she says she wants to "be drug free" for her children's sake. But she also admits that "what I want and what I do is two different things." She enjoys the feeling of being high and does not expect to be able to shake the habit: "I even go as far as to say, you know how they say your life is written, you know, everything as you come up is already set up in the big book. I said this is it. I'm destined to be a addict."

For these women, drug use colors every aspect of their lives. Their relationships with intimate partners fall apart because of their joint commitment to drugs and hustling. Their children, both born and unborn, suffer from their use of substances that no one can control. Their family relationships, tenuous in some cases before their drug use, are now even more strained; parents, who themselves are often marginal, have little patience for the additional problems their daughters bring to their lives. These women have burned many bridges and have few supports left to connect them to the "straight life," as Virginia calls it. Within this inundated world they express their agency as women and find meaning on the other side of life.

For most of the women, sex work is the dominant means by which they get crack-cocaine for their pipes or straight shooters or cocaine and heroin for their syringes. It is not their sexual feelings that compel them to work but the lure of money and drugs. Having sex is easier and safer for Tracy than shoplifting. Her clients live in the same public housing community as she does, and so, as she puts it, "What fucking trouble can you get in for having sex?" Margaret sticks to her regular customers or to guys in the neighborhood who are looking for girls.

Charlie is the only one of the five who works the streets. After being arrested several times for felonies, she switched to the sex industry because the crimes she was doing carried hard time. Convinced by a friend that her white–Puerto Rican features were unusual enough to make her a successful member of the street-walking culture, she learned to walk that walk and talk that talk. Armed with a shot of heroin, she overcame her initial aversion to fellatio and, by her own account, became much sought after on the stroll. Spurred by the new competition from "crack whores" who have deflated the price on the street, Charlie now offers a "money-back guarantee." Her success has earned her the enmity of some of her fellow prostitutes. Besides living with the fear of being killed or robbed that is common to all sex workers, she has been warned, "Watch your ass, Char, because there's a couple of girls out here that want to cut your face."

In the sex industry, life becomes a revolving door, swinging one way for customers and another when police corral sex workers into paddy wagons that speed them from dark streets to the "safety" of jails. In their world, "tricks" and other drug users help during the hard times. As Margaret proclaims, "They never forgot me and I appreciate things like that. They never forgot me when I was down and out."

Sex work is often the only crime that many criminologists think of when they consider women at all. Moreover, many criminologists believe that, if women enter into crimes with male partners, their role is secondary and, in fact, men would not choose to enter into partnership arrangements with them (Steffensmeier, 1983). As I have pointed out elsewhere (Pettiway, 1987), these arrangements are more complex, and the accounts here corroborate the diversity of female crime participation. They show that, although women may lack the physical strength to commit certain crimes independently, they plan and execute a wide range of offenses, in some instances employing men to carry out the more physically difficult parts of the operations.

The ego lives in history and strives for self-definition and self-valuation in the face of the interlocking dissonance produced by race, class, and gender oppression. The power of these five women to make qualitative distinctions between desires and motivations marks their agency (Taylor, 1996). If we examine their evaluative vision, what do we see? They do not reject being "normal" because some contingent or circumstantial issue conflicts with other goals; nor does being "deviant" compete with other desires or alter these women's circumstances in such a way as to prevent them from pursuing other goals. When criminologists talk about "deviance" versus "normalcy," they seem to imply a second dichotomy of "degradation" versus "dignity." Is it possible for us, given the criminological discourse and the dissonance created by oppression, to define these women as making choices that speak to their desire for dignity and their will to survive?

I think the answer is yes. There is dignity in assuming responsibility. For example, as a drug user, a person may rely on others to support her habit or she may assume responsibility for her needs herself. In this regard, all these women choose to be responsible. Margaret understands this burden when she says:

> My reasons for doing it [going out and getting money herself, rather than waiting for her partner to supply her with drugs or money] was because I am a drug addict myself—me, myself, and I—and I don't think nobody have to take care of my habit, you know. I wouldn't put that on nobody 'cause that's a burden, you know. It's a burden to me myself and it's my habit.

Similarly, a user may blame outside circumstances or other people for her drug use or she may accept responsibility for her own choices. Again, all these women take responsibility for their lives. Virginia refuses to blame her crack use for the things she has done wrong: "I don't worry about stuff . . . because I done been through the changes as far as being slimy and conniving, and I done been through all that. . . . I ain't gonna use the pipe as an excuse for my wrongdoings anymore." She has also learned to take care of her personal responsibilities before she allows herself to play.

These women are reflective evaluators of their social worlds, their lives, and the lives of others. In considering her life, Margaret wonders whether human decency and drug use are compatible. She echoes Matthew 6:24 ("No man can serve two masters: for either he will hate the one, and love the other; or else he will hold to the one, and despise the other") when she says, "I'm tryin' to be a decent person and a drug addict at the same time. And I've started to believe that you have to be one way or the other." Likewise, given what she has witnessed, she questions her mother's religious conviction that it is possible to love everybody.

As I suggested at the beginning of this introduction, these are women who understand the images and meanings of their physical environments. Tracy has learned to traverse the dangers of the public housing project where she lives: "When you grow up in the projects, man, you gotta stay away from the boys raping you. You got to duck gunshots and somebody getting stabbed and then the drugs is there staring at you. And it was a survival for your life every goddamn day you woke up."

These are only a few of the ways these women are reflective evaluators of their social worlds, and it is within the context of their social worlds that they set boundaries for themselves and others. In their commitment of crime, time is money and boundaries must be established. Margaret explains: "When I turn tricks now, I do it like I'm gonna give you two or three minutes and if you can't get it in that bit of time, sorry. You know, before, I was aiming to please them 'cause the money was like that. But now the money's not like that so it don't make me no difference whether they come or not." Charlie agrees: "I light a cigarette and I tell them when the cigarette is burnt down, your time's up. If you want more time, that's more money. If you want to touch me, that's even more money."

These are proud women driven by their sense of duty. Often this sense of duty makes them silent holders of pain but knowers of truth. Though they admit to having low self-esteem, they also admit to being independent, sensitive, caring and helpful, compassionate and loving, and social resisters. They may not have given much thought to their future, but they are defiant defenders of their identity. They have chosen to terminate pregnancies and to allow fetuses to grow inside their bodies, they have chosen to leave abusive relationships and resist violence, they have chosen to shoplift or to sell their bodies based on their individual constructions of need, and they have recognized their intelligence but in some cases have chosen not to use it. In these ways they proclaim their personhood and their agency.

In the end, they are self-realized, and they merely want to be accepted just as they are. They have resisted many individuals in order to do their "own thing," to be their own boss, and to be in control. They accept life and they lack self-pity and do not, for the most part, blame others. In this book, they speak for themselves.

In reading these accounts, some readers will want to find a kind of chronology. But these women do not present their lives in a linear fashion. Time is measured in terms of relationships, and what emerges is a chronology of intimacy.

The first challenge of reading this book is to learn to approach the language of the stories. The language takes some time to get used to. I recommend that you read slowly. Your learning curve may improve significantly if you begin by reading passages aloud so as to become familiar with each narrator's cadence and style. Being attentive to the language will bring insights into a way of life.

They use language in creative ways. Laquita describes herself as living in an "abandominium"—an abandoned house where she took up residence when she and her partner became homeless. They casually use expressions such as "Couldn't carry a note in a pail" and "I was becoming a L7, a square," as well as "throwing her every which way but loose." Instead of having the ability to fight, one has the ability to "rumble." Their voices are powerful and their imagery sure. Tracy, for example, reflects on her life by saying, "The shit I had to endure, it was a whole chumpy of misery," where "chumpy" refers to that thing which has no name or cannot be remembered. Choices in life, the decisions that one makes, are conditioned by "whatever is clever," because "it won't no thang at all." Sometimes a person gets a "double bubble," not one insult but two. If there is no support or one does not have the energy to be bothered, one simply "steps off," leaves.

Although we may be troubled by acts that offend our individual and collective senses of humanness, we must not fail to recognize the intrinsic value of each woman as she tells her story of problems faced and choices made. She may seem to be separated from her own humanity by acts of "deviance," but the core of her humanity, the self, lingers and waits for conversion while the ego lives in time. The self, the core of being and humanness united with a spiritual universe that is beyond comprehension, exists whether the person has access to it or not.

When we do not listen to "outsiders," when we construct their lives only as theoretical notions locked in a disciplinary discourse, we deny their humanity. When we fail to listen to the mistakes of our own lives, our understanding of the lives of "outsiders" becomes clouded with the fog of our own weaknesses. When we fail to listen to our social and political beliefs that are steeped in self-interest and conditioned by misogyny and racism, we forget where we stand and how those views color our voices and shape our humanity.

In climbing life's hills and taking one's burdens, there are mountains of failure before one glimpses success. Margaret, Charlie, Virginia, Tracy, and Laquita tell their stories, recalling the troubles and the tragedies of their lives. They live in imperfect days, but maybe, in the spirit of the old Negro spiritual, we will all understand them better by and by.

Notes

1. Moreover, these accounts are edited versions of the raw transcriptions of the taped interviews. In some cases, substantial amounts of original material were deleted to reduce the length of the manuscript and eliminate redundancies. Some materials were rearranged for readability since some themes were revisited at different points in the interview process. In removing and rearranging materials, however, I took care not to diminish the essential narrative expression of the individual or break the original chains of thought and the original conception of the chronology. In all instances editing was done to retain the uniqueness of the speaker and the essential flavor and texture of the interview.

2. Each person was interviewed over a two-day period. For each of the life history interviews, participants received twenty dollars. The length of the interviews varied, depending on the individual's attentiveness. In conducting the interviews, I always began with a qualitative guideline, but in many cases it became clear that that method was too restrictive. Some people's lives just did not fit the guideline. In those cases I crafted questions based on the unique attributes of the person's experiences.

Legal protection for respondents was accorded by assurances of anonymity and a grant of confidentiality from the National Institute on Drug Abuse, which guaranteed that project employees could not be compelled by any court or law enforcement agency to reveal information sources or questionnaire data. In the accounts in this book, all information that might readily identify the participants has been deleted. In addition, I have changed personal identifiers such as the individual's code name, the city in which the research was conducted, place names and the names of establishments, the neighborhood and street names where their activities were conducted, as well as the names of the people they talk about.

3. Within this framework, the discipline confirms a woman's "deviant" identity (Becker, 1963). Even when imposing a pathological label on women, some criminologists believed members of the criminal justice system act chivalrously toward women. They believed police and court officials had been duped as to the real nature of women (Pollak, 1950).

4. Through certainly all people have basic similarities, by identifying individuals simply as "typical" or "deviant" human beings, researchers, both men and women, lose sight of the idiosyncrasies that divide people into groups and often give them their own perceived identities. The history of modern humanism has promulgated both the suppression of differences and the oppressive denial of differences. For example, there has been a denial of female difference as well as a denial of differences in sexuality and difference of races. (On humanism, see Harding, 1986; Soper, 1990; Johnson, 1994; Heller and Fehâer, 1991; Foucault, 1986; McCarthy, 1987.)

5. Much of the research on female criminality focuses on explaining women's crime participation in terms of theories devised to explain male criminality (Laberge, 1991; Leonard, 1982; Smart, 1976), theories developed and tested using male samples without any concern that the results may be gender specific. In differentiating the frequency of crime, criminologists have identified theoretical concerns that find their origin in Marxist theory (power control, socialist feminist, and neo-Marxist) but have failed to recognize the manner by which gender and race operate within social classes (Simpson, 1991).

6. This line of reasoning has been sharply criticized (see Daly and Chesney-Lind, 1988; Miller, 1986; Smart, 1978; Chapman, 1980; Datesman and Scarpitti, 1980; Gora, 1982; Heidensohn, 1985; Steffensmeier, 1978). Chesney-Lind (1986) and Miller (1986), for example, have argued that gender differences remain significant even when women share men's social and cultural opportunities. But the practice continues. Simon and Landis (1991) raise the question whether the offending patterns of women will mirror those of men as they break their traditional and historic roles. In drug research, Brownstein et al. (1995) addressed this issue by considering the opportunity for economic liberation afforded by women's participation in the drug market.

7. Though some criminologists have tested theories derived from male-only samples to determine whether they apply to females (Cernkovich and Giordano, 1979; Datesman and Scarpitti, 1975; Giordano, 1978), many criminologists fail to recognize

the generalizability problem that confronts the discipline. When the issue of generalizability is viewed alongside the "gender ratio problem," which centers on the relatively higher rates of male criminality (see Box, 1983; Hagan, Simpson, and Gillis, 1987; Steffensmeier, 1983; Wilson and Herrnstein, 1985), it is not surprising that many researchers have employed qualitative research methods to address these issues (see, for example, Chesney-Lind and Rodriguez, 1983; Rosenbaum, 1981a, 1981b; Miller, 1986; Bell, 1987). More important, the feminist imperative calls criminology to understand the problem of gender within the context of the production of knowledge and the implications of men's and women's construction of theory and research.

8. What has been studied extensively is women's use of their bodies as a resource in the commission of sex work (see Goldstein, 1979; Inciardi, Lockwood, and Pottieger, 1993; Hunt, 1990; James, 1976; File, 1976; Miller, 1986; Rosenbaum, 1981a; Richie, 1996; Winick and Kinsie, 1971). There has also been an attempt to create a literature on women as crime victims, particularly as victims of rape and domestic assault (see Dobash and Dobash, 1992; Richie, 1996). Feminists have considered the relative treatment of women vis-à-vis men in the criminal courts (see Chesney-Lind, 1986; Kruttschnitt, 1982) and the effect of race and class on sentencing outcomes (Daly, 1989, 1993).

9. The lower ratio of water to total body weight causes women to metabolize alcohol and drugs differently. Marijuana, for example, is slower to clear a woman's body than a man's (Braude and Ludford, 1984).

10. This deviation from a woman's expected gender role is said to be reflected in behavioral rates such that "illegal drug use is even more deviant for females than it is for males, and the greater the illegality, the greater the deviance from expected— and typically enacted—behaviors" (Inciardi, Lockwood, and Pottieger, 1993:23). Alcohol and drug abuse carry far more stigma for women than for men (Inciardi, 1986; Sandmaier, 1980; Sterne and Pittman, 1972; Gomberg, 1982; Child, Barry, and Bacon, 1965; Rosenbaum, 1981b; Waldorf, 1973). According to these researchers, even a limited number of drug-use episodes severely affects "a woman's entire social identity, stigmatizing her as wild, promiscuous, unstable" (Inciardi, Lockwood, and Pottieger, 1993:23). Therefore, drug-using women are believed to be more socially isolated from conventional society and more disconnected from immediate family members and children than are drug-using men.

11. For example, Messerschmidt (1993) observes that social structure affects individual behavior such that behavior mirrors class, gender, and racial position. For example, relationships with family and peers have been shown to be important fac-

tors related to delinquency. Parental attachment, conditioned by intimate communications and strong familial control and supervision, is generally believed to inhibit delinquency. Researchers hypothesize that parental socialization and family ties vary across both racial and gender lines. Family variables appear to be more important for whites than for African-Americans, but identity support inhibits delinquency across all racial and gender groups. Thus, increased supervision and control appears to inhibit delinquency for African-American males and females, but family conflict, perhaps generated from issues of supervision, appears to increase delinquency among white females (Cernkovich and Giordano, 1987). Moreover, researchers have shown that associating with delinquent friends increases the likelihood of delinquent activities regardless of gender (Giordano, Cernkovich, and Pugh, 1986). It is possible, however, that delinquency is "a by-product of having close friends with few life ambitions" (Simpson and Elis, 1995:70). For Simpson and Elis (1995:73), "differential access to and influence of these structures [the household, culture, and social class] leads to the development of oppositional and accommodating masculinities and femininities (i.e., doing gender) that dictate whether and what types of crime are committed by males and females, blacks and whites."

12. Taken from the original, unedited transcript.

13. Informal family social control and its three salient dimensions (discipline, supervision, and attachment), or their absence, are central to the criminological discourse associated with deviance (see Sampson and Laub, 1993). These characteristics serve to link children to society through emotional bonds.

References

Adler, Freda. 1975. *Sisters in Crime: The Rise of the New Female Criminal*. New York: McGraw-Hill.

Becker, Howard. 1963. *Outsiders: Studies in the Sociology of Deviance*. New York: Free Press.

Behar, Ruth, and Deborah A. Gordon. 1995. *Women Writing Culture*. Berkeley: University of California Press.

Bell, Laurie. 1987. *Good Girls/Bad Girls: Feminists and Sex Trade Workers Face to Face*. Seattle: Seal.

Bourgois, Philippe. 1996. *In Search of Respect: Selling Crack in El Barrio*. Cambridge: Cambridge University Press.

Box, Steve. 1983. *Power, Crime, and Mystification*. New York: Tavistock.

Braithwaite, John. 1981. "The Myth of Social Class and Crime Reconsidered." *American Sociological Review* 46:26–57.

Braude, Monique C., and Jacqueline P. Ludford. 1984. *Marijuana Effects on the Endocrine and Reproductive Systems: A RAUS Review Report*. NIDA Research Monograph 44. Rockville, Md.: National Institute on Drug Abuse.

Brownstein, Henry H., Barry J. Spunt, Susan M. Crimmins, and Sandra C. Langley. 1995. "Women Who Kill in Drug Market Situations." *Justice Quarterly* 12(3):473–498.

Cernkovich, Stephen, and Peggy C. Giordano. 1979. "Delinquency, Opportunity, and Gender." *Journal of Criminal Law and Criminology* 70:145–151.

———. 1987. "Family Relationships and Delinquency." *Criminology* 25:295–319.

Chapman, Jane Roberts. 1980. *Economic Realities and the Female Offender*. Lexington, Mass.: Lexington Books.

Chesney-Lind, Meda. 1986. "Women and Crime: The Female Offender." *Signs* 12:78–96.

Chesney-Lind, Meda, and Noelie Rodriguez. 1983. "Women under Lock and Key." *Prison Journal* 63:47–65.

Child, Irwin L., Herbert Barry, and Margaret K. Bacon. 1965. "Sex Differences." *Journal of Studies on Alcohol* supp. 3:49–61.

Christian, Barbara. 1985. *Black Feminist Criticism: Perspectives on Black Women Writers*. New York: Pergamon.

Collins, Patricia Hill. 1986. "Learning from the Outside Within: The Sociological Significance of Black Feminist Thought." *Social Problems* 33:14–32.

———. 1990. *Black Feminist Thought: Knowledge, Consciousness, and the Politics of Empowerment*. New York: Routledge.

Colten, Mary Ellen. 1979. "A Description and Comparative Analysis of Self-Perceptions and Attitudes of Heroin-Addicted Women." In U.S. Dept. of Health, Education, and Welfare, *Addicted Women: Family Dynamics, Self-Perceptions, and Support Systems*, pp. 7–36. Rockville, Md.: National Institute on Drug Abuse.

Creed, Barbara. 1995. "Lesbian Bodies: Tribades, Tomboys, and Tarts." In *Sexy Bodies: The Strange Carnalities of Feminism*, ed. Elizabeth Grosz and Elspeth Probyn, pp. 86–103. New York: Routledge.

Daly, Kathleen. 1989. "Neither Conflict nor Labeling nor Paternalism Will Suffice: Intersections of Race, Ethnicity, Gender, and Family in Criminal Court Decisions." *Crime and Delinquency* 35:136–168.

————. 1993. "Class-Race-Gender: Sloganeering in Search of Meaning." *Social Justice* 20:56–71.

Daly, Kathleen, and Meda Chesney-Lind. 1988. "Feminism and Criminology." *Justice Quarterly* 5:497–538.

Datesman, Susan K., and Frank R. Scarpitti. 1975. "Female Delinquency and Broken Homes: A Reassessment." *Criminology* 12:33–55.

————. 1980. "Women's Crime and Women's Emancipation." In *Women, Crime, and Justice,* ed. Susan K. Datesman and Frank R. Scarpitti, pp. 355–376. New York: Oxford University Press.

Davies, Margaret. 1994. *Asking the Law Question.* Sydney: Law Book Company.

Derrida, Jacques. 1981. *Positions.* Trans. and annot. Alan Bass. Chicago: University of Chicago Press.

Dobash, R. Emerson, and Russell P. Dobash. 1992. *Women, Violence, and Social Change.* London: Routledge.

Elder, Glen H., Jr. 1985. "Perspectives on the Life Course." In *Life Course Dynamics,* ed. Glen H. Elder, Jr., pp. 23–49. Ithaca: Cornell University Press.

Estrich, Susan. 1987. *Real Rape.* Cambridge: Harvard University Press.

File, Karen N. 1976. "Sex Roles and Street Roles." *International Journal of the Addictions* 11:263–268.

Foucault, Michel. 1986. *Power/Knowledge: Selected Interviews and Other Writings, 1972–1977.* Ed. Colin Gordon; trans. Colin Gordon, Leo Marshall, John Mepham, and Kate Sopher. New York: Pantheon Books.

Freud, Sigmund. 1923. "Fragment of an Analysis of a Case of Hysteria ('Dora')." In *Case Histories I.* Pelican Freud Library, vol. 8. Harmondsworth, U.K.: Penguin.

Freund, Matthew, Terri L. Leonard, and Nancy Lee. 1989. "Sexual Behavior of Resident Street Prostitutes with Their Clients in Camden, New Jersey." *Journal of Sex Research* 26:460–478.

Frye, Marilyn. 1983. "The Problem That Has No Name." In *The Politic of Reality: Essays in Feminist Theory,* pp. 41–51. Trumansburg, N.Y.: Crossing Press.

Giordano, Peggy C. 1978. "Girls, Guys, and Gangs: The Changing Social Context of Female Delinquency." *Journal of Criminal Law and Criminology* 69:126–132.

Giordano, Peggy C., Stephen A. Cernkovich, and M. D. Pugh. 1986. "Friendships and Delinquency." *American Journal of Sociology* 91:1170–1202.

Glynn, Thomas J., Helen Wallenstein Pearson, and Mollie Sayers. 1983. *Women and Drugs.* Rockville, Md.: National Institute on Drug Abuse.

Goldstein, Paul. 1979. *Prostitution and Drugs*. Lexington, Mass.: Lexington Books.

Gomberg, Edith S. 1982. "Historical and Political Perspectives: Women and Drug Use." *Journal of Social Issues* 38:9–23.

Gora, JoAnn. 1982. *The New Female Criminal: Empirical Reality or Social Myth?* New York: Praeger.

Gottfredson, Michael, and Travis Hirschi. 1986. "The Value of Lambda Would Appear to Be Zero: An Essay on Career Criminals, Criminal Careers, Selective Incapacitation, Cohort Studies, and Related Topics." *Criminology* 24:213–234.

———. 1990. *A General Theory of Crime*. Stanford: Stanford University Press.

Hagan, John. 1989. *Structural Criminology*. New Brunswick: Rutgers University Press.

Hagan, John, John Simpson, and A. R. Gillis. 1987. "Class in the Household: A Power-Control Theory of Gender and Delinquency." *American Journal of Sociology* 92:788–816.

Harding, Sandra. 1986. *The Science Question in Feminism*. Ithaca: Cornell University Press.

Heidensohn, Frances M. 1985. *Women and Crime: The Life of the Female Offender*. New York: New York University Press.

———. 1994. "Gender and Crime." In *The Oxford Handbook of Criminology,* Ed. Robert Reiner, Rod Morgan, and Mike Maguire, pp. 997–1039. Oxford: Clarendon Press.

Heller, Agnes, and Ferenc Fehâer. 1991. *The Grandeur and the Twilight of Radical Universalism*. New Brunswick, N.J.: Transaction.

Hill, Gary D., and Elizabeth M. Crawford. 1990. "Women, Race, and Crime." *Criminology* 28:601–623.

hooks, bell. 1981. *Ain't I a Woman: Black Women and Feminism*. Boston: South End Press.

———. 1989. *Talking Back: Thinking Feminist, Thinking Black*. Boston: South End Press.

Horwitz, Allan V., and Helene R. White. 1987. "Gender Role Orientations and Styles of Pathology among Adolescents." *Journal of Health and Social Behavior* 28:158–170.

Hunt, Dana H. 1990. "Drugs and Consensual Crimes: Drug Dealing and Prostitution." In *Drugs and Crime,* ed. Michael Tonry and James Q. Wilson, pp. 159–202. Chicago: University of Chicago Press.

Inciardi, James A. 1986. *The War on Drugs: Heroin, Cocaine, Crime, and Public Policy.* Palo Alto, Calif.: Mayfield.

Inciardi, James A., Dorothy Lockwood, and Anne E. Pottieger. 1993. *Women and Crack-Cocaine.* New York: Macmillan.

James, Jennifer. 1976. "Prostitution and Addiction: An Interdisciplinary Approach." *Addictive Diseases: An International Journal* 2:601–618.

Johnson, Pauline. 1994. *Feminism as Radical Humanism.* Boulder, Colo.: Westview Press.

Katz, Jack. 1988. *Seduction of Crime: Moral and Sensual Attractions in Doing Evil.* New York: Basic Books.

Kruttschnitt, Candice. 1982. "Women, Crime, and Dependency: An Application of a Theory of Law." *Criminology* 19:495–513.

Laberge, Danielle. 1991. "Women's Criminality, Criminal Women, Criminalized Women? Questions in and for a Feminist Perspective." *Journal of Human Justice* 2:37–56.

Leonard, Eileen B. 1982. *A Critique of Criminology Theory: Women, Crime, and Society.* New York: Longman.

Loeber, Rolf, and Magda Stouthamer-Loeber. 1986. "Family Factors as Correlates and Predictors of Juvenile Conduct Problems and Delinquency." In *Crime and Justice,* vol. 7, ed. Michael Tonry and Norval Morris, pp. 29–149. Chicago: University of Chicago Press.

Marcus, George E., and Michael M. J. Fischer. 1986. *Anthropology as Cultural Critique: An Experimental Moment in the Human Sciences.* Chicago: University of Chicago Press.

McCarthy, Thomas. 1987. Introduction to *The Philosophical Discourse of Modernity,* by Jürgen Habermas. Cambridge: Massachusetts Institute of Technology.

Messerschmidt, James W. 1993. *Masculinities and Crime.* Lanham, Md.: Rowman and Littlefield.

Miller, Eleanor M. 1986. *Street Woman.* Philadelphia: Temple University Press.

Morgan, Peggy. 1988. "Living on the Edge." In *Sex Work: Writings by Women in the Sex Industry,* ed. Frederique Delacoste and Priscilla Alexander, pp. 21–28. London: Virago.

Moynihan, Daniel P. 1965. *The Negro Family: The Case for National Action.* Washington: U.S. Government Printing Office.

Murphy, Sheigla, and Marsha Rosenbaum. 1995. "The Rhetoric of Reproduction: Pregnancy and Drug Use." *Contemporary Drug Problems* 23:581–585.

Naffine, Ngaire. 1996. *Feminism and Criminology*. Philadelphia: Temple University Press.

Patterson, Gerald R. 1980. "Children Who Steal." In *Understanding Crime: Current Theory and Research,* ed. Travis Hirschi and Michael Gottfredson, pp. 73–90. Beverly Hills, Calif.: Sage.

Perkins, Roberta, and Garry Bennett. 1985. *Being a Prostitute*. Boston: Allen and Unwin.

Pettiway, Leon E. 1987. "Participation in Crime Partnerships by Female Drug Users: The Effects of Domestic Arrangements, Drug Use, and Criminal Involvement." *Criminology* 25:741–766.

———. 1996. *Honey, Honey, Miss Thang: Being Black, Gay, and on the Streets.* Philadelphia: Temple University Press.

Pollak, Otto. 1950. *The Criminality of Women*. Philadelphia: University of Pennsylvania Press.

Rice, Marcia. 1990. "Challenging Orthodoxies in Feminist Theory: A Black Feminist Critique." In *Feminist Perspectives in Criminology,* ed. Loraine Gelsthorpe and Allison Morris, pp. 57–69. Philadelphia: Open University Press.

Richie, Beth E. 1996. *Compelled to Crime: The Gender Entrapment of Battered Black Women*. New York: Routledge.

Robbins, Cynthia. 1989. "Sex Differences in Psychosocial Consequences of Alcohol and Drug Abuse." *Journal of Health and Social Behavior* 30:117–130.

Rosenbaum, Marsha. 1981a. "Sex Roles among Deviants: The Woman Addict." *International Journal of the Addictions* 16:859–877.

———. 1981b. *Women on Heroin*. New Brunswick: Rutgers University Press.

Sampson, Robert J., and John H. Laub. 1993. *Crime in the Making: Pathways and Turning Points through Life*. Cambridge: Harvard University Press.

Sandmaier, Marian. 1980. *The Invisible Alcoholics*. New York: McGraw-Hill.

Shaw, Clifford R. 1930. *The Jack-Roller: A Delinquent Boy's Own Story*. Chicago: University of Chicago Press.

Shimkin, Demitri B., Edith M. Shimkin, and Dennis A. Frate, eds. 1978. *The Extended Family in Black Societies*. Chicago: Aldine.

Simon, Rita J. 1975. *Women and Crime*. Lexington, Mass.: Lexington Books.

Simon, Rita J., and Jean Landis. 1991. *The Crimes Women Commit, the Punishments They Receive*. Lexington, Mass.: Lexington Books.

Simpson, Sally S. 1991. "Caste, Class, and Violent Crime: Explaining Differences in Female Offending." *Criminology* 29:115–135.

Simpson, Sally S., and Lori Elis. 1995. "Doing Gender: Sorting out the Caste and Crime Conundrum." *Criminology* 33:47–81.

Smart, Carol. 1976. *Women, Crime, and Criminology: A Feminist Critique*. Boston: Routledge and Kegan Paul.

———. 1978. "The New Female Criminal: Myth and Reality." *British Journal of Criminology* 19:50–59.

Soper, Kate. 1990. "Feminism, Humanism, and Postmodernism." *Radical Philosophy* 55:11–17.

Stack, Carol B. 1974. *All Our Kin: Strategies for Survival in a Black Community*. New York: Harper Colophon Books.

Staples, Robert. 1973. *The Black Woman in America*. Chicago: Nelson-Hall.

Steffensmeier, Darrell J. 1978. "Crime and Contemporary Woman: An Analysis of Changing Levels of Female Property Crime, 1960–75." *Social Forces* 57:566–584.

———. 1983. "Organizational Properties and Sex-Segregation in the Underworld: Building a Sociological Theory of Sex Differences in Crime." *Social Forces* 61:1010–1032.

Sterne, Muriel W., and David J. Pittman. 1972. *Drinking Patterns in the Ghetto,* vol. 2. St. Louis: Washington University.

Straus, Robert. 1984. "The Need to Drink Too Much." *Journal of Drug Issues* 14:125–136.

Sutherland, Edwin H., and Chic Conwell. 1937. *The Professional Thief*. Chicago: University of Chicago Press.

Taylor, Charles. 1996. *Human Agency and Language: Philosophical Papers,* vol. 1. Cambridge: Cambridge University Press.

Walby, Sylvia. 1990. *Theorizing Patriarchy*. Cambridge, Ma.: Basil Blackwell.

Waldorf, Daniel. 1973. *Careers in Dope*. Englewood Cliffs, N.J.: Prentice-Hall.

Walker, Alice. 1982. *The Color Purple*. New York: Pocket Books.

Williams, Patricia. 1991. *The Alchemy of Race and Rights*. Cambridge: Harvard University Press.

Wilson, James Q., and Richard J. Herrnstein. 1985. *Crime and Human Nature*. New York: Simon and Schuster.

Winick, Charles, and Paul M. Kinsie. 1971. *The Lively Commerce: Prostitution in the United States*. Chicago: Quadrangle Books.

Workin' It

"Now it's really hard for me to hold on to that little bit of

Margaret that my mother had, that my mother raised, and still be

this drug person. . . . I'm trying to be two people at one time. You

know, I'm trying to be a decent person and a drug addict at the

same time. And I've started to believe that you have to be one way

or the other. . . . You can't straddle the fence."

Margaret

When I was growing up, my mother wanted me to grow up and meet a nice guy, marry him and have babies and be happy. I feel I disappointed her. I'm sorry if she's hurt, but I've already done that now. When I sit down and give it serious thought, I feel real bad because I know better, and because I know better, I know that she knows I know better because she taught me better. Sometimes I sit down and think about, well, maybe I need to change my life so she could at least see me in a different light before she goes. Now all I need is the. . . . How do you do this? What is the first step? What do you do first? To start changing it, you know, what do you do? Except for just trying to just do it on your own, 'cause I'm not good at that at all.

When I was growing up, I thought I wanted to be a nurse for a long time, but I never went into that. I never went that way. So when I started working, I was a secretary. I likeded that line of work, but my dreams and stuff, if I had any, I think they died. I don't know when those dreams died because, after I grew up and started working, I wasn't really working towards anything. I just went and picked up a skill and I used it. So I never really set out to become anything other than what I was being at the time.

So I wanted to be a nurse, and no, I never said I was gonna be a drug addict. What I did want to be coming up as a child was to get married and have a husband and have my own house. I did want that. I wanted to be a married person with kids, just happily married at home with my husband, living the homey type life. It's what my mother wanted too, you know. My mother thought that if you were good enough for a man to go to bed with him, then you should be good enough to marry him and have his kids, and that's how she raised us. That's not how all of us turned out to be, but that is how she raised us. To be faithful to a man. Be a good wife to him. Be a good mother.

I admired the type of person that my mother is. But when I was growing up, I didn't say that. My mother . . . seem like she wasn't aware of the bad things, you know, because she never lived in the world. She never mingled with the worldly people. So that's the only thing I would want to be different between me and my mother, to be aware of all the bad ways people can be and things that people can do to you. She told us all how to be good and how to live right, but she never told us how . . . what not living right was.

My mother is very religious. So religious. That's how she survived. That's the only thing that's been in her life since my father. See, she's obsessed with religion, but it's not a bad thing, but that's how she lives. She goes Tuesdays, Thursdays, and all day on Sundays, unless they're having a revival. Then she go every night. When I was born she did the same thing. We went Tuesdays, Thursdays, and all day Sundays, unless there was revival. When I was coming up, we had Joy Night on Saturdays. So we went on Saturdays, and if it was revival, we went every night too.

She's a Christian, you know, holy sanctified and filled with the Holy Ghost, jumping and shouting, those kinda people. She's one of them. She raised us by the Bible instead of any other kinda way. She'd tell us that we shouldn't tell lies. We shouldn't bother other people's kids. We shouldn't steal. She grew us up. My father wasn't religious at all. He didn't even believe in God—at least that's how he talked.

My mother was beyond strict. We couldn't wear pants. We couldn't dance. We couldn't listen to rock and roll. We couldn't go to the movies. We couldn't go bowling. We wore dresses all the time, even as kids. So we couldn't like jump and run in the streets. We couldn't do that because we had on dresses. And then if our dresses were up over our head, you get your behind beat, you know. You have to sit down like a lady when I was a child. We jumped a little rope, played a little hop-scotch, but that was about it. We couldn't get in the water plug, you know.

As far as I know, my mother didn't go to school at all. I don't know about my father, but I don't think he went either. My mother did domestic work, you know, washing white people's clothing and cleaning their houses and stuff like that. And then she worked on a farm a couple times picking blueberries and stuff like that.

They were born in Phillipsburg, South Carolina. My mother came to Jefferson when her and my father separated. My father never came to Jefferson, though. We came here because my oldest sister was living here.

I was six when my mother and my father separated. I don't remember much about him when we were all living together as a family. Only thing I know is what I heard. So I don't really have any feelings about the times my mother and my father lived together. But after we came up here, he used to come and visit. He would seem to be the same mean, grouchy old man that I heard about. So I was fine not having him in the house. I would rather not be with him than to be with him. He wasn't willing to take care of her or us.

My dad was an alcoholic. He drank every day. He made corn liquor. When they were together they fought all the time. They fought about my father coming home, feeling guilty 'cause he done did what he done did. And my mother would be sitting there meek and humble, and he would take it out on her or one of the kids. He just was used to find reasons to argue from what I hear. Then after they was separated, we go back down there, he still be the same way. He would find things to argue about. Argue about her taking us away. Like he didn't really care about that, you know. And he would just be the type that would get drunk and wanted to fight.

I know my father has been in jail for shooting someone, and for making liquor. Different times, of course. He shot this guy and the guy didn't die right away, but it was because of this, you know, because of the gun wound that he did die eventually. So my father got charged with homicide and went to the chain gang.

I really don't know how I felt about my father. I don't . . . I don't hate him because I don't feel no hateful hate, but I don't feel anything else either. What I hear about him, I don't know how anybody can love him. I think I was twenty-one when my father died. He had lots of illnesses. He had cancer. He was a diabetic. He had syphilis. He had a lotta diseases when he died.

Well, he was sick for a long period of time, you know. My mother had moved back down there to stay with him. He was diagnosed as terminal in the middle of the summer, and in October he passed away. When he died, I went to the funeral because he was my father. I don't remember crying, you know. He was my father only in the sense that he made me.

My mother never got into another relationship. She just went to church. I have never seen another man in my mother's house other than my brother's friends or my brother-in-law and his friends, my nephews and their friends. I don't even remember a deacon coming over for no reason at all. So even now that all the kids are gone, it's still no man coming around. There must be some kind of dark family secret because from what I hear about how bad my father treated my mother, it's like she had to do something sometime. I never heard her curse. I've never seen her do anything wrong. I mean, it was just incredible for her to be like how I describe her.

My mother raised us by the Bible, like that. She told us what was a sin and what wasn't a sin. How to treat people, treat people right, and . . . you know . . . she raised us like that, which wasn't really the real world, after I got out into it, 'cause you can't love everybody. You have to don't like somebody, okay? 'Cause if you love everybody, then everybody and things they do will be all right with you. And it's not that way. She didn't tell me about, you know, how people . . . how strong some people's minds are and how wicked some people's minds are and how some people would treat you like you're dirt and you don't have to be doing nothing to nobody. All she told me was to love everybody and treat people right and what was a sin and what wasn't a sin, and you shouldn't, you know . . . she never said what you don't let people do to you. It's just what you don't do to people, you know.

I had eight sisters and three brothers. Three sisters who are dead now, so that leaves me five sisters. Two brothers are dead. One passed away in '72, and my other brother passed away in '73. My brother got stabbed in the heart. His girlfriend stabbed him because he was cheating on her. She was charged with involuntary manslaughter and she got probation. The one that died in '73 we found him in a river. So we never knew what he died from . . . I mean, how he got in the river. They just wrote it down as suicide, 'cause they said he didn't have any bruises or anything like that.

Three of my sisters have died too. One died in '81, I think it was. One died in '82. And one died a couple years ago. Two died of cancer and the other one had lupus. One of my sisters that is living now has some kind of infection on her spine and it caused her to be paralyzed. I wasn't that close to the three sisters that died. I'm more close to the one that's ill now.

All eleven kids didn't come to Jefferson. Most of them were grown when I came up here. My mother brought . . . let's see, five girls and one boy? No, wait a minute, she brought me, Mildred, Carol, Trudy, and Tommy. She brought five of us with her. And she left Marilyn, Slim, Frank, and John Boy down there. So that's nine, and my other three sisters were already grown and married and one was living in Philadelphia, one was in New York, and one was living in Jefferson.

Well, when we came to Jefferson, we moved onto Hering Street. When we left Hering Street, we moved to Barr Street. Lots of crime. I grew up around Twenty-second and Barr. A lotta gang wars, a lotta burglaries, a lotta dope selling, a lotta dope doing. Cars and clothes, materialistic things, were important to the people in the neighborhood I lived in. When we left Barr Street, we moved to Baker Street. When we left Baker Street, we moved to Oberholzer Street, and from Oberholzer back to Barr, and then I got married out of that house.

My mother was very clean. The house was very important to her. Because we all had to do it. And we had to do it. She was also a good cook, as long as there was something to cook. You know, say, if we was doing a little bad and we had to eat something like cornbread and fatback, I don't think she enjoyed that. But when she . . . you can tell how people feel about cooking 'cause it's the meals that they make, and we always had big meals, lots of meat, lots of vegetables.

When I was coming up, she couldn't afford to dress nice. So she was more particular about how we looked than how she looked. She tried. She looked the best what she could. But we came first. If it was between her getting a pair of shoes and us having a pair of shoes, we got the shoes and she would wear a pair of my other sister's shoes, you know.

We had to wash clothes by hand. We had to mop the floors. We had to wash dishes, scrub the woodwork, ordinary chores. Nobody had they own room. So everybody had to clean up the rooms. You come out from school, you do your homework. You change your clothes and you go outside and sit on the steps or whatever, unless you're going to church, unless it was a Tuesday and church night. If it was church night, you ate and got ready for church. And when you finish eating, whoever turn it was to wash the dishes, washed the dishes. Got your school clothes ready for the next day. And that was the day. We used to have prayer meetings in the street and stuff sometimes, but that wasn't very often.

As for school, I didn't play hooky until after I went to high school, mostly when I was a senior. If I went to school and I didn't feel like staying, I went home. She asked why, I would tell her why. And that would be that.

Well, once I got suspended—I was in junior high school—'cause they told my mother that I had got drunk in school, right? Which was the truth, but because my mother raised us like she raised us, and she never seen no signs of it, she didn't believe it. And they couldn't smell anything on my breath because I had squeezed lemons and stuff, sucked lemons and stuff. So she didn't believe them, she believed me. But it was the truth. I did get drunk in school.

I didn't get into any fights in school. Hardly none until I got in junior high school. Not often at all. Maybe six or seven fights. Girls that didn't like me, 'cause I always wore dresses or something. They used to talk about me.

My older sisters went to school to see how I was doing, but my mother never went. I didn't receive bad grades. I mean, I got C's, but I never got E's and F's. I did when I got in high school in gym. I failed gym for two years. My mother didn't say nothing. I used to think up lies and tell her that I didn't want to take off my clothes in front of people when I got in high school. I really didn't feel like jumping up and down and all like that. I did used to have a lot of trouble with my stomach, which I found out later why it was, and so she didn't really jump on me about gym. Just when I got in twelfth grade.

I was disciplined sometimes with an extension cord. But she would always tell us why she was beating us. I didn't get beatings that often. Not with an extension cord, though. She might pick up a shoe and hit us, or something, but then my mother, she's real religious, plus she's countrified, all right? So she didn't understand a lot of the things we were saying. If she was helping me with my homework or something like that, like my spelling words, and I would spell the word and the word had a "w" in it, she thought I was trying to be smart 'cause she don't say "double-you." She thought I was saying "u," you know. She'd say, "dubb-yah" and "you." So she would think I'm being smart, so we got our little beatings 'cause she didn't understand. Honest mistakes, but she thought we was being smart.

The most severe non-physical discipline was when she told me I couldn't see the guy I wanted to see. She just told me she ain't want it. Like he used to come to the school and meet me and walk me home. She ain't wanna see me walking on the same side the street with him, you know. And if she did see me, in the house—"Here I come!" you know. Doing that in front of him. Stuff like that.

That really made me feel bad because I thought . . . I didn't feel like a child, you know. I felt like I was supposed to see this man because I wanted to. I loved him, you know. And I didn't feel like she would have to worry about me going to bed with him and getting pregnant 'cause I wasn't. That's not what I wanted.

I had my period when I was eleven. Well, when I got sixteen and seventeen, that's when I heard more talk about it. So when I had my period my mother didn't say anything to me. She told my older sister to give me one of them things. It was like the same way with sex. "Don't let no boys fool with you." I really wanted to carry it on a little further, but I knew what she was talking about 'cause I heard her telling my other sisters, "Don't let no boys fool with you."

But that is not the proper way. . . . When my mother was thinking I was thinking about sex, I really wasn't. But I was in love with that nigger, though. I was in love with that nigger, but I wasn't thinking about no sex. And when she didn't think I was thinking about it, that's when I did it. When she had . . . after she had used up and was letting it be like it was being, that's when I started having sex. But she always said, "If you're good enough to lay down with a man, you're good enough to marry him." And that's how I grew up.

And I couldn't hardly date him. I had to go through I don't know what just to walk down the street holding his hand. Yeah. My mother done jerked me in the house by my collar many a times for standing in the door talking to that man. Threatened to beat me up and everything. "If I see you talking to him again I'm gonna wale on your behind like I'm waling on a snake."

I never did get pregnant. So I guess that was a worry she didn't have to have. I had my first sexual experience at fifteen or sixteen. She let me go spend the night over my sister's house and then I called my boyfriend up and asked him to come over. And he told me a little lie, something about something was wrong with him, he was having trouble, and the doctor told him to try and see if he could have sex.

I didn't use any protection 'cause I didn't know. I just didn't. I didn't know where to go get it from when I first did it 'cause birth control pill wasn't that much talked about. A little couple years after that it was. A little later girls could go to the clinic and get them without their parents knowing about it and all that. But I never used birth control. My mother never told me anything about that. She just told me don't let no boys fool with you. That was her way. I learned about where babies came from on my own. From growing up, having sisters, and just common knowledge. And going to school and having hygiene classes.

What I didn't know at the time was that he had VD. He had the clap. And I did it and I got burnt, but I didn't know that till years later that I got a venereal disease from him. That's the only man that I ever had sexual intercourse with until I had to go to the hospital. And that's when I learned. I had gonorrhea for a long, long, long time and I didn't know it. So I got a pelvic infection disease from that. And I believe that's why I can never have any children.

I think my mother loved me when I was growing up, but my brother was my mother's favorite, the one that's living now. And that was because he was a little effeminate coming up, you know. So he got beat up a lot and they tell me as a kid my dad used to beat him up a lot, you know. They always said that, you know, my father didn't like my brother because he didn't look like the other fellows, the other boys in my family.

When I was growing up, I was closest to my sister Marilyn. She's a drug addict now. Well, before I knew what she was really into, she had a good job. I likeded the way she dressed. She had cute boyfriends with nice, pretty cars and she used to get dressed up all the time and go out and stay places and have fun. And she used to buy me stuff. She's about ten years older than me.

I idolized my sister Marilyn, but that died too after I learned lots of things about her. Then I didn't have any more idols. I learned that she was a drug addict all the while. She still maintained a job and everything. After the job went away and she started going to hospitals and stuff and then I was getting older, she started letting me know certain things. We shared the same bedroom. So she started telling me certain things about herself and then I stopped looking at her like I looked at her and so I didn't have any idols left. Marilyn is still a drug addict and I never, never see her. 'Cause I never go where she is and she never come where I am. I miss the closeness with my sister, but once she learned that I was a drug addict, we didn't get along anymore.

My brother, however, did everything right. He was a good child, he never was a sinner. He grew up in church and he stayed that way.

My sister Carol used to play the good child, the one that thought she was better than other people, but she did lots of bad things. You know, not bad things, but danced and partied and did those things before she gave her life to Christ. She was the only Miss Goody Two-Shoes. She played good.

And my sister Trudy, she didn't play the good child, she just simply was a good child, and she did everything right except she got pregnant before she got married, and then my mother made that right. And you know what, she's still with her husband. Yeah, her oldest kid is coming out of school this year. My mother made that right. She told him point blank, "Oh, you gonna marry her."

Well, with my two older brothers, it was hell most of the time. My one brother, oh God, he was crazy. He used to beat us up. He used to get drunk and just curse and fight and just cause all kinds of hell. Find things on fire. So we was kinda scared of him. So I guess my brother was the black sheep or the troublemaker in the family. He was sick. He was mentally ill. He couldn't help hisself. He really had a problem, really he did. But I guess you call it the "rams" when people be drinking. Just lose their mind and want to fight and stuff.

No telling what my sisters and brother are doing right now. No telling. My brother, he's a chef and he's a preacher. My sister, my baby sister, she's going to school. She going to Community College. My other sister has moved back to the South now. She's a nurse's assistant. She's going to nursing school still. And my other sister, she's a registered nurse. And my other sister, of course, she's in the hospital right now. She's sick, she's a drug addict. And my other sister's a drug addict. So they don't work at all. The one's that's in the hospital is paralyzed from doing drugs. I don't know what she did wrong but, you know, she was a mainliner too, and I don't know if she hit a nerve or something but anyway she got real sick and she's paralyzed from the outcome of her doing drugs. And my other sister, she's still on drugs. She been doing drugs ever since I been knowing her. She's still on drugs, doing good. She look all right. She's like forty-two.

I guess I wasn't supposed to know what my sisters were doing, but I did. So if someone asked whether prostitution was foreign to me when I got into it—no. I was really aware of it because I knew my sisters was doing it, you know. They might have tried to make it seem like that's not what it was, but that's what they were doing, and I was around them so I knew what they was doing. And the same way with drugs. I didn't grow up and then get into it. I grew up into it. Do you know what I mean?

I don't know what attracted me to my husband. I was a child, eleven years old. He was a nice guy. He was fourteen, and he was in high school 'cause I wasn't. Perhaps I was attracted to him because he was real black and bow-legged. And then I got to know him a little bit. He always had a job. Even as a kid, he always worked, and he just seemed like a nice guy. And then by the time I got sixteen, we got engaged. By that time I was madly in love with him 'cause he took real good care of me. I wanted to stop going to school 'cause I couldn't dress like other people and stuff like that. He stepped right in there and made sure I was dressed like other people. There was plenty of times when we didn't have the money and this man gave it to me and didn't expect me to go to bed with him 'cause he understood, you know. Made sure when I went to school I had money to spend for lunch if I didn't want the free lunches. And things like that, things that meant the world to me, you know. And he did them things.

After I got engaged, the relationship turned sexual. You know, he lied to me. He told me that the doctor told him that something was wrong with him down there. The doctor told him he had to try to have sex to see if it could happen, and I gave in. It wasn't a pleasant one. Our sexual life was the pits, to me. 'Cause he was kinda rough there, in that way. You know, if he was sucking on my breast, he would be biting and it would be hurting, you know. And his hair was rough and I would get bruises on my face from him rubbing it, you know. I mean, he wasn't trying to be rough. It was just the way he was. So mostly when we had sex, I would have sex totally for him. The pleasure I got out of it was pleasing him. He never brought me to orgasm. Never. I only experienced an orgasm through masturbating. That's the only time, that's the only way. I never reached a climax with a man till after . . . I think I was . . . I don't know how old I was but my marriage was over and everything before I ever reached a climax with a man.

He had a reputation with the girls on the street. He had plenty of girls, always had plenty girls with him. Never bothered me. Even when we got married, he had girls. It never bother me. I don't know why, but it still don't bother me.

I got on my own when I got married. My mother was neither-nor. It was all left up to me. She cared, but she didn't tell me to get married or not to get married. I was eighteen and he was twenty-one. Before I turned nineteen, I was separated. I guess he just didn't want to be married. Started beating me up and all this kinda mess. So that's why we separated.

He hadn't done that before. He was a heavy drinker. . . . And I harassed him a lot. I didn't know a lot then. So I didn't understand a lotta things he did. He stayed out a lot and he drank a lot, and to me that was really, really, really bad. He did do some drugs, but mostly he drank. And at the time, I grew up in the church, so that was really bad to me. So I stayed on him, stayed on him, stayed on him, and that's probably why he beat me up. We separated. He left. Then I was all on my own. I guess being alone frightened me most when I was growing up. 'Cause I just never was by myself. There was always somebody around. I never did like to be alone. I still don't.

Our marriage ended slowly. He never really moved out 'cause he never took his clothes. So he always felt like he could come back, right? But he never really came back either. And then when he found out I was doing drugs, he just . . . that was it. Never got a divorce. He was fine except for the beating me up part and he stayed out an awful lot.

Him and I never went out, and I didn't really hang out. I stayed at home mostly 'cause that was all that I knew until, like I said, until we got separated. That's when I started socializing with different types of people. So I got in the fast life after my marriage . . . you know, after we got separated. Up until I was eighteen I was in church doing the proper things. Then I got married and everything changed. Well, I stopped going to church and I started going out to parties and clubs and stuff like that. I started seeing other guys and then, couple years later, I started doing drugs.

Oh, well, when I first started doing drugs, I was about twenty-one. Seriously doing drugs, you know. Shooting and stuff. Before I got married I didn't even drink. In my marriage I did a little drinking. Creme de cocoa and milk, things like that. Took a diet pill every now and then, smoked a joint every now and then. But nothing serious until about twenty-one.

When my husband left me, right, about a year later my job moved to North Carolina. I had oil heat and I couldn't afford to buy my oil. So there was this girl over my house named Jackie. I was cold. I was boiling pots of water and stuff like that, had on a lotta clothes. So she told me, she said, "If you wanna keep warm, I got some monster." She said, "If you put some of this in your coffee, you'll be hot." I put some in my coffee and I was sweating.

So that's when I started doing drugs. I started doing speed then. Then time went on and I got another job at OIC and I was working, but I still was doing monster. Although I had a job, I still was doing monster, but I was just snorting it and drinking it.

I worked at OIC for a year and then I resigned. I resigned to go down there to be with my father before he died. So I resigned and by this time I'm twenty-one. So I goes down there and I stays down there for a while, you know. He dies, I come back home. I stayed in South Carolina about three weeks. I didn't have nothing to come back to. I still had my apartment, okay? 'Cause I move from Quincy Street and I moved down to High and Ridge to an apartment. My husband still gave me money. He paid a little bit of rent for me, stuff like that, but he stopped 'cause he found out I was doing drugs. That's when I just . . . everything just started changing. I didn't have a job. I started, you know, turning tricks.

So when my husband left I started hanging out with people that . . . wild girls, you know. To me they were wild. They hung around a lot of men. They used to smoke angel dust and trip and stuff like that. I never did smoke angel dust but I started doing the drugs and I started drinking and, you know, turning tricks. I really don't know if it's because I was hanging out with them or not. I don't know if I woulda did it anyway or what.

There was this girl named Dawn and this girl named Elaine. Dawn had about five kids and she . . . just like I say, she stayed in the street a lot. She didn't take care of her kids. She didn't take care of her home, and just spent the checks on her, doing drugs and stuff like that. Dawn lived on the block that I moved on when I first got married. But I never did socialize with her until after me and my husband had broke up. Then I, you know . . . I started socializing with her. And Elaine lived up the street on the same block. She had one child. She took a little better care of herself and her child. I don't know if it was only because she had one or what. But they dressed real nice and they looked real good, but they just didn't take care of their kids, you know. And those are about the only two people that I hung with for a while then.

I grew up around drug addicts. My sister . . . my older sister's a drug addict, my older brother was a drug addict, the other one was a alcoholic, so the drug scene wasn't new to me at all. It was like the doors opened . . . all I had to do was just walk right through it. And with an open door, you'll normally . . . you'll walk right through it.

I realized that it wasn't all that bad from what I could see. They still took care of theyself. They still had nice clothes. They still kept their hair done. Now, my brother . . . I never wanted to be an alcoholic, you know. I mean, I never wanted to be a drug addict either, but I don't think I would ever become a . . . well, he was a wino instead of an alcoholic, you know, he didn't . . . he stopped caring altogether. But my sisters, they didn't stop caring. So it didn't look all that bad to me.

I can't say that I was forced into it 'cause I really wasn't, and nobody pressured me about it 'cause nobody did. Whatever I did, I did it because I wanted to do it. But I didn't set out to be strung out on drugs. But after you do it, you know, first you do it casually, but there's no casual drug addict. Then you're doing it . . . if you do it often enough, it becomes a way of life before you know it. And that's what happened to me. When I stopped snorting and drinking it and I started mainlining it, it became a way of life before I knew it. Then when I woke up, you know, in the morning, I didn't feel right, okay?—my body didn't feel right—and then one day I realized I didn't feel right 'cause I didn't have no drugs in it, you know. So you go get some drugs and it goes on like that. Before you knew it, ten years done passed by and you're a drug addict and you're strung out and you're a real live drug addict now. And you never knew you was becoming a drug addict till you became one.

Then, it was monster. I never did use heroin. Yeah, started mainlining monster at twenty-one. I did that until the fad wore out, and that was like after I went downtown. Well, they call it meth in the Metro Center. I think I still did meth for a couple years. Yeah, the fad changed. All the people in North Jefferson was getting busted and stuff, the meth labs and stuff, when it was hard to find. And when you found some, it didn't get you . . . you got high but it didn't last. Like you could do a twenty dollar bag of meth—not even a twenty dollar bag, you could do a dime bag of meth—and you stayed up for two or three day, all right? That's how we, you know, that's how we stayed up and made our little money turning tricks. Was in good spirits and not all worn out and stuff, right?

And then I couldn't find it no more and I was slowing down from turning the tricks 'cause I was leaving from downtown and stuff. And then I just went up North Jefferson one day and everybody was buying coke so I bought some coke. And I did it and I still didn't like it that much but it . . . it took the edge off of not having meth. And I didn't never like cocaine. If somebody give me cocaine, I'd give it back. But now I'd take all you can give me, right?

Cocaine I've been familiar with for about seven years, I guess. But cocaine is much, much different than meth, you know. This cocaine thing is much worse because you get such a little bit for your money and it lasts such a little bit of time. A five dollar bag of meth would last you all day . . . the high will. You take a five dollar bag of cocaine and you ain't even satisfied with that one hit.

The first time I used cocaine I felt this rush. Meth is a milder rush. Cocaine hits you like . . . boom!—like that. It hits you real hard and real fast. With meth you feel it coming on. It's ṣmooth, but it lasts so much longer than cocaine. Meth is more mellower. You get a rush in your head, but you can stand it. You get a rush from cocaine, you have to sit down for a minute.

When I first started using meth, I didn't ever worry about becoming a dope fiend. Didn't worry about becoming addicted either. I didn't feel as though I was addicted until I started doing cocaine, really. That's true. Sure, I craved for meth but it didn't bother me like this here stuff bothers me. So now that I'm not doing meth anymore and I'm doing cocaine, and I see the difference in how I feel now, now I think, "Cocaine! I'm strung out on cocaine!" I did meth, and because I mainlined it for lots of years, I guess I was addicted to it, but I didn't started making money before I started doing drugs, okay? Now I turn tricks to get drugs.

I was turning tricks anyway. I started out turning tricks for survival. To pay bills and stuff. Now I turn tricks only to buy cocaine. In the beginning I bought the meth to help me stay up so I could do what I was doing. But then I was living in the best hotels downtown, wearing the best clothes. I was doing those kinda things with my money. Now, all I do with the money is buy cocaine. Then I was working. I got up and went to work because that's what I did. Now I get up and go do it 'cause I wanna hit.

I didn't learn any skills from anyone. When I started really, really turning tricks—I mean, for money—I went downtown on my own 'cause there wasn't no money noplace around. You know, I have been with different guys and stuff, they were selling drugs and stuff like that, but it was never mine. So I went downtown, on Eleventh and Mill. You know, sat around, watched what was going on. And then I had one friend down there who was a guy, and he told me, you know, you gotta fix yourself up, buy you a wig, buy you these kinda clothes. So I did that and I started making money. I was twenty-three then.

I didn't start turning tricks until I was like two years into my addiction. I was past twenty-one when I went downtown, about twenty-two, twenty-three, something like that. I met this guy down there. He had girls, but he was a drug dealer. He was a drug dealer and that's why he had girls, because he had the drugs. He wasn't like a pimp. No. No, he rode a bike and wore sneakers and stuff like that. So we became friends. Later on we became more than friends and I was sorry about that. I hung around him a lot and I seen the girls—they was giving him money—and how they dressed and how they looked and how much money they was giving him, so I learned like that. And then I started turning tricks and then, 'bout three, four years after that, me and him started going together. He broke my jaw and I was very sorry I ever met him. But for years I was just downtown, Eleventh and Mill. Staying there from hotel to hotel, making money. Then I left Jefferson and I went to Charleston, West Virginia, and I worked down there some. Then I went to Florida. I went a few places, turning tricks, just working that way and doing drugs.

Turning tricks came natural. That came naturally, you know. Men always was hitting on me and it just came natural. You know, wasn't nothing that you had to know how to do that you didn't already know, that a woman don't already know. Except for when you call yourself a professional. Then you have to learn how to suck, you know, things real good and stuff like that. How to make them hurry up and reach a climax and stuff like that.

I've exchanged sex for drugs. Sure. Well, this guy that I know, he's a dealer and he wanted some head. So he gave me an eight-ball, which all the time they don't offer you that much, but he gave me one. I've been knowing him since I was a child. That's probably why. He gave me a eight-ball and I gave him a blow job. Other times, guys done gave me like four bags, three bags, and I done gave them a blow job. These are five dollar bags and I done gave them a blow job, but that's mostly what I do. I don't really fuck a lot. That's what I mainly do is give blow jobs.

It usually happens in a car. In their house. Or we have this little area where we go where you can't lay down or nothing but you do stand up and it is outdoors but nobody can see you 'cause it's real tall trees and stuff around. And you might go back there since I'm only giving a blow job and it's all right to me. It's not a park. It's like a lot, a vacant lot. It's an empty lot. So you go up in there, and it's just like I say, they stand up over top of you. So I can go in there, but most of the times it be in their car, or in their house, or in somebody else's house.

If I'm turning a trick and I know he got more money, I might take it. I might dip . . . dip in his pockets. I'll do that in a minute. And if I'm desperate enough, I'll do it to somebody that knows me and I know I'm gonna see again. But usually they be understanding about it, you know. They'll tell me, "Well, I know you wanted that hit that bad, but give me my money back." Then I'll pay them back when I get it, you know, so that's probably why I ain't get hurt yet, 'cause I have done that to people I know. Sometimes I be feeling safer with doing it to somebody that I know than doing it to a stranger, 'cause you don't know if you gonna get caught at that, you know.

One time I took a couple hundred dollars from this man out of his house, but he was telling me he only had five dollars. I went upstairs, he had fifteen one hundred dollar bills on the bed. I supposed I shoulda took it all, you know. But I couldn't get outta the house with all of it 'cause he wouldn't let me. He had a shotgun. So I just peeled a little bit off and put the rest of it under the bed. Told him that's where it was at the whole time, on the floor, right? But you shouldn't treat people that way. If you got . . . least he coulda gave me twenty dollars. You got fifteen hundred dollars there and you gonna tell me five dollars? Yeah, I took it! Old man! A old man!

Some of the guys are really bummy. But you know what? A lotta guys that look bummy, they don't be stinking or nothing. You know, you check their penis and stuff and, because that's what I do is give blow jobs, I could tell just before I get too close to it whether or not I wanna do it, you know. Most times I carry through with it. If I say I'm gonna do it, I'll do it even if I got to go home with them and wash them up and stuff like that. 'Cause if you stink, that doesn't mean you got no disease. No. But you got more of a chance of having one than a person that's well kept. If I can't stay down there, if the odor is so bad so I can't breathe . . . where you got to breathe through your nose, I can't do it. I just couldn't do it.

I try to use rubbers. If you could be slick enough to put the rubber in your mouth and just grab their dick and put the rubber on it while you're doing it, like that, then you all right. You know, you put it in your mouth and put it on their penis and while you're doing it up and down, you know, you just slide the rubber on there. They don't feel it 'cause it's all wet. It's all wet, and you hold it down the bottom where the tight part is. If they're real big then you can't get it on there.

But lots of guys, even though AIDS is going around, they don't want to use no rubber. They refuse to use a rubber. And then it be hard. I'm not gonna lie. It's real hard. It's hard as hell to walk away from a guy that got ten dollars or five dollars in his pocket and want it real bad and only thing stopping you is a rubber. You want that money so bad. And sometimes I'll go for it. Most of the times Shaft'll be around. I'll tell him, you walk up on me . . . give me a chance enough to get the money, you come and get me, you know. Be times like that. Then they might get outta hand, and then I'm thinking they gonna fuss or fight and I have to give their money back. But Shaft will come up and say, "What you doing?" Acting like he don't know what I'm doing, and stuff like that.

I'm living in my apartment, eighteen hundred block of Bartlett Street. It's between Cumberland and Fisk, Nineteenth and Twentieth. I've been there I guess ever since the first of the year. I don't really like the neighborhood there. It's all ran down and stuff, you know. It's a bad neighborhood. A lotta drugs in the neighborhood, a lotta breaking in people's houses, a lotta violence and stuff. It's okay living there as long as you mind your business, I guess. I'm living with Shaft there.

Shaft is lazy. He don't like to do anything. He's used to that, though. It's how he was brought up. He never had to do anything so he still don't do anything. He gets a check and that's about it. So, to me, I'm just giving more than I should be giving for him just to be a man of mine—he's not my husband or anything like that—you know, for us not to have any kind of commitments. I'm doing really more than I ever should think about doing because today or tomorrow he can walk out of my life and there's nothing I can say or do about it. You know, 'cause I don't have any . . . we don't have any obligations to each other.

Why do I do it? I don't know. Every day I say, "He can leave if he want to." But it never happens, he never leaves. We argue a lot, fight a lot. I guess it's just 'cause we don't . . . neither one of us have any inspiration or motivation to do anything else.

I don't think it's a good relationship. Both of us on drugs, you know.

That's all we do with our money. I manage to pay the rent and I never pay the whole amount, but I manage to pay enough so I can stay there, keep the lights on, and buy a little bit of food, you know. Mostly we pay rent and stuff and buy food with my money. With his money, he does what he wanna do with it, and what he usually wants to do with it is spend it all. So that's how it goes, and I have to go out and turn tricks and he acts like he don't know what I do but he knows what I do 'cause where else would I be getting money from?

I feel like he's less than a man and I treat him the same way. I have no respect for him. Not at all. I don't treat him bad but I treat him like a person. . . . If we're walking down the street and if I knew I could go and get some money from the guy over here, I would say, "Excuse me," and I'd go get the money and it's like that. If you don't want me to do that, then you get the money. But he's not getting any money so ain't no such thing as disrespecting you. I'm disrespecting myself by having you in my life, you know.

He's just lazy. He's not afraid to hustle. He's not afraid to do anything. Don't let that fool you. He's just lazy and don't wanna do it. When you robbing another person, you can go to jail. When you put your hand on other people, you can get locked up. He don't mind doing that. He doesn't mind doing that at all. He doesn't mind taking things from his mother, stealing from her. You can get locked up doing that. He doesn't mind doing that either, but he knows that his mother's not gonna do anything to him and I'm not gonna do anything to him, and that's why he does it.

I think the man is to take care of the home. As far as intimacy, I think however you were when you were going together that made you wanna marry this person, you know, if they were affectionate with you, if you hug and kiss a lot or if they buy you flowers or always send you cards or pay you compliments or whatever, never change that. If the woman wants to be home, cooking and cleaning and this kind of mess, then she should. I believe if she wants to work in the home, as long as there's no children involved, then the home is their responsibility, the cooking, the cleaning, everything, it's their responsibility. I don't believe in no such thing as a woman supposed to take care of her man. I mean, not like I do with Shaft . . . not take care of him like you got a child. You gotta cook . . . you know, cook dinner a certain time and clean up this way, you know. I don't get into that. I never did. See, I'm prejudiced. I do believe that a man should. . . . I have to put it this way. If they're married, I believe that the bills are the man's responsibility if he can do it. A woman works 'cause she wants to, that's how I look at it. A male works because he has to. I don't know if that's right or wrong, but that's the way I think. That's all I've known. A man works 'cause he has to. A woman works 'cause she wants to.

When I met Shaft—oh, God—I was in one of the worstest places I ever lived in in my life and I should have known from that. I was living on this dead-end street. The whole block got two houses on it that people live in. So I was sitting on this little shanty out there where they used to sell barbecue and stuff at. I was sitting out there. He walks up to me one day, say the magic words, "You get high?" I say, "What?" "You get high?" I say, "Uhm-uhm, wanna get high?" "Sure, why not?" That was it. From then on, we started being "get high" buddies for like a couple months.

He didn't move in right away, because I wasn't living all by myself then. I was living with this other guy, but we wasn't going together or anything like that. I was paying my way there. So Shaft wanted to come over there one day and the guy didn't really like him, right? So this guy I was staying with . . . he worked on a farm. He was a drinker so he didn't like drugs that much. He was putting up with me 'cause I was paying the money. So Shaft wanted to talk to me one night. I didn't wanna talk to him. So he tried to break in the house, right? And the man cut him from here all the way around there, cut him up real bad. Cut him across the forehead and on the ear.

He was really hurting, you know. He had something like a hundred and something stitches. He got cut up pretty bad, but he brought it on hisself. You know, he went and got a stick and tried to pry the door open. He was trying to get in the house 'cause he wanted me, and I wasn't coming out. He told me to come out, and I wasn't coming out 'cause we had already argued. So I told him I was going in. It was only gonna lead into a fight, so I went on in the house. He kept calling my name, calling my name. Now, while he's outside, I'm hearing him tell these people, "I'm gonna fuck that bitch up." I'm hearing him say this. So I'm supposed to go out then? I said, "If he come in here, this is your house, you do what you supposed to do."

Now that's what he did. He went and got a stick and he pried that man's door open, so the man told him, "If you come in here, I got something for you." He came in anyway. Then he start arguing with the man. So the man just cut him. And he hollers to me, "Margaret, get this man off of me!" Honey, hush! He brought that right on hisself. I ran and got the police. But I wasn't trying to get in the middle of no knife. I ran and got the police, by that time.

Oh, he scared me so bad. He was having blood running all down his face, looking like Halloween, right? "I'm not going nowheres without getting me a hit." I couldn't believe it. This man is bleeding to death. "I'm not going nowheres till I get me a hit." Then I have to run around try to get five dollars real quick before this man bleeds to death. He got the hit, went straight to the hospital. I couldn't believe it. I was so scared, I thought he had really lost his mind. I'm telling him, "Right, if you hurt like that, how you gonna think about a hit?" But that was all he was thinking about.

So I moved out. That's when I lived with my sister and I told her I'd only be there for a couple weeks and then I found a place of my own and that's when he moved in. He moved in my house. So we've lived together ever since January.

I didn't know him, I didn't know him in the beginning. So the bad things that I know now, I didn't know then. He was attractive to me. I likeded the way he looked and he kept hisself real neat. I'm looking at him and I'm saying, "Well, to be a drug addict, he seems to keep hisself up pretty good," you know. He buy clothes. He lookeded nice. So I . . . well, that's all you got . . . what else you got going for you? I already know he's a drug addict so he don't have no job, you know. He seemeded to have schooling 'cause he talked all right and we got along pretty good. So if I was gonna be intimate with someone, I'd rather be with someone that I was attracted to physically. And that's what it was. And now I'm not attracted to him at all anymore. But I mean, you know, he's still "Shaft" to me. Like I called him by his real name after we got intimate, but now I'm calling him "Shaft" again. So that just shows you that that's gone away. It's wearing thin.

I just wish he could just get up and do something sometimes. And then he gets violent, too, and he don't have a right to. I mean, he gets violent over things that don't belong to him. He gets violent over things that belong to me. Like my money, you know. He gets violent over that. I'm *supposed* to do things for him, you know. If I'm doing something for myself, I'm *supposed* to do it for him too. If I'm buying me anything . . . I mean, from a pair of shoes to a hat, if I'm getting it, he's supposed to get it too. Not if you don't get the money.

In the beginning it was all right. He was hustling. He was getting money. I don't know. He would have a hundred dollars here, a few dollars there, and then it wasn't a strain on me, you know. 'Cause he was paying. It was never enough for him to take care of me with, but it would add to it, so that was a help, but then all that changed. I guess when he seen that I would go out and get some money and come back and break down with him, that just made him say, "Well, I'm not gonna do anything anymore." That wasn't my reasons for doing it. My reasons for doing it was because I am a drug addict myself—me, myself, and I—and I don't think nobody have to take care of my habit, you know. I wouldn't put that on nobody 'cause that's a burden, you know. It's a burden to me myself and it's my habit.

Yeah, well, most of the other relationships I had have been with drug dealers. So that wasn't a problem, but I still made money and I paid for the drugs. Whenever I spent money, I got more than my money's worth, you know. I just gave him a little money and he gave me a lotta drugs. That meant I had a very large habit. That's right. That's why it's such a burden to try to take care of someone else. And he's been on drugs for twenty years. So his habit is far worse . . . greater than mine. Where two people might get high off a hundred dollars, it's gonna take us like two or three. And that's a lotta money to be having . . . to make out in the street.

We share drugs and that's it. And besides each other there is no recreation in our lives. The whole world revolves around drugs. Drugs, drugs, drugs. Do I have friends? Drug addicts. They might come over to our place or we go over their place, or whatever.

So in the beginning he would sort of share the responsibility in getting high, but then the burden more or less fell on me. Yeah. I don't understand. . . . It's still that way. He still don't go get money. Because I'm forced to sort of play that role, I don't have much respect for him and he don't have much for me. Because I turn tricks. But it's probably both. We're fine as friends. When he wants something other than friendship outta me, I tell him just like this, "I fuck for money and you spends that. Now I ain't got to fuck you, too."

But he still fights me though. He still does that. We fight about my money. My drugs. My whatever. That's the only time we fight. When he gets a little check, we have a nice day. Whenever I get money, we have a miserable time. When he gets his check, he shares it with me. Well, I can't lie on him. He's bought me a couple pair of pants. He bought me a pair of boots last year. But other than that, it's about it.

Fights start because he would ask for something and I would say, "No." And then he would try to take it. Here a typical example. One time I came home with only enough drugs for me. But that was all I had. That was all I could get. He's in the bed. "You don't have enough for me?" "No." "Oh, you don't?" "No." Bam! But he waits till after the drugs get in me. All right, then I'm all . . . really hysterical then. Then I'm tripping more than I would be tripping . . . especially when he's ready to hit me or something. When you high, you don't know how you gonna act. So I really goes off, and then we be fighting for hours 'cause I'm really scared now 'cause I'm high. More scareder than I would be if I wasn't high, you know. Jumps up out of the bed and hit me right here. This is the last time. See this scar? Hits me right there. Busts my eye wide open just because I didn't have enough.

When we rumble, I'll hit him with my fist. Then I pick up anything I see. Then we fighting. Rolling on the floor fighting. That's right. Rolling on the floor fighting, rolling, breaking down the beds, breaking down the chairs, falling all over everywhere. That fight lasted until I found out I was bleeding. That's when I ran away, you know. I felt this warm stuff running down my face, then I looked in the mirror and I seen all this blood and I ran away. Went to the hospital. They didn't put no stitches in it. They just patched it up. Well, I called the police. Then they took him to the precinct. They told me they was gonna keep him 'cause he had a bench warrant. Half an hour later, he was right back, came back home. Everything fine, like nothing ever happened. He apologized once or twice, but who wants to hear it when you bleeding and stuff.

Yeah, in the beginning, I had that dumb thought in my mind that, you know, if the man slaps you, you just take it. I don't feel that way anymore. But if I still wanted him in that way, I probably wouldn't feel that way. If I wanted him, I probably would take more than I take now. But I don't care nothing about him that way no more, as being my man and stuff like that. So if he try to hurt me, I'm gonna try to kill him. And that's a shame, but it's like that.

Honey, we argue every other day, but, fighting, we fight about two or three times a month. There's gonna be a bruise to let somebody know that they've been hit. Drugs is the thing that upsets us, period. It's never nothing other than drugs. We don't argue about nothing except money, which is one and the same. That's all we argue about. He'll put jealousy in there as the reason, but it's never that.

Afterwards he say, "I'm sorry." Well, we used to have sex. To me that's like raping somebody, you know. I don't like that neither, but it's happened a couple times. Once we had a real bad argument and he wanted to have sex. Not a real bad argument—we fought. He wanted to have sex, and when I gave in, then he said, "I don't want you now." I'm saying, "What?" "I did want you when I asked but I don't want you now." And that really, really hurted me. That really, really hurted my feelings. And so after that, if we fighting, we fighting. Just have to wait till a week or two weeks or whatever it is till I'm, you know, feeling like we could do it.

Most of the time after the fights, he'll lay down and go to sleep, and I'll sit up or I'll sit on the steps. When it's warm out, I'll sit on the steps until I get sleepy, or I'll go to one of the speakeasies and get a bottle of wine and drink it and go to sleep. The next day he wake up and he acting like ain't nothing happen, but all inside of me, it's still there. It ain't going nowhere. I'm act normal, but I'm still feeling the way that I feel.

Well, when I was married, fighting was killing me. That's why it didn't last very long, 'cause it was killing me. Not my physical body but my inner self. It was killing me. But you know what, after I started doing drugs, all that changed. I could take a whipping like nothing. Me and a guy like Shaft we could fight, like we do fight now. It bothers me when it's happening and I still keep it inside me, that he did these things to me, but I can go on with the same guy. And he's not dead yet and I'm not dead yet, you know. I ain't tried to kill him yet, you know. I did try to get him locked up once.

You know it doesn't affect me the same way as it affected me when I wasn't a drug addict and I was getting beat up. I just couldn't understand why I was getting beat up, although I was nagging a man, my husband. I didn't think I was nagging then 'cause I just wanted the best for him. That's how I was looking at it. That's all I wanted for myself and him as well. Now, I realize that I am a drug addict, and I do . . . not that I'm supposed to get beat 'cause I'm a drug addict, but this is the kind of things that happen to people like me, you know. This is the kind of lifestyle that most people are used to living.

The worst fight I've ever had with a man was when I got my jaw broke. I was downtown then with the guy that was such good friends of mine. I got with him and he broke my jaw. He said I was being too nice. I never did understand that. But he was at this hotel with this girl and I went around there and all I did was ask him what time he was coming home. That was bad. To him I came 'round there to catch him doing this, but that wasn't why I came there. How was I 'posed to know he was there with her, you know? But in his mind, I came there for that purpose, to find something, you know, that he was doing wrong. Hit me with his fist and broke my jaw. He's not a big guy but he's strong. He's muscular like, you know.

I stayed in the hospital from like January to June because it kept getting infected. I mean, my face was messed up. I came out once and had to go right back because he hit me again in the same place and I had to go right back. So they just said, "Well, we gonna keep you here because we have to put a piece of metal in here." They operated on my face three times, trying to set it back so it would grow, you know, where it be normal, and it still not straight, but it's better than I ever expected to see myself 'cause my face was totally, I mean, you know, it was . . . I mean, you know, it was twisted. It was messed up.

Then I kept . . . people were still bringing me drugs at the hospital, and I didn't know long as you do drugs that you won't heal. I didn't know that. Then one day, the doctor say, "Are you still doing drugs?" And I say, "Yeah." He say, "As long as you do drugs, you're not gonna heal. We might as well send you home." I said, "Don't send me home, not with my face like this. Not with my face like this. I won't do the drugs." I stopped doing the drugs. . . . That's another time I stopped doing the drugs. Then I started healing up. They put a hole under there to drain the infection and stuff. But my face was really . . . I didn't even know myself when I looked in the mirror 'cause it was all, you know . . . all this up here was twisted around, you know. It was just all twisted.

It wasn't no way I could make money then, you know, but I tried. I went out there wired up and everything and it was real difficult for me then. I had a nice apartment and I lost that 'cause I couldn't pay the rent, you know. And I didn't want him back, right? So I didn't go home. I didn't go to my mother's 'cause I didn't go when I was well, I wasn't going then neither. But I made it . . . I made out all right. I had a few tricks that was relatives of mine and they took care of me. When you become a prostitute, your tricks is your best friends, you know.

My tricks sort of helped me through that very difficult period. That's right. They're the only ones that did. My sister came to see me one time in the hospital and that was that. My tricks helped and other drug addicts who I helped get on their feet and other guys that I helped get started, like they mighta needed a thousand dollars to buy their first package, helped me. I mighta gave them five hundred to help them out. They never forgot me and I appreciate things like that. They never forgot me when I was down and out. They came, you know.

Besides my husband I've never been in a relationship with someone who I could say I really loved. So I really don't know what love is. I wouldn't mind having a man that didn't do drugs, that worked for a living. Perhaps he's an ex-drug addict, 'cause then he would understand, you know. If he never did drugs, he would never understand a person that do do drugs. You never felt the way they feel so you can't understand it. But if you've been on drugs, then you can understand somewhat. I'm not saying that you have to go along with it, but you would understand. So I think I would like to have a man that's been on drugs before but has recovered, not only because he could understand me, but then it's something to look up to, you know.

If I wasn't a drug addict, I don't know what kind of man I would want.

Probably a stiff-necked man. You know, real proper one, one that didn't do anything but go to work and buy nice things and stuff like that. Real square. If I was in recovery, . . . I don't know if it's true or not, but I've been around a whole lot of people that's been on drugs and not on it anymore, they still keep some of their dope fiend ways. There's still something about them that you can tell, if they don't do drugs, they used to do drugs. There's something, you know, it's something, and so I guess I'll always have that trait from now on. I would hope the person that I would be with would be able to understand that, like I said. Only way to understand that is to have a whole lot of knowledge about drug addicts or you've been one yourself. And not many people favor drug addicts.

I do like black, real dark-skinned guys and bow-legged guys, but I have more physical attraction to females than I do to males. And I like nice-looking girls. Girls that wear dresses and heels and things like that. I might see a guy and he's cute, black and bow-legged, but he don't do that, you know, that little thing, that little tingle. I don't get that with guys, but looking at some women, I get that.

I would consider myself bisexual 'cause I have been with a woman before. Girls make you feel different. Although this one woman, we fought a lot, too. But I feel better as a all-around person, I feel better. I do. I do better when I'm with a woman than when I'm with a man. I don't know why. I guess 'cause men don't really like me, see. They really don't. They act like they do until they get me, and then once they got me, they act like they hate me. And that's the truth. So I don't know if I bring that out in them or if that's just how they are.

Oh, I was grown, fully grown and separated and everything from my husband when I had my first relationship with a woman. In my twenties. Well, this is when I was living around there at Quincy Street. She was living around that way and I met her around there. And I felt like I wanted to be with her. She let me know how she felt and everything. And I did it. So I met her by just being in the neighborhood, speaking, saying hello to each other. Then I started going over there all the time. She was having this girl named Regina babysit for her all the time and I used to go over there with Regina to watch the kids and stuff. And she told me she was gay, and I was interested.

And so we started being friends and then one day she kissed me and it went on like that. My family knew. I told my family and everything.

So give me the woman! It just feels better! Everything about it is better. Ain't nothing going up in you, making you uncomfortable. All right? It's just your body and her body and it feels better. It's softer. When she touch you, ain't nothing hurt, nothing at all hurts. There's nothing that's gonna give you any kind of discomfort, any kind of pain, any kind of "Oh, you gotta do that." If she's like sucking your tittie, you don't feel like she's biting you. She's use her mouth and not her teeth. It's just all around better.

Do I think of myself as being gay? I don't know what to consider myself. That happened once in my life, and I haven't practiced it since then. Although there have been times when I was in the street—not like I am now, before I got strung out, when I was downtown working—it's been plenty of times when men wanted to see two women, and that was no problem, you know. Even right now, if a guy spend enough money, he wants to see two women, it's no problem with me. I guess I would consider myself bisexual because I do still have relationships with men. And although it's the same way with a male or female, it's hard to find a woman that's a square, that doesn't do drugs, that would take time to be with you if you strung out on drugs, especially female. They seem to have stronger feelings about that than men do.

I don't know any homosexual men that's drug addicts. I know a few lesbians though. Drug users treat them all right, but the guys don't like them 'cause . . . 'cause they be saying she thinks she's a man, you know, and because half of they manhood is already taken away by the drugs, . . . that really intimidates them.

I only started drinking like here lately, like a year or so. I never really drank. If I went out to a bar or something, I might have ordered, like I said, a creme de cocoa and milk, but I never got high off the alcohol, you know. Then I did diet pills. Popped a few diet pills here and there. I smoked joint a little bit. But when I started doing drugs is when I started drinking and snorting that monster. So from drinking and snorting that monster, I started shooting up. I started mainlining 'cause I moved from one place to another. The next place I moved, the people didn't snort. They was banging.

First time I banged I was over this . . . it's a whole family that lives in this one house, right? It was a lotta kids and everything, but we used to go in the basement. I was still drinking it and snorting it, right? So then I was watching everybody do it. Banging. I told Stella . . . say, "Stella. Hit me." It's no problem. No questions asked. Nothing. Right away she hit me.

Then like a week later I was home and this guy came over my house and I wanted him to hit me 'cause I didn't know how to do it in the beginning, right?. . . . There's lots of kinds of syringes, but I had the ones they call these buffalo things, right? They real short but they real fat. By me not knowing a lot about this stuff, I didn't know that what you had in a little skinny, regular syringe, when you put it in the big works, it look like you ain't got nothing in there. But it can be a whole lot. It just look like a little bit 'cause it's in a fat thing. So the guy asked me for something, I told him, "Naw. Look at all that I got." I mean, it was like this, but it was still a whole lot in those fat syringes. Said, "No. This is all I got." I said, "You gonna hit me?" Boy, when he hit me with that shit, he ran it straight in. I heard bells ringing. I couldn't see, and this went on for like a hour. I got in the shower just so I could, you know, bring myself around and stuff. And he told me, "See, that's how you get kilt." That's what he told me, "That's how you get kilt. You be greedy. That's how you die." But I didn't know.

So ever since then I got me a pair of works. I went in my room. I put a stocking around my arm. I look for that vein. I found it. I went in it, and I was hitting myself ever since. That's how he taught me. You're supposed to hit your own fucking self, especially if you don't wanna give nobody nothing for doing it for you, you know. 'Cause if you don't wanna pay them, they might fuck you up.

So over the course of a week or two I learned how to mix it up, draw it up, and put it in. This is with the monster. It's pretty much the same with all drugs you do except for now, with this cocaine they selling, you got to cook all this cut off of it because the cut is what was making people sick—these different cuts they put in them—so usually I cook as much of the cut off of it as I can.

How many hits do I take like during the course of a day? A day? Oh, boy, many as I can get, but I'd say about nine, ten, and would have spent about fifty, sixty dollars, and that's just for me. There wouldn't be any time between the first shot and the second shot if I got five dollars in my pocket. If I could get it all at one time, it would be enough to satisfy me. Now with this cocaine I want a drink after I do it because I be feeling real jittery and you be nervous and anxious, you know. So you drink some wine and it'll calm you down and mellow you out, or take a drink of any kind of strong liquor. I'd rather wait till I'm not gonna shoot up no more to drink or I'll drink because I don't have any more to shoot up.

After I shoot up, it lasts about five or ten minutes, really. You know, the rush that you get from it. But there's stuff they selling nowadays, I don't know what they putting in it. It makes you bug a little bit. Like I never bug like that. Stare in one place for a long time, stare one way or just be looking down on the ground. I never did that till I started doing cocaine here lately. And then I noticed that it'll last for like fifteen or twenty minutes. You be realizing that you looking like that, but you can't stop. Yeah, you schitz longer than the high lasts. As a matter of fact, you don't schitz while you rushing, you know. While you feeling the rush, you feeling the rush, then after the rush go, you start schitzing.

I don't wake up wanting drugs 'cause I don't usually wait till I want them. Like there's a routine. I usually just go on and get it. I feel cotton-mouth though. I gets up early in the morning. I get up about eight or nine o'clock, sometimes earlier than that—I been babysitting for three weeks so now I get up six o'clock, okay?—but before that I'd get up at eight or nine o'clock 'cause I can't sleep. I have my first shot about twelve. I might eat breakfast and I won't eat no more until nighttime.

So the routine is get up, watch the morning stories—I watch "Santa Barbara"—eat, then I might watch "Wheel of Fortune." Okay? Then that other word game, you know, the "Family Feud" thing, watch that one. And by twelve o'clock, either if I didn't . . . if I don't already know where I'm gonna get five dollars from, then I go out and I find someplace to go get five dollars from. I go get high and then between that time and the time I go home, that's when I'm steady doing, getting high or getting the money to get high.

After I get my first hit I go back out and get more money and come back and get high and do that all day. And that's what I do all day long. As far as getting in? Oh, man, 'bout normally I would say . . . I guess about eleven or twelve o'clock. I could go home if I wanted to 'cause by that time I done had a drink and I'm calmed down. I always end the evening with a little wine. Every time I go home, if I don't have a drink, a bottle to take with me, I'm going to a speakeasy and they gonna give me a drink, that's all.

I never have money left from the day before. I might have two or three dollars, but it's no way people gonna let me come in the house with five dollars. Ain't no way. That five dollars is gonna stay in that house. And if I do come in the house with five dollars, the only way I'll keep it is that Shaft don't know nothing about it. And since he's always out there looking and make sure he don't miss nothing, he always know.

Now I'll go on Sixteenth Street to cop. Before that I was going to the projects. Twenty-second, Twenty-first and Ludlow, and Twenty-first and Hering, those projects. But now they're gone. They got locked up. They was on television when they ran up there and busted them boys outside. So now I go on Sixteenth Street, and if not Sixteenth Street, it's in the neighborhood where I used to hang out, where I first met Shaft. This little street called Cardinal Street. They selling drugs again. They got three dollar bags on Tuesdays and Thursdays and they be the regular nickels but they just sell them for three dollars on Tuesdays and Thursdays. So on Tuesdays and Thursdays, that's where I go. So where I could get one bag for five dollars, I can get two for six. So that gives me a break. And that's where we usually go on Tuesdays and Thursdays. But every other day we be on Sixteenth Street. If you're a dollar short, they let you go anyway. I could really make out on Tuesdays and Thursdays, if I had a lotta money. Man, yeah.

Never been in shooting galleries. I'm a drug addict, but I'm scared of a lot of drug addicts all in one place at one time. I'm scared of them because I know what a lotta ways people think, you know. And usually they think prostitutes have a lot of money, but that's not the case all the time. I know how sometimes I'd be fiending and I'd be wanting me a hit real bad, and if they think I've got the money, I know they gonna take it from me at all costs. No, I don't go to shooting galleries, and I don't go to smoke houses.

I don't mind being around other drug users as long as it ain't personal, you know. If they come to my house, I don't have nothing that they might wanna

steal, but they disrespect places so bad, you know. Like when you're using
. . . when you clean up the syringe, ask me for something. If I don't have it
right there for you, just don't squirt the blood and stuff on my floor—just
take it for granted that that's where I want you to squirt it at. 'Cause blood
stinks after it sit for a while. Don't just take for granted that you could just
pluck the ashes on the floor. You know what I'm saying? Just don't take these
things for granted. I could see if you seen blood and cigarette butts all over
the floor, then I could see you doing that. But you don't see that.

I stay pretty much by myself. Me and whoever I'm with. 'Cause things happen to you in them places. See, people think just by you being a drug addict
these things can happen to you. It's not always the case. Sometimes you put
yourself in that predicament where it can happen to you. If I'm home shooting
up, I ain't expecting nothing to happen to me in my house. But if I'm in a shooting gallery where any and everybody can come in who gives the man two dollars and they got guns and knives, anything could happen to me, you know. I
know it's not much protection but I try to put at least that much on myself.

Money determines how much drugs I'll do. Now, say on a check day . . .
usually it's his check day . . . on his check day, we spend more money in a
hour than we spend all day, any other day. Do you know what I mean? If
we have a hundred dollars this day, it'll all be gone in an hour on check day.
But if it's any other day, we might spend a hundred dollars or a little more,
but it will take us all day to spend that. You following me? 'Cause you got
it right there in your pocket, you spend it all right away. Now I don't agree
with that 'cause I be wanting to wait sometimes 'cause I know I be wanting
another hit. When it's your check day you feel bad when you gotta go out
there right away and turn a trick and you just got the check.

I carry my works all the time. Yeah, if I know I'm coming out. Yeah, all the
time. If not, I'll go 'round the corner and I'll get a pair for a dollar. I never
know who I'm gonna see or who I'm not gonna see. When we go to his
friend's houses, his friend sells works, so we usually get a set from over there.

A lot of needle sharing is going on. Maybe not as much as used to be, but
it's still a lot of it going on. People aren't cleaning their works with bleach,
not like they should be. Since bleach is supposed to be the only thing that
kills them.

I share my works with him. We clean them, but not with bleach but with alcohol. As far as HIV, you know, you just put it in your mind that your partner doesn't have it, so it's just in my mind that he doesn't have it. Although I don't think about what he does when I'm not around. I don't think about maybe he used somebody else's works, you know. I don't think about that. I've been tested not too long ago. Negative. I got tested last Thursday again because, when you take one test, it does not . . . what they say . . . it's not proven. You can always have it and, you know, you should take another test. Well, we took that one, both of us took it. We took the second one so. . . . Yeah, because you know Kim, right? You know the one— Dude's daughter's mother? She supposed to have that and Shaft used to go with her too. When I heard she had AIDS, I got concerned then.

You know what's good on the streets 'cause that's where everybody goes. You can see the line standing there. You watch the traffic. Whichever way everybody's going, or even you see one of your friends and you say, "Where's it at?" And they'll tell you.

I haven't been given garbage that often, but a few times. You won't know till you shoot it up, and how you feel from it. It's been a couple times when some people OD'd off the same thing I done shot, you know. And I be saying, "How? We did the same thing. How could this. . . ." You know, it don't be the potency of the drug, it be your body. Sometimes your body rejects the stuff and so if it's one of them times where your body just doesn't want it, it rejects it and your brain does the same thing. You're just unlucky, but you never know when that might happen.

It's not that the drug is that good 'cause they don't sell that good of drugs on the street anymore, you know. You have to know somebody to get drugs like they be saying eighty percent pure and all this kinda mess. The drugs we shooting right now is less than probably forty percent pure. It's probably less than that, 'cause that's why you have to shoot so much of it.

So you really don't know till you put it in your body. It could be like aspirins or something, or sugar or something, and you put the water on it and you try to cook the cut out and it like thickens up and it like you cooking some kinda food, you know. It lumps up or something, you know. Then you know it's garbage. But if whatever they selling you dissolves just like cocaine when you put a little heat to it to cook the cut away and it just leaves a liquid, you won't know until you shoot it. Somebody could be giving you acid, and you won't know. But if your body is feeling . . . you can tell when you don't feel right. Okay, you might be jittery or you might feel a little light-headed. If you're light-headed, I think you should wait for a little while, you know. I've had a lot of seizures. I'm an epileptic anyway.

Since you don't know how strong it is either you inject it very slowly, very slowly. Sometimes you be wanting a hit so bad, till you just push it right on in and those would be most of the times when I have seizures. 'Cause when I want it I'm running it straight in without stopping and waiting, you know, like you go halfway, then you wait, then you feel a little rush, then you know if you can take the rest of it. But sometimes you want a hit so bad, you just rush it right on in.

I feel that one day eventually everybody that does drugs is gonna die from it. How long can your body . . . since it's something that's not supposed to be inside your body anyway. You always hope that you never die from it or hope that one day you might wanna stop because you're doing it, you know. But I believe that everybody that does drugs, especially as regularly as I do, something is gonna happen to them.

I did try smoking a pipe when I first came back to Jefferson, right? Couple years ago. When I started smoking a pipe, I didn't wanna change my clothes. I didn't wanna wash up. I didn't wanna do nothing. And still I haven't gotten back to the way that I used to be, far as doing my hair and this kinda of stuff. . . . Whereas I would never come outside like this with my hair like this, if it wasn't done up—I'd put a scarf on or something—now I'll come outside with it all going back, with a big forehead. And I know that's just me being slack, you know. So it do take an effect on that.

Because of my drug use I don't worry about my health and I don't worry about OD'ing. I don't worry about being arrest. Not anymore. I don't do nothing to get locked up for anymore. And the little bit I do do outside in the street, it's no cops, since it's not a main stroll. I stay away from most people that I knew before I started doing drugs and, like I said, everybody that I socialize with now does drugs. But I worry about things like this: I have another sister, the one that's a nurse. I've never stolen from her, but she rather me not be in her house if she's not home, okay? That bothers me because she don't have any reason for that, but I guess she don't wanna have a reason for that, you know.

I see my mother . . . well, every other day. She has been sick here lately. So I've been seeing her every day. See, I talk to her every day, and I might come down and see her, you know, if I'm . . . the days that I don't get too high, I go see her. 'Cause I don't go around her if I'm doing drugs. And so I do drugs mostly . . . mostly every day, maybe four days out the week, and the other three days, I go and say hello. You know, sit and talk to her for a little while. I mop the floors or whatever she might need done.

As a matter of fact, I think I'm more closer to my mother now than I was when I wasn't doing drugs because I didn't . . . I know how it sounds, but I didn't need her as much when I wasn't doing drugs and not only for money or nothing like that, but to talk to her, 'cause there be a lotta times when I just have to talk to somebody that I know loves me. No questions asked. I know she loves me and I be feeling down and out and crying up a storm 'cause I'm depressed, and I just go see her and talk to her and I feel better. She'll pray with me for a little while and I feels better so . . . I think we're closer now. I'm closer to her anyway.

I have seizures. So I'm eligible for welfare. I don't have to go through that much. They don't care how much your rent is, they only gonna give you a certain amount of money. In other states where they don't have a common-wealth, they pay your rent. No matter how much your rent is, they pay that. But here in a commonwealth state, you go to a whole 'nother monotony for really little or nothing.

Welfare nowadays, it's good for people that got kids, but if you're a single person, all they can do is buy you a high. It can't do nothing else. I get a hundred and five dollars in stamps. Now they just went up in stamps. Say I get a hundred and two dollars every two weeks. My rent is a hundred and fifty. So I go take seventy-five dollars out of one check, seventy-five dollars out the other check, and pay the rent. That means I can only keep one of my utilities, my gas or my electric, you know. I can't have them both. So in the wintertime you keep the gas and in the summertime you keep the electric. And in the wintertime I use candles or I use the people downstairs' electric by using an extension cords, you know. Then in the summertime, I use my own lights.

So that's how I had to do it in order to make ends meet. It's not possible for somebody to be on welfare in Jefferson and live decently. Not a single person, unless she gonna go someplace and get a room, one room, where you don't have no cooking and all this kinda mess, where you go get a hot plate and you cook like that. Usually when you get a room, you don't have to pay no utilities, and when you don't have to pay no utilities, then people don't want you using all their electric to be cooking and having a refrigerator and all that kinda stuff.

Welfare is just a formality for me. I go and I give them my doctor's thing and they take it and I'm outta there. But before, you used to have to . . . you know, just ask a lotta questions, that's all. They invade your life. They ask you all your life. They be asking you if you're a drug addict and stuff. And they ask you how you been making ends meet before you wanting to get on welfare. If you give them something to pry into, they gonna pry, but if you don't give them anything, then they won't pry, because there's nothing to pry about. They say, "How you been making out?" "The best way I can." And ain't nothing else you can say about that.

Now they got a new system now. Everybody's eligible for welfare once a year, for three months. And they're eligible for food stamps for six months. If you're on the drug program, you're eligible for welfare. If you have a handicap or something like that, you're eligible for welfare. If you're under a doctor's care and long as the doctor say you're under his care, you're eligible for welfare, if you need medication. If you don't need medication, then you probably can get welfare for three months and food stamps for six months.

The regular medical cards are blue. You get a green one and you can't get no medication with that. You can only go to the hospital and stuff with that. So in order to get a blue medical card, you have to be on welfare. So if you need medications to live . . . like I have to take Dilantin for the rest of my life. They say I probably take it for the rest of my life because of the seizures. So they have to give me the welfare 'cause I need the blue medical card. And all of them takes it because they overcharge the government or the state or whoever it is. But I've learned that if you don't have medical assistance or nothing like that, they will still take you. Like when I got admitted in the hospital for my jaw and my stomach, they admitted me and they took care of me, but while I was there, they got a social worker that'll hook you, to get you hooked up on welfare, and you pay like that.

Using drugs is a way of living for me now. It's not that I never think about me in another way. Sure I do. Sometimes I'm just sitting down, you know, I'll flash back in my mind when I wasn't doing drugs. How I lookeded then. How people treated me then, you know. When I went places, how men looked at me then that don't look at me now. Sure, men still look at me but it's a different type of men that's looking at me now than used to look at me, you know. I used to have nice, decent, respectable men looking at me, but they don't pay me any mind anymore. Now it's these little, you know, ten or fifteen dollar bums that's looking at me, you know. But that's the kind of life I'm living now. So, sure, sometimes I wish I was like I used to be, but that wish doesn't stay there very long, you know. Evidently, I haven't missed it enough that I would stop or try to grasp it again, you know. I'm a drug addict and I don't wanna be one but I'm one. So I'm just being that. Whatever it takes to make you say, "I'm stopping," I don't have it.

Before I started doing drugs, if a man wanted to talk to me that was . . . say when I was working at OIC . . . if a director wanted to talk to me, you know, get to know me personally, I felt like this, "Why you want to talk to me?" You know. What could he possibly want with me? Okay, so I didn't have very high, whatever you wanna call it . . . self-esteem.

Yeah. I didn't think very much of myself then. I didn't know then that I didn't think a lot of myself, okay? But I can look back now and I say I didn't think very much of myself because if the best wanted me, I wanted to know why I was wanted by the best, okay? I never felt like I was the best, so that might be why it never even crossed my mind to think that way. I always felt small, less than them, and wondering what could they possibly want with me. Now that I'm less of a person than I was then, which I am, but I don't feel less about myself. I know this sounds crazy but I don't feel less about myself because I don't come in contact with anybody that's doing anything other than what I'm doing. So I feel just fine. Oh, that's horrible, but I feel just fine. There is no reason to change because I feel just fine.

The only thing bothers me is my mother. That's the only thing bothers me. It doesn't matter how my sisters feels 'cause they're only my sisters. Now my mother, she might not think so, but she means a whole lot to me and how she think of me means a whole lot to me. And I do want her to be happy and I know she's not happy with me being like I am. That's the only thing that bothers me. My mother is seventy-two. And that's the only thing that bothers me. Other than that, nothing else . . . nothing else. I'm all right.

I think using drugs is like committing suicide. Only you doing it slower. I never thought of that before until just now. Instead of taking a gun and blowing your brains out . . . it might take you a lotta years, but eventually it's gonna kill you. If it don't kill you, it's gonna lame you or something, it's gonna do something to you that changes your whole life.

Get off of it? Like I said, thoughts come to my mind but they don't stay very long. Mainly because I wanna get high again. I don't know what it will take. I'm telling you, when my sister got bad off sick like that and I went to the hospital to see her, I went there every day to see her. Just today me and her, we're getting high together, and tomorrow she's dying, you know. Now she can't walk. And she'll never walk again. And I'm saying, if that don't make you change, what is it gonna take?

I don't know what it's gonna take. Do I think I have to hit bottom? I have. If this is not it . . . I think I'm more out there now. Really I do. Oh, God. Perhaps, perhaps it'll probably just take that—either die or you get up, you know, 'cause everything else has done happened to me, I think. I done been beat up. I done been hurt up. I done had guns, you know. I done been close to death. Not hurt so bad till I almost die, but I mean death has been facing me lots of times, you know, like with tricks about to blow my brains out if I don't do what they want me to do or somebody taking my money.

Like it was one time I was with this guy in a car and I don't know if he woulda used the gun. I don't know. That's just it, you never know. And he wanted to have anal sex and I don't do that, but that's what he wanted. So after he paid me, that's what he was gonna make me do. No, that not what he . . . that's what he *made* me do, only because I didn't wanna take the chance of whether he was gonna shoot me with the gun or not. I didn't know. But I know I had a gun in my face and I wanted out, you know. So I did it. After that he took his money back. He took not only his money, he took all of the money that I had. I got out of the car. I felt like a heel, but I was glad to be out of the car, you know. There have been a few other situations like that. A few, not many. A few.

I usually have somebody watching my back. Now with Shaft, I doubt if he'll do anything. And, damn, somebody took my money once, but they didn't beat me up, I'm looking for him, and he's someplace else probably getting off, you know. I'm looking for him to come and help me or come and get my money back or something. But he's not that . . . I don't think I've never known him to fight a guy. I know he might shoot somebody or stab somebody or something like that, but he don't own a gun so, you know, I've never known him to fight any guys.

There're things I wish I had not done. I wish I would never started doing drugs. Well, to tell you the truth, I'm not much on stealing things, you know. I've taken money from . . . like I said, from tricks . . . but that's mostly how I get money, period. I don't go selling things or nothing like that. I've never been into that. Now I have sold my things. Like if I had a television, I mighta sold it. But we did do one thing, though. We did take somebody's television that was living in that place that we was living at, and I'm sorry I did that. It really wasn't worth a whole lot, and that's the only reason why I'm sorry. I'm not sorry that I did it to the person that I did it to, though. There was just a little bit of money we got from it. We got like twenty dollars. It was a nineteen-inch color television. Wasn't nothing wrong with the television.

I've never done anything to my family to get drugs or money. I always got my own. Even when I was in a relationship with men I still went out and hustled. Because you know why? They treat them women . . . I be seeing them . . . I be looking at it. They be treating them girls like they ain't nothing, just to get one. . . . If the girl don't go out . . . even if she's with a drug dealer and her man got all the drugs, if she want one bag of cocaine, he got to talk to her like she's nothing. Or he got to smack her around or something and she just sit there and wait patiently for him whenever he feels like giving out that one bag. You can't do that. My habit can't wait for you to feel like it's time for you to get high now. See, I be done killed somebody, see, you know, 'cause I'd rather just go out there and turn my little tricks if that's what I'm doing to get my money. Turn my tricks and come back and give you the money. When I give you my money, give me them drugs, you know.

Well, I can't say that I regret turning tricks, because I really don't. But what I do regret is the ways that I turn them now. I used to make good money, you know. Fifty and a hundred dollars, like that. It's quite different now, you know. I don't even know where those girls are now, but now I get five dollars and ten dollars. I might get twenty dollars every now and then. I'm not gonna lie. Except for those two guys that have a house that I go to regularly—they give me forty, fifty dollars. That's only because I'm the only girl that they do see and we're friends, like that. But other than that, five dollars, ten dollars, six dollars, seven dollars, that's how people wanna give you money. And so that's why girls have been changing and don't usually give guys what they really want. So I regret doing that. And I regret letting a lotta people . . . like I've been abused a lot physically by guys, and I regret that.

The only thing I learnt in the streets was how to put the rubber on without them knowing, how to go in their pocket without them feeling, and that's all. I think that's all. I go in their pockets by pressing your body up against theirs, and going in the pocket at the same time so they don't know what's being touched. Sometimes they have their pants on. Most times they pull them down. And that's the best time 'cause I can dip them then. Well, in West Virginia, that's when I learned mostly how to walk up to a man. He could be standing straight up in the street and you just rub on him and when you walk away, you got the wallet. The only way he knows his wallet's gone is if you start running. If you don't start running, that man'll go right on about his business and go away, and you might have some trouble the next day if you stand in the same place. He might come back. Don't even know his wallet is gone 'cause he's also into that good feeling, you know, that rubbing, wanting to be all like that. So he ain't even paying that no mind.

And then you learn how to encourage them. Like all that old talking. I never did like that. You know, how you got to encourage them. "Fuck me" or, you know, or "All this big dick," and all this kind of shit. I never did like that 'cause I'm not much of a talker when I'm doing that. Moaning and groaning and all this kinda mess, you know. You learn that you gotta play with their balls 'cause that enhances, you know. All that old mess. I picked up these rules by just being around. Just by being around.

Some men will say, "Baby, do it like this." Yeah, they the best kinda tricks there is, 'cause then you know what to do. And other times, they won't be satisfied, you be wondering, "I wonder why he won't stop for me no more?" 'Cause he didn't like the way you did it, you know.

The only thing I never learned and I'm still learning about is how not to get needle marks. Some people don't have none. Shaft don't have none. He goes right here in his leg though. But then after he go there it be hard like a brick. But I don't have that vein right there in my leg. My sister, she don't have none. She goes right here, it's black and it look like a real big corn, you know. But they don't have no needle marks nowhere on their body. No tracks or nothing. I don't know how they do that. White boys, I know, they use tattoos to cover them up.

The most unusual customer was a man that wanted to eat my bowel movement. I'm pretty certain that was the most unusual one. He paid good money, though. See, those weird people, they pay the best money. Wanted me to shit in the toilet or shit on the floor, on a piece of paper, whatever. He ate it. He could tell you what you ate. Your meals, you know. He could tell you if it had onions in it. Everything. Everything. He could tell you all that. He was a white man, downtown, driving a nice car, one of them office executives. Paid two or three hundred dollars. So what the hell. If I couldn't shit, give me a enema, you know. Make me shit. For two or three hundred dollars—that's a whole night's work.

Well, I done met people that wanted me to beat them, but I'm not into that. Then I met this one guy, he had this ink pen, right? And he told me to stick the ink pen in his navel real hard. I can't do them kinda things. I try it but I can't do them, you know. Something just stopped me from doing it 'cause I'm scared of them kinda people too. 'Cause if they like pain, ain't no telling how much pain they think I could take, you know.

The most unusual guy I met, he just like to grind with all your clothes on. And that's the best date I ever had. With all his clothes and all your clothes on. He just liked to grind. He paid me about twenty dollars. Not much. Twenty dollars.

And there's this other guy, he liked to see you smash lemon Tastykake pie. Yeah, he liked to watch you smash them. He put a piece of paper on the floor and you smash the pie on the floor. You gotta have flat leather shoes and have on stockings and stuff and just smash them. And he'd be getting off and I'll be smashing them with the bottom of my feet with these shoes on. You could leave your top on. All he wanna see is this part, you know, your legs. I mean sometimes if you're hungry, you'll be hating to smash them pies.

I had this one white guy—I don't like to talk about this 'cause I was ashamed myself—but he ate my . . . he ate . . . he went . . . he had oral sex with me when I was menstruating, and this was a good trick. This was the one that put . . . he put. . . . You know Belaire House downtown on Mill Street, Eleventh and Mill, between Mill and Allman? I think it's that little street. It's Cook Street. Okay, he moved me in there one time and this was a good trick. Well, he worked right on Southbourne Street, the State Building or something like that. Okay, he put me in there. He liked to have oral sex when my period was on. And this man get up and look like I don't know what, with all this weird stuff on his face, and to me that's very weird. I was just like . . . like I say, I was just a little ashamed 'cause I let him do it, but you don't be thinking about, you know, being ashamed until you see him, and then you say, "Oh, my God! Look at you. Look at you."

First I was staying at the Fraser on Eighth and Sussex, right? He was paying by the week there. Then I wanted my own place so he paid . . . he put all the money down on the apartment in Belaire House, and the reason why I had to leave was because I was a prostitute and they didn't want me in there 'cause they seen me standing on the corners and stuff like that. I stayed in there for three months 'cause he had to pay two months' security and a month's worth of rent. So I stayed there till all that went out and then I moved. I seen him the whole while I was in Metro Center. Even when I left and I was staying with one of my sisters, he used to come over there sometimes and see me. And I used to make up little lies, like I have to go to court and pay a five hundred dollar fine. He used to just give me the money.

But the kind of tricks I've turned have changed. It changed when I came back to Jefferson this time. When I came back home a few years ago, I was about this big and I was in New York then and I was still turning forty, fifty dollar tricks. Okay. When I came back, the piper done took over everything, right? And the tricks just wasn't paying no money. Nobody was downtown on Eleventh and Mill anymore. The majority of the people that's up there now are homosexuals, faggots. They're up there, but I don't know where the girls are. They must be in North Jefferson somewhere. And then I had started smoking a pipe a little bit. So that's the trend that I got caught up in. They just not gonna spend the money anymore 'cause they can get whatever they want, and it's not only bummy-looking girls out there that's doing it. You have very clean girls out there that's nice-looking that do keep their hair done and do change clothes every day, and they still turning tricks for five and six dollars. It's because that's how little bit the drugs cost, and when you smoking the pipe, or even when you shooting up, and you want the hit so bad, especially if you've had one, you'll do that.

When I was in Metro Center, working in Metro Center, I hung out with this one black girl named Black Girl. That's the only person I hung with here. That's all you need. 'Cause if you hang around with a different girl all the time, they'll be taking your money and you won't be knowing nothing about it. So you find you one girl that you could trust, that when y'all go and get some money, you know, if she gets it, she's gonna break down with you, and if you get it, you gonna break down with her. Other girls, they'll be taking money, you won't be knowing nothing about it, and the trick'll be beating you up and you be wondering why. All because this girl done took his money, and you don't know nothing about it.

Say if a guy wanna take both you girls, right? And y'all wanna take his money, and one girl sit in his face while the other girl take the money out of the pocket, you know. But you might be with a girl that you don't know and that you can't trust. If you sit in this man's face, she's gonna take his money and you ain't gonna know nothing about it, 'cause nine times out of ten, she got a pimp she gotta take this money to.

And I've never really had a pimp like that. Had a pimp once and that was in Charleston, West Virginia, but it was the greatest pimp I ever seen. Only thing I had to do was . . . he had like a whole lotta white girls, right? He had like fifteen white girls. He was . . . this is how he worked. He took them to whorehouses. I met him in Jersey. He took them from down South and brought them up here to the whorehouses. And all he wanted, and since it was up my alley, all he wanted was for a girl to be with some of his girls sometime. And that's what I did. The money I made I kept it. I was with the girls for performance, for them to get sexual satisfaction. And I kept all my money, paid my rent, and, you know, I didn't have to give him none of my money or nothing. Just pay my rent and buy my clothes. That didn't last very long. The feds came and locked him up. And down there is where I first learned how to . . . how to live good, being a prostitute. How to live in a great, you know . . . a real nice apartment and have real nice clothes. That's where I first learned that at.

When I turn tricks now, I do it like I'm gonna give you two or three minutes and if you can't get it in that bit of time, sorry. You know, before, I was aiming to please them 'cause the money was like that. But now the money's not like that so it don't make me no difference whether they come or not. I'm gonna do what I do and then I'm done. I ain't making love to you, you know. They be wanting it sometime, they be saying, "Well, you gotta play with my. . . ." "I ain't gotta play with your titties. No, I don't. I'm sucking your dick. That's all I got to do." Then they be saying, "Well, lick the balls." "I'm not licking no balls. I don't have to do none of that. I be here to suck your dick. That's what I'm here to do and that's what I'm doing." And then I took all the thrill out of it then, so half the time they don't want it no more, right? So that be fine with me 'cause they ain't getting no money back.

There was a time when I would do more, like make love and all of that. Yeah, I would. Yeah, I did it. I played with their nipples and, you know, lickeded a couple times, suckeded and lickeded and caressed them, yeah, I did it. But it was well worth my while. Now, that doesn't mean that I did the same thing with them that I did with my intimate partner. No. I would do all the things 'cause I would suck they dick and I would fuck them and so that's all I do with my intimate partners. Only thing is I feel different with my intimate partners. So the physical kind of stuff is the same, but the feelings aren't. Although you act like they are. You be screaming, hollering and all that kinda mess, but you really don't be feeling that.

I go out looking for tricks now. You just go where you know they be. If you know they riding up and down Hillside Avenue—and that's the closest to me now, Hillside Avenue—so you go up Hillside Avenue and it is always people outside that you could talk to or whatever, and if you walk long enough up Hillside Avenue, somebody's gonna stop you because somebody's gonna want something. I start off at Hillside and Nineteenth, Twentieth, and I walk on up to Hillside and Pendleton if I have to. But I never usually have to walk that far.

Like people that got the stores and stuff, they trick too. You go around there like five o'clock in the morning when they first come to open the stores up, they'll trick with all the girls. And you depend on them. Then it's the restaurant around near there that I can go and get money from him because he, you know, loans out money. There's a lotta little, you know, things like that I do. Go to Charlie's and get twenty, twenty-five from him. Pay him back. He don't charge no interest or nothing. Just pay him back.

I had two regular guys which were older guys that I seen . . . you know, I still see them, I see them all the time, all the time. But sometimes I go outside and I see guys that's out there, just looking for girls on the street on Hillside Avenue or on High Street and check them out and go from there. Most times they approach you in some kind of way, or call you or something. Usually you be . . . you be in neighborhoods like . . . you be talking to people and everything, you know. You walk to this corner for a moment and look, and then you come back, where everybody else is standing at, like that.

You know cops, they not out there like that. Now, when I was really downtown, there was no way that you could know unless you stood there and you watched how many times he rode around the block, just them in the car, and never see a girl in the car with them. Then something's wrong then, you know. Or you just look at the kinda car they drive and, if they driving a unmarked car, they still got some kinda lights or something on them cars the other cars don't have on them. But I got locked up a lotta times downtown by not knowing who I was getting in the car with 'cause they have cops in Cadillacs and everything down there. Looked good, too. You know, they have them Italian cops down there, looking real good. "Hey, babe." One time he said, "Hey, babe. Where you going?" I said, "With you." Went right to jail. Got a short leather jacket and looking real good.

In New York I got locked up, it was this black guy. He had rotten teeth and everything. Now you wouldn't think a cop gonna look like that, right? He had all these rotten teeth, right? So I figured he was a good one. He lookeded like a little nerd or something. I just knew I was gonna get all his money. Take it to him, 'cause he lookeded like that type. We in the car. I done told him how much money I wanted and everything was fine. At the light . . . we got to the light, this woman on this side, I thought they was hookers. They was dressed like them. Tell me, "Get out the car. You're under arrest." I said, "I be damned!" Two women. They got real good vice in New York.

The most unusual incident with a cop . . . one of them took me to a hotel and tricked with me and let me go. That was unusual, 'cause I didn't know he was a cop and I didn't know until after he showed me the badge and stuff. He picked me up. This was in Jefferson, but I think he was using me to find out where the girls go to the hotel—to bust the hotel or something, right?— 'cause he took me there and he kept me and asked all these questions about the rooms and how many rooms, all this kinda shit. But we did date and he gave me fifty dollars, and then he showed me his badge and everything, and I felt like . . . oh, boy. He told me he was a cop but he wasn't going to lock me up 'cause he said, "I could tell you don't know what you're doing." I said, "Thank you." He didn't lock me up. But not too long after that the hotel had got shut down. So I'm saying he probably used me 'cause all the rest of the girls probably knew who he was, you know, and I didn't. You can get in a lotta trouble like that by not knowing who cops are and people see you with these guys and then something happen not too long after that, they think you have something to do with it. And which you do, but you don't be aware of it.

Six months was the longest time I was in jail. I was up to County Road. It's fine up there. I know how that sounds, but it's fine. It's nothing like people try. . . . See, I've never been to a penitentiary. I don't know what it's like in a penitentiary. But those places are just . . . them girls go there to have fun. Nobody . . . you don't have to fight if you don't want to. You do have studs walking around with men's underwear and stuff like that, thinking they really are men, but if you don't want to be bothered with them, then they don't wanna be bothered with you. You know, you use it to get healthy. Lotta girls go to jail on purposely to take rest periods and stuff. Yeah, and they get all the antibiotics that they need to clean they system out and stuff like that. Lotta people go to jail just for that purpose. So it wasn't all that bad. I got a job working inside the jailhouse so I could have, you know, commissary money and stuff. I was working in the kitchen and then I worked in the garment shop.

There were little fights, fighting over a chair in the mess hall or fighting over the television or the telephone and stuff like that when I was in jail. Never seen anything serious happen in jail. I never even heard of no girls getting . . . like they been saying, girls be getting raped and stuff. I never even heard nothing like that. The only thing that's bad is that you can't go outside. But six months wasn't that long to me 'cause it went fast, kinda fast. I wasn't expecting to get out then 'cause they had a probation detainer. I had a couple of them, as a matter of fact. I hired a lawyer and nothing was working, but this thing called *Jackson vs. Hendricks* or something like that—it was some kinda organization—they got me out.

I've been locked up lotsa times. Lotsa times. Lots and lotsa times. So many times I can't count them. They do this like every day downtown. They ride around and lock all the girls up, but you don't go to the Police Headquarters or nothing. They just give you citations. And so, you know, we'd get locked up two or three times a week.

You know, people feel so bad towards the drug dealers, right? I know that it's doing a lot of wrong to people, but I look at it like this: If he don't sell it to me, I'm gonna be mad as hell at him. Maybe I feel like this 'cause I am a drug addict. I don't knock them for doing it. I knock the ones that's selling people stuff that's not drugs that's supposed to be drugs, the garbage, or somebody that done sells somebody something that's too pure when it shouldn't be as pure. If you sell to somebody something that's strong enough to kill him, I don't think you should do that. But long as they making a living I don't look at them hard. Well, my mother said to me, she say, "This man walk around with all this gold and all these big cars and you walking around looking like a bum 'cause you give him all your money." Yes, but I'm giving him all my money 'cause it's by choice. He's not making me give him all my money, you know. He don't even ask me to give him my money. I just walks up to him and be mad if he don't take my money, you know.

If you legalize drugs, everybody might be drug addicts and we don't need that. It's gotta be somebody here to do something, right? If they legalize drugs, everybody would be doing it. Kids would be doing it. Although there's kids doing it now, but kids would start doing that at a much younger age. I don't know how the world would be like since it's like it is now and it's not legalized.

I won't buy drugs from kids. You do have kids that sell drugs, but I won't buy drugs from kids. Kids twelve and thirteen years old, I won't buy drugs from them. Yeah, you even got some younger than that. I won't buy drugs from them, you know, 'cause if that was my son or my daughter, I wouldn't want one of my girlfriends to go buy their drugs from my baby. If my baby out there selling, you come and tell me, you know, and I'm gonna make sure my son or daughter don't be out there selling it. But nowadays that's what everybody's using. That's what the white men is using. I don't care how much money black people make, it's really a white man behind this mess because they the ones that got all the access to the stuff and that's what they using now. They using the minors because the minors can sell it all the time until they turn a grown-up and never go to jail. They wanna recruit the youngest ones they can to sell drugs so they don't have to worry about going to jail.

I don't really think the government is doing anything to get drugs off the street. I really don't. Seems to me like they could stop everything else. Now, if they could stop food from going inside other countries, they could stop drugs from coming in ours. Now, don't you think so? I mean, they should be able to do that. Do something. 'Cause locking these drug dealers up, it doesn't matter, if you could lock up every drug dealer that's out in the street right now, five minutes later it's gonna be somebody else out there with the same drugs, from the same person, whoever they're getting it from, at the same corner selling the same thing.

I think the government really got a hand in it. I do. I really do because it's so widespread here. And then here lately you been hearing about so many crooked government officials, you know, doing so many crooked things. And it's hard for me to believe that as greedy as they are, they gonna let this . . . all this money. . . . 'Cause it's a whole lot of money being made. By the time it get to a person like me that, if I start selling drugs, if I could make a couple thousand dollars a day, imagine what them people way up there is making, right? And with that much money being made, how they gonna just let it go past them and they don't want none of it? That's all they really, really be into is the money thing.

The black community, I think . . . the ones that selling it think it's great. 'Cause they finally got a chance to get them cars and all that gold. That's a nice way to get rid of us, 'cause it is doing that. I mean, they think that the next war gonna be with guns and stuff. It might not be 'cause the drugs is about the best killer I've seen. And it's definitely doing that in one form or another. If it's not for the money, it's for the high. And a lot of us are leaving here just that way.

I think straight people look down on me because I am a drug user. Straight people look down on any drug addict 'cause they're a drug addict, but see that's only because they . . . they only looking at me as a drug addict. They not looking at me as a person. To them you don't have a person anymore, but it's not true in all cases—in most cases, but I don't even know if it's in most cases. Some people do still have a heart. Some people do still have morals. See, like I say, all the detrimental things I've done were only to this person right here. It never went outside this person right here. Perhaps that's the worst way to be in the world.

I don't know, but it's not too many people that I go to and they'll turn me down. Okay? Because they don't have a reason to turn me down. My family of which my two sisters are the most people that turns me down. Like I said, people that's gots stores and stuff and I can go to them and get anything that I need. You know, you don't run it in the hole but, if you need something, you can go out and go and get it. And that means a lot to me, you know. But all in all, they look down on you. Now, there's a couple of store owners that, if I woulda went in there about ten years ago when I was twenty-one or twenty, they woulda been wanting me to be their woman. I go in there now, they do anything for me but that, you know. So it's different. They look at you quite different.

I would tell people for them not to come this way. It's been like . . . not even like a roller coaster. It's been like living somewhere where you don't know nobody and all you know is drugs. And all you live for is drugs. And everything that you do and every day that you wake up, everything that you do to get anything, the only thing that you try to get is drugs. After you do drugs for such a long bit of time you block yourself away from everybody and everything else that doesn't do what you do. The only people you come in contact with is your family, if your family. . . . Most people can't go around they families anymore. All you wanna do is get high. Sometimes you wanna eat. Sometimes you don't, you know. I'm not the exception, but every now and then I go to church, sometimes, to regroup this person that I am, you know. I go to church and I cry and I pray and I cry and I pray. Although I'm not repenting for my sins. I just feel the need to do this so that I can keep on going, you know. But I don't have a lotta guilt. The only time I have bad feelings is when I think about my mom.

But all in all, my life hasn't been good. It hasn't been great, it hasn't even been good. It's been liveable. It's been liveable only because, I guess, I choose not to deal with my person, who I am, who I really am, because when you start doing drugs, you start being somebody else automatically. Now it's really hard for me to hold on to that little bit of Margaret that my mother had, that my mother raised, and still be this drug person. It's real hard to do that and sometimes I guess that's why I have a lot of problems 'cause I'm trying to be two people at one time. You know, I'm trying to be a decent person and a drug addict at the same time. And I've started to believe that you have to be one way or the other, you know. You can't straddle the fence in this thing unless you have means of getting money other than doing criminal things.

I don't see a future if I keep going the way that I'm going now. I really don't see one. And, like I said, whatever it takes for you to, you know, to buckle down and straighten out, I still haven't gotten that yet.

"In the beginning, like I said, this was fun. The Avenue was fun. The drug game was fun, you know. The pursuit of finding out where the best drug was and getting high was fun. Now, it's scary out there, you know."

Charlie

All my life I've tried to buy my mother's love but . . . she just won't. . . . You know, I guess mothers have different loves and different ways and I'm just not the one, you know. I called her one time Thanksgiving. I called her and said, "Happy Thanksgiving. I love you." She said the same to me but—I was talking to my favorite sister, Phyllis—she got back on the phone and said, "I just had a moment of emotion. What I just said to you I didn't mean." And I was like—you know, I didn't say it out loud or anything—but where did that come from? Why did she have to do that to me? "Happy Thanksgiving, I love you," and then come back and say, "I didn't mean what I said. I was just struck by a moment of emotion." I mean, "Wow!"

Like I've always tried to do the special things and stuff. You know, I'm not gonna tax myself with it anymore. I finally found a guy who treats me like a person and accepts me for myself and I'm happy. The rest of my family is miserable and they want us to break up because they see how happy I am. I was never really happy till I was thirty-five, and I am now.

I just don't think my mother knew how to say she cared. So I think there's something inside me that says, "Yeah, she cared in her own way." I think she wants things just to be better for us, to get more out of life than she did. Not have, as she called it, to slave, you know, be degraded and all just to make a little living to put food on the table or whatever. I think I disappointed her and she lets me know that I disappointed her too. 'Cause it's just constantly, you know, "I got your kids. You're a whore. You're a junkie." That used to hurt. But I've just like—poo!—blocked her out. I've got my own problems.

I grew up in Warminster. It's a white-bias, prejudice, low-life white people, you know, low income. If you say to a white person, "I live in Warminster," they consider you like a low-life. You're nothing. That's like the ghetto whites, you know. But it's not true with all of us. That's the brand we have. You had to fight if you grew up in Warminster. You had to be tough. You know, the other white kids feared you if you say you're from Warminster, and . . . boom!

There was a lot of crime there—burglaries, drug dealing, you know—but it was important to people that families stuck together, neighbors sticking with each other, like them against the cops. In most families the men worked. We were told to respect our parents and stuff. Nothing like these kids these days are. We just learned about family first, stick with your family. We were taught to dislike blacks and Puerto Ricans. Well, not taught that, but it was always said, you know, "That nigger, that spic" or "They have balls coming around here."

Now, it's not like it was. Warminster today is . . . oh, it's terrible! The kids don't respect their parents. They don't respect anything. They don't even respect themselves. They graffiti everything. They curse you out. You wouldn't believe the way they curse. Like truck drivers. The girls look sleazy. Like, you know, when we were younger, we weren't into makeup real heavy and our hair all hookerlike, you know. Some of the clothes they wear, they're either all tight or they're into this genie-type, "I Dream of Jeannie" shit. You know, with these pants that their crotches are all down here. They're just bad. They don't fear nothing. They'll kill you for five dollars, and I think that has to do with the crack.

I grew up white, but in reality I'm Puerto Rican and white. I met my father when I was eighteen. So it like really fucked me up because everything she had taught me, the prejudices and all I had about Puerto Ricans. . . . And I couldn't believe she had lied to me all them years. I finally understood why like my hair is wavy, you know. My sisters have long, straight hair and stuff. In the summer I'd get darker, and the kids used to spit on me and call me "nigger" or "spic." So it got to the point when I was little I would . . . even in the summer, I would wear normal clothes so I wouldn't get darker and I'd iron my hair trying to make it straight.

My father was born in Puerto Rico, and my mother was born in Jefferson. There's two versions of when and how my parents met. My father told me that my mother was like a hot little bitch back in the early fifties. At that time it was really shameful to go with another race. They were at a party and she was just "hot to trot." You know, built, and she had big knobs and shit, and they, you know, fucked. She found him attractive and she happened to get pregnant. Her version is he raped her. I tend to believe him now.

I don't know much about my father. I met him. I seen his mother and I seen his brother once. I met his four daughters, but I wouldn't know them if I seen them now. Last time I heard he supposedly is a captain or something down at Sixth and Commerce, but he's an alcoholic. He drinks like you wouldn't believe. I don't know how he got in there.

They didn't live together and they weren't married. As a matter of fact I have a sister that's three days older than me. So all together there is six girls, but it's three different women. That antagonized me against him. I said to him, "Why did you marry her mother and not my mother?" He said, "I'll tell you the truth. I asked your mother to marry me and she said no. So I married Bernie." So he went on to have four other girls with Bernie and then there's another woman that has one girl with him. So he has six girls all together and no boys. Me and Penny, you know, are the oldest of his children.

My mother had six other children. I have three sisters and three brothers and I am the oldest in that crew. There's four girls and three boys from five different men. So my sister next to me has one. My sister next to her has one. Corrie and Eddie have one. Pat and Timmy have one. Five. Jean Marie is three and a half years younger than me, then after that Phyllis is four and a half, Corrie's five and a half, Eddie's six and a half, Pat's seven and a half, and Timmy's eight and a half. By the time I was eight years old she had all of them. No more after that. She had a hysterectomy.

Then that's when she had the nervous breakdown. I'd say when I was about ten she had the nervous breakdown and all the kids were taken, you know. The one next to me was bad. I mean she was a bad little kid. They put her in a home with me. Phyllis, Corrie, and Eddie went to their fathers, and Pat and Timmy went with their father.

It didn't seem to matter that my father wasn't there. I just felt sorry for her. You know, other kids' mothers were home with them and their fathers were out, you know, bringing the food home. My mother didn't have that and I didn't understand why because she was so pretty. I knew it was why she had to struggle like she did. So I remember feeling sorry for her when I was a kid and really loving her more because she could have just got rid of us. That's what I thought in my mind, "Man, she could have just put us away or something and just forgot about us, but she didn't."

I finally found out about my father because he chased my mother down on Dryer Street one day. I told her, "Mom, somebody is trying to get you to stop." We were in a car. But she wouldn't stop. She obviously could see who it was, but he was better than her and he just came around. Zoom! As soon as he got out of the car, I knew. I felt like I was looking in the mirror except he was a lot darker than me. And his hair was more curly. And I just felt . . . like I looked at her and I'd just opened the car door and I got out and he said, "I'm your father." I said, "Oh, no! What are you? A spic? A nigger? What?" You know. I looked at her and she said, "Charlene, let me. . . ." I said, "Oh, I hate you." I said, "Why didn't you ever tell me? All these years the kids have been spitting at me. I said, "You lived in a white neighborhood, and let me. . . ." I said, "I hate you!" I just ran.

You know, then I started shooting dope. That's when I first got into shooting really. Then I started going out with Puerto Rican guys. All my life I've only gone out with one white guy. I had my first two kids by him. I was a virgin until I was fifteen. I ended up having two kids with a white guy. All the rest of my life I've been going with Puerto Rican and black guys. I found out that I like them better and they treated me better than white guys. I didn't have to be worried about being called names.

I was born in prison in the Falk Corrections Center and my mother for years had me believing that it was my fault that she was in prison. I just found out in 1988 why she was in prison. She had told me back then if you're under eighteen and got pregnant, and you didn't put your kid up for an adoption or abort, that your parents put you in prison, and for years that was on my conscience. It was my fault that she was in jail. So she was supposed to be in jail for two years until she was eighteen. She got pregnant when she was fifteen. I was born when she was sixteen. But she had a fight with one of the CO's—matrons—in jail and she got two years more in Irwin. For four years I lived with my grandmother and I didn't know anything about her. Finally, in 1988 I was in jail. I did ten months there. I went to Female Offenders for three months, and then I went to Petersburg for a month. Finally, October nineteenth '89 I got out again, you know, but I worked in the admission this time and I had access to records. I went back to 1953 and found her name. She was in there for burglary. As I was getting older, the story she told me didn't sit right, you know. Didn't even sound right. Damn, how many people would be in jail if that was the truth? Because you get pregnant you go to jail? Come on.

I lived with my grandmother till I was four. Then, when my mother got out of jail, she liked snatched me from her, you know. So I lived with my mother until I was eight years old and then I went to court and I told them I didn't want to be with her. I said I wanted to live with my grandmother. My grandmother said, "I can't take care of her. I'm getting old and I have a bad heart," and that just like flabbergast me—like, "Wow!" you know—'cause she was the one who told me, "Tell them you don't want to be with your mother." And I did. And I thought if I said I wanted to be with her I would, and then she turned around and said that. I was like. . . . So they put me in a home in Georgetown. At the time, it was called Bethesda, at Remington and Waverly, nine-ten Waverly. It was a home for broken families, a Catholic home. Run by nuns. And looking at things now I feel like they were my four best years.

I liked it there. It was nice. There were all different reasons kids were there, you know. For their families broken or the state took them. My mother was paying some money to them. She had to. I guess for my keep. They said I was a very hyper child and they start giving me . . . what the hell . . . Thorazine and she signed papers for it. You know, sometimes I believe that may have started my addiction from age eight. They had me on Thorazine, you know, to keep me calm. Not that I was bad. I was just too nervous.

So I was in the home when I learned about my mother's breakdown. I was ten years old. All I knew was Jean Marie came with me and I was told my mother had a nervous breakdown and that all the kids were taken off her. Finally, a couple years ago, we did get to meet our younger brothers, but the youngest one said, if he ever seen my mother, he would spit on her. So God only knows what their father told them. The one next to the youngest we met him, Pat. He like looks more like us than his other side. Timmy, the youngest one, looks just like them, you know, but Pat looks more like us.

My grandmother died in '87 and I regret it now. She died of cancer of the lung. She wouldn't take the medicine or nothing. Like I was her favorite grandchild and I just couldn't go to the funeral. I guess I couldn't accept that she was dead. Before she died she was just asking to see me. Like she had gone back in her mind. And I did go to see her before she died, but I didn't go to the viewing. I said I was going to go and my uncle even paid the owners to keep the funeral home open an extra hour. I should have went, you know. Like I was her favorite grandchild. I couldn't go and I didn't go and my family didn't talk to me for a long time. They just don't understand it. It's not that I didn't want to go. I don't like funerals.

I don't know why I was close to my grandmother. Maybe 'cause she had me for the first four years and I don't remember being beat up or called names. My grandfather died in the war in a plane crash. I don't know what war, but my grandmother never remarried. I just remember she was with this man, Frank Bronsky. Even after my mother got me back, he used to meet me on the road when I went to school and he'd give me a dollar, take me to the candy store and buy me chocolates. I like snow caps. They were chocolate, these little white things. I loved them. He used to buy them for me.

I don't remember my grandmother ever hitting me or anything. I just remember happy things with her. One time, it was the worst thing I did. She had a little can of stuff to feed the fish. I thought they were hungry and there was a bunch of them and I put all of it in and they all blew up and died. She didn't even beat me then. You know, she just said, "Bunny, did you feed the fish?" I said, "Grandma, they were so hungry. I could tell. So I just put all that in. It was just a little can." She said, "They blew up, they're all dead.

Fish will keep eating, they don't know." You know, she didn't hit me or nothing.

My mother dated during that period when I was between the ages of four and eight. I remember her with Fred, with Patrick, and then finally John. I never had any problem with the men that lived in the house with my mother and us. I didn't like the last one, the two youngest boys' father. That was Patrick. He was in high school when my mother was like in her late twenties and you know it was so ridiculous to me. I felt embarrassed. You know? But I liked Fred, the one that has two kids, Corrie and Eddie. I liked him because I knew he really loved my mother. At that time we had a nice house. One Christmas he built us this doll house. It had electricity and everything, you know. He was with my mother and his sister was with my mother's brother. You know what I'm saying? So it was like . . . them two families interweaved.

She was with John for twenty years. He ended up hanging himself. I believe near the end of their relationship she firmly put in her mind that they—Tom and Tiff, who are my kids—were hers and John's. She could never conceive again after the hysterectomy she had and she really wanted a baby by John and here comes Tom. I was eighteen years old. She snagged him. He was born three pounds, nine ounces. He had a lot of problems. And he still has asthma, you know, bad heart, and she'd love him to death.

And Tiffany—I kept her with me. She was born when I was nineteen or twenty, but I kept her with me until she was about six months. I was into the heroin so bad I couldn't take it. I called one day and said, if somebody don't get this kid, I'm just gonna leave her somewhere, you know. And I never realize it but she was malnutritioned and stuff. I just knew that I didn't want the state to have her. I wanted to try and keep her with the family and to this day my mother, like when she's mad at her, she tells her, "I never wanted you anyway. I just kept you because Tom was so attached to you."

When I was younger, I was really naive and a good kid. My mother had a lot of expectations for me. She worked two jobs. Like she put me in Our Lady of Mercy Catholic school. She had got it in her mind that she wanted us to be Catholic 'cause she thought Catholics really were strict. And if you came out of the Catholic school you were more respected than if you finished public school. I didn't skip a lot of school. I liked school. My mother checked up on our homework and all. I never brought home bad grades. She'd go to school to visit and monitor my progress, and she got along well with the teachers. They were nuns and that made a difference. You know, maybe if it was someone without a habit, a female or guy, she would have less respect. She would listen to what the nuns had to say and all. She just wanted us to do better than what she had been and she figured if we had educations that maybe we wouldn't end up like her. I was the one who was going to become something 'cause I was an A, B student, but then my father . . . when that happened. . . .

When I was about fifteen I was already experimenting with acid and stuff. By this time she was sending us down to the old guy. That was Phyllis's father. So she was sending us down to his house on the weekend, to get rid of us, right? And it was great! No supervision. He'd give us all kind of money. We were running around wild down there. That's where I met Tom and Tiff's father. That's when I became not a virgin. I was hanging with the little crowd down there and I wasn't really bad yet. I never got locked up when I was a juvenile, but since I turned eighteen, every year except—knock on wood—since I met Darrin, my current boyfriend, I've been in jail every year even if it was for a couple of weeks for something, 'cept this year I haven't been, you know.

My mother was pretty. She's five foot two, you know, she like thirty-eight C or D, real thin waist, nice ass. You know, she was just nice-looking, nice wavy hair, and she flaunted it. So she was a waitress. She was working two jobs. That's how she met John. I remember times he used to give her a black eye so no guys would look at her, you know. When you're a waitress, that's your livelihood . . . that's how you make money.

Once she met him she didn't deal with nobody else. He was running around on her a lot. Like everybody knew it, you know. There was a lot of physical abuse and stuff with her and John. He came into our house at ten and I told him one day, "One day, John, I'm gonna get you. We're all gonna get you. We'll jump you. We're little now, but we're gonna get you one day." And I did. One day he was hitting my mother and I was like in my twenties and I took a baseball bat and busted both of his kneecaps. He was begging me for mercy. I broke them. I just kept . . . bam, bam.

There were a lot of fights with John. He would accuse her of running around on him and shit, which she wasn't doing. She was working. She didn't have the time. But I do remember sometimes we'd go to the corner bar, she'd take us down there, you know, and she'd be drinking. She'd be up on a stool and there's this bottom part, we'd all be sitting there, and guys are trying to hit on her. They'd give us quarters or buy us potato chips and give us money to play music and stuff. Sometimes the guys would give us dollars and stuff and she'd take them, you know. That's how she kept her drinking going. But she never took any of them home or anything.

I was expected to look after the kids. When she worked, that was my thing. She had a list up, our morning chore, our afternoon chore, and our after-school chore. Like on the weekends she do all the cooking, pre-cook, and I would just have to open the vegetables and, you know, maybe peel the potatoes or prepare the noodles or whatever for that day. The meat was prepared. I just have to heat it up. So she would write, "Monday, this is breakfast, this is lunch, this is dinner," you know. She was a good cook. All of us can cook. Eddie too.

We were like little soldiers, you know, when I was under twelve. We knew what time to go to bed. Then sometimes she'd be down at the neighbors' or something and we'd be in our rooms throwing pillows at each other and stuff. You know, goofing off. But that was usually on the weekends. Like we had a routine during the week. School days we had dinner at a certain time, breakfast at a certain time. You know, we're up and dressed, our beds made and everything, and downstairs for breakfast 'cause she made our breakfast before she went to work. When we came home, I was responsible for lunch and dinner. I was responsible for getting that on the table. By the time she got home, dishes were done. We were all either sitting down doing our homework or the ones that were done with their homework were watching TV. At a certain time, hit the bed about nine o'clock, I think— eight, nine o'clock, I don't remember.

After she'd give us breakfast she'd be out to work. We would go off to school. Then she'd come home maybe for a little break, maybe an hour or little more to clean up, clean herself up again to go to the next job, which like four or five hours at night, you know. Then she'd come home. We'd all be done our homework and in our pajamas and stuff. And sometimes she might want to go out to the bar and get a few drinks. I guess it depended on what bills were paid or if she knew she could spend four or five dollars. She also knew that men would buy her drinks at the end of the night, hoping that they were going home with her. Sometimes she'd go to the bar by herself and end up calling the house and saying, "I want yous to come around. I'm having some problems with this guy, you know. He's just not taking no for an answer." But once he sees all the kids, he'll back off her, you know.

She kept the house real clean. Very clean. Sunday was the . . . like the rest day, you know, for real, like the church says it is, that's the way she'd roll. She worked five days a week, but Saturday was like "GI Day." You got to clean your rooms and the kitchen and the stove. I always had the refrigerator 'cause I did it the best. And she thought I really liked that job. I hated it. So everybody had a chore and I was like the enforcer 'cause I was the oldest.

Most of our lives we lived next to the railroad and I remember this one place we lived up around First and Jenkins, two thirty-nine East Spivey, and it was so close to the railroad tracks. We used coal, that's how we heated the house. A lot of trains would stop there for a couple of days and we would go up and fill pillowcases with coal to help her. We would steal like institutional-size cans of peaches and peas. You know, anything to help out. Like there used to be this store called Brenan's and she'd take us in there every year and she told us, "What Mommy's going to do is wrong but I have to do it because there's too many of you," and she'd trade our coats and we all walk out in new coat on and our shoes. She'd come in with us. And she might purchase a couple little items in there. Back then shoplifting wasn't as . . . you know, people didn't suspect as much and there wasn't all these gadgets and all. She would just make sure she took all the tags off everything and that's it. Put our new shoes on us and we'd all be good to go for the year.

From twelve to sixteen, John was there . . . we liked him sometimes 'cause it was real cool. He'd drive us around on his motorcycle. By then my mother was dealing pot. Things started to get better. It started out that Jean Marie was dealing the pot and my mother was still working these two jobs. Jean Marie had been a runaway a lot. She'd bring pot to my little brother Eddie and he'd sell it and she'd give him like whatever. I think it was . . . selling nickels and dimes at the time and she'd drop in every once in a while. Pick up the money, give Eddie something. He thought that was cool. You know, he's a little kid. Leave him another package. So I just told my Mom one day, I said, "Mom, there's things going on this house." And I just broke it down to her. I said, "Jean Marie's using your house, and if anything happens, you'll go to jail. We're all minors." You know. There was so much traffic where you wouldn't believe it. I said, "I'll tell you the truth, Mom. All these years you've been working, I think since it's already doing it, you should take the business over." You know, she thought about it and she did.

We were making . . . oh, man! you wouldn't believe it. She'll buy five, six bundles at a time and they were like cubed, you know, pounds. We learned how to clean it, bag it. All the kids worked. We were all in it. She had hideouts, like a step cut out, you know. We went through busts with police officers and a couple stickups, you know. People come and rob us, you know. It was just wild. Things got out of hand. All of us started getting into using drugs. I started selling at about fourteen.

She would go through these rampages. Her and John would fight. Oh, we didn't care. We were all high, you know, on our various drugs that we liked. All of us were smoking pot, you know. We were allowed, you know. Eddie was about six then. He was smoking pot and dealing it. Like customers come to the door, I want five "nicks." We knew where the stash was, right under the step. I finally told her about that too. I said, "Mom, too many of the customers are seeing where we go to get the pot. You know, we could get busted like by a snitch or something." And eventually it happened. Then they came up with some hideouts up in their room, in the floor, you know.

When the dealing started, people came through with clothes. If they didn't have money, they would come with all kinds of stuff. She bought hot stuff too. Meats. Like good meats, steaks and stuff. Any little deal. Clothes, you know. You know, even till this day she buys a lot of hot stuff.

We didn't live in any place for a long time and it just seemed like after every three years we moved. When you get in a neighborhood, people don't like you till they know you. The kids used to tease us because we had hand-me-downs. And all of a sudden we start selling drugs. We had control.

You know, it was like power. Now like all these kids that used to tease us and all, now we had everything. We were even above them and they'll have to come to us. Like sometimes they would be short, you know, for a nickel and we'd make them beg us and shit 'cause of what they had done to us.

Man, between getting busted and between getting called for him beating her up, like domestic dispute or whatever, the police were there at least every month. And finally, when I was fifteen and a half or sixteen, I rolled. You know, I got out of it. And I'd drop in occasionally, every few months or so, you know, just to see how they're doing or what's happened, you know. It was just too taxing on me.

I don't feel happy about how my mother treated me at all. I mean she burned me. She abused me mentally. She lied to me. Oh, I have values and scruples, but I believe what I have I acquired on my own or from going through different phases. Like, you know, going through. . . I've been in . . . like I've lived with every different race. You know, I've been involved in everything, you know. Especially when you're involved with drugs and living on the streets. You just learn a lot. You pick up a lot on your own. Things you won't do and will do.

But she taught the girls that they shouldn't depend on a man. Never trust men. Use men, 'cause all the men want from us is to fuck us. Always be able to get your own. And really, if you can, you wear the pants. Don't let the man be over you. Where the man can't say, "I'm taking care of you in this house, bitch," or something like that. She was the boss.

When I was growing up, the thing that I learned most was to respect your elders, speak when you're spoken to, try and learn in school because you don't want to end up like Mommy, having to . . . you know, being a waitress to make tips to keep food on the table, you know. She also taught me to dress decently, you know, not to run around like a slut, cleanliness, you know, as far as yourself and where you live.

Sometimes my mother would just freak. It could be something small, something big, something she heard. We took something out of the refrigerator we weren't supposed to or lying to her. At any given moment, she could explode. Yelled at us. Curse us. "That's what I get! I'm out working for you and this is the way you pay me back." Sometimes she would say, "I would have been better not having you to begin with. I never really wanted you, but you came out of me, so it was my responsibility." When she was drinking, she'd get depressed and say, "If I didn't have you, I could be running around doing anything I wanted. I'd probably have a decent man. No man wants to settle down with me. I got five kids already."

She totally beat me one night. She used to do stuff like make us get naked and wet and then hit us with the catty nine tail. The catty nine tail was this rope, not like that you hang on your door, not the cloth, it had plastic over it. She'd make like a knot and whack us with it. We had welts sometimes. Sometimes we'd have to bend over, hold our ankles, and we'd get hit with the bread board. If you moved, you got three extra. You know, stuff like that.

She told Fred to beat me one time. I did something wrong and he beat me. The next morning—she always made lunch, he was an electrician and he liked her to make his lunches— I asked her, "Can I make Daddy Fred's lunch?" She said, "Yeah." I did this I know because I remember doing it. I killed two shad roaches and put one on each of his sandwiches. Thank God that before he ate the sandwich obviously he'd looked at his sandwiches to see what my mom made. He called her at lunch. "Who made my lunch?" She said she told him I made it. So I got it good that night again. But you know I was like satisfied because I got him back for beating me the last time.

I remember her burning me when I was six years old. I still have the scar on my knuckles. She says that I took rent money off the table and went out and bought all the kids in the neighborhood candy and stuff. Well, she didn't actually burn me. She put my hand over the fire to scare me and I pulled it and I burnt myself. But I was six years old. Common sense would tell you a six-year-old kid is not stronger than an adult. I remember it like it was yesterday.

During a month she would lose it maybe ten or twelve times a month. No one was ever severely hurt. No authorities were called or anything. Except my burn's about the worst thing she did. She might ground you for a week or whatever. With me, if it was something I liked, she might take my record player and my records away or no phone calls.

She would never embarrass me in front of anyone else. Not when we were kids. No. As we got older . . . now like she more like talks, telling different people family things about us and trying to make people feel sorry for her. "Oh, poor Phyl, with her kids that put her in a home." The martyr.

When she was saying these kinds of things it didn't make me feel good, you know. I'd just sometimes block her out. I'd say she's drunk. She has a lot of shit that she goes through. So I imagine she has to take it somewhere. I don't know why she did it. 'Cause from what I understand, her mother didn't raise her either. Her grandmother raised her and her uncles and stuff. I don't know what the deal was. She never really, really quite explained it. Her and my grandmother were not close until almost near when my grandmother was dying. My grandmother died when she was seventy-nine. And about two years before that her and my mother finally got close. My mother couldn't do enough for her. But I just figured maybe she was treated like that when she was younger so she just thought that was the way to do it.

Up until I was fifteen I listened to my mother. When I was fifteen and a half that's when I had sex for the first time. And I felt guilty about it. She didn't know yet. I didn't get pregnant or nothing till I was seventeen. I respected my mother, but I wouldn't want to be the kind of person she was when I was growing up because she used her children like puppets. Like puts us against each other. If she's mad at you, nobody else is supposed to talk to you or they get shunned.

She was always taking in kids. When my uncle's marriage was getting ready for divorce, my mother took his three kids. All through my life my mother's been the type. . . . We have this kid, "Jack Ass," we call him. She took him in and he calls her Mom and all till this day. You know, comes and brings her presents on Christmas. You know, just take in different people off the street where she would like want us to be jealous like. If it was a boy and he's calling her Mom, my brother Eddie would hate him because, "Yeah, you're really my mother." If it was a girl all of us would freak out. Till this day she pushes buttons. Like gets a fight going with us, you know. Like we're little puppets, you know.

I dropped out school in the eleventh grade. Jean Marie dropped out in ninth or tenth, same with Phyllis. Corrie dropped out in the twelfth, and Eddie dropped out in about ninth or tenth. Some of them have GED's though.

When I was in Our Lady of Mercy and I wouldn't adapt to algebra because to me it didn't mean . . . I can add, subtract, multiply, divide, fractions, percentage, great. But to me putting letters with numbers didn't mean anything and I wasn't gonna use it in my future and I didn't want to learn it. I didn't like it, and I flunked it. I don't know it till this day. And for that I was put out of Our Lady of Mercy and that hurt her. Number one, after that she took all the kids out of Catholic school and put them in public school and I felt so bad for that. You know, . . . well, Jean Marie would never fit or Phyllis, but Corrie was a brain. Corrie may have been the one, you know. What my mother did was wrong. Just because I failed she pulls them all out and so Cor, to get back at her, went up to twelfth grade and like two or three months before school's over she dropped out. And she called herself getting back at her, but she knows now that it hurt her.

She wasn't particularly concerned about the kids I hung out with because I hung out with a pretty nice crowd. But my sisters Jean Marie and Phyllis hung at Rogers and Clarke, and they were some bad kids. They used to rob factories. The cops were always on the door about Jean Marie and Phyllis.

If someone called and told her that I was seen somewhere else getting in trouble, she would either ask us if it was true or she'd jump in the car and go find out if we were there. I've known her to drive Jean Marie, Phyllis, and Corrie off corners. Like they'd be so embarrassed. They say, "Oh, God, here she comes," you know, and they couldn't get away quick enough. Then they might get grounded for a couple of nights or a week.

Me and my brothers and sisters got along all right. We stuck together. If one was in a fight, we all were down there. We all got along great together as kids. Except, like I said, the one next to me, I never like. . . . She tried to intimidate you and . . . you know. She lived in Washington, D.C. and she was a dancer, a call girl. She only dealt with judges and senators and doctors and she had a condominium, a limo service, and couple of hotdog carts. And she was into snorting. She used to constantly put me down because I was a "street whore," as she calls it. She would never belittle herself to trick for twenty dollars for blowing a guy or something. I was disgusting, you know. I told her, "Don't ever say never," and sure enough she's out there. She's a piper now. She lost everything and she's out on the same route I'm on. I mean, it's a shame.

Phyllis's back with Mom. It's a shame. She don't want to be there or anything, but that's besides the point. She's on DPA. Her daughter is with the father, and she has a son. Oh, she's got a little thing going at night. Some hot telephone thing. I don't . . . I'm gonna talk to her more about it. At first my brother's girl was doing it, but he got out of prison and he found out. My mother has no scruples. Like Deborah lost her job at Taco Bell. She was an assistant manager. Deborah had bought her a brand new refrigerator, had been paying every week to stay there. My mother just don't give an inch. "You gotta do something to pay me to live here" and all this. So Deborah got into this phone shit. You know, talking to guys. They call her from twelve to eight in the morning and she's got this private number. So now Phyllis's doing it. Supposedly from what I understand she's still doing it in Deborah's name so welfare won't find out that she's getting that check.

Corrie is next to her in age. She lives in Warminster too. She live at Warminster and Wicomico. She just got over a piping addiction, her and her old man. She has three kids. She's the closest to what my mother was. My sister Jean Marie gave her son to the grandmother. My kids are with my mother and two of them are with their father. Phyllis—the one kid's with his father and the other kid, from what I'm hearing right now, somebody has. So Corrie is most like my mother. She has her children and is taking care of them, but Corrie is very sloppy. Her house is a mess. But, you know, she tries. Like her oldest, little Irene, basically we all helped raised her. Corrie was young when she had her—she was about eighteen—but everyone pitched in and helped her and now little Reeney basically is doing what I was doing with the kids. She helps her mother with little Ellen and Georgie. You know, a lot of shit gets put on her. She's only ten years old.

Eddie is next to her. My brother was sent to prison for burglaries and drugs. Maybe eighteen when he went to jail the first time. That was my mother's son, so she was getting him out, you know. But then after a while she got tired of it. And a couple of times he ripped her off. Finally, she turned him out. Now this time he did about two years in jail, and they sent him to this program. I called there the other night to try to talk to Phyllis. He picked up the phone and said, "Whoever this is, I want you to know I'm in the picture now." So that told me he must be out. He's living there with him and his girl.

My mother, now she's got balls behind her . . . she can't hardly walk. She's got emphysema, asthma, she's got a breathing machine in her room, so she always wants at least one of us be living there to keep up the house. You know, she's still into a clean house, you know, food on the table at dinnertime, somebody to wash and do the dishes, water the plants, and she always needs at least one of her kids there because Tiff and Tom, my two, these kids ain't into being clean. She's even paid me to clean their rooms. They are slobs. I never . . . they're nothing like we were. This generation. These kids are different. I mean the girl wears her hair up. She uses a can of hairspray a day. She carries it around with her. She's real pretty, too. She looks just like a model. I haven't seen her since she had the baby. Oh, she's wild. When my mother learned I had my period she didn't tighten up on me. No, she trusted me. Because I had been good up until that point in my life. I found out mostly about sex from Jean Marie, the sister next to me. My period came on when I was at school one day. I was embarrassed. I didn't know what it was. I hadn't heard before that. But my mother just told me how to deal with it and basically it was once a month where we had to get rid of bad blood and after that we cleaned ourself out with douches. I went to the nun and told her . . . I was sitting on my desk and I was bleeding. She told me to go down to the nurse and, you know, not to come back to the class for the rest of the day. You know. Go home and talk to my mother. And my mother told me that now . . . she asked me . . . she said, "I don't think you're doing it, but are you having sex with boys?" And I said, "Oh, God, no, Mommy!" And she said, "You know, now if you let a boy do something to you, you can have a baby. 'Cause now you're a woman."

I was fifteen and a half when I had sex the first time. We were down Phyllis's father's house and we were staying overnight and my boyfriend . . . it was late, and he told Dan, that was Phyllis's father, that he couldn't go home, could he spend the night? And I knew he was lying. Dan said, "Yeah." Phyllis and Corrie were asleep on the cot. I was asleep on the couch, and Scott was supposed to sleep on the chair. My boyfriend came over. I don't want to yell to upset Corrie and Phyllis. I always believe that the old man engineered that, like watched or something. He just penetrated me and that was it. I wasn't happy with it. I didn't have orgasm or anything. I stayed with him until I was about nineteen, and I have two kids by him.

He wasn't the one I really liked. The one I really liked was Jay-Jay and like I felt he looked too good for me to try to go with so I settled for Scott 'cause Scott looks a little like Jay-Jay. Scott and I were going together at the time. I don't know if he expected me to have sex with him. I don't know if I expected it. I knew he tried a lot. And I'd "No, no, no." But something inside me that night told me if Uncle Dan let him stay there something is going to happen. I didn't want to make any noise because Corrie and Phyllis were over right across from me and I didn't dare want to let them know anything.

I was in my late twenties when I learned about contraception, contraceptive measures. Once I had my first baby. I had a baby when I was eighteen, nineteen, and twenty-one. I had two of them and a set of twins. And I had the last two when I was twenty-nine and thirty and then I had my tubes tied. I was also in my twenties when I learned about venereal diseases. All the stuff I learned about sex I learned in the streets.

I've had one abortion. It was a payback. I had twins. I got raped and I was also having sex with this other guy that I really liked. So I wasn't sure who the father was—if Scott was the father or if the guy I was really liked, Jay-Jay, was the father or not. I gave them to the state. When I had the twins he said they weren't his and I wasn't really sure and then when I got pregnant again I was sure it was his baby. He really wanted it. So I called myself paying him back. Got an abortion.

I have six children and none of them were trick babies. I know who all their fathers are. Tom is eighteen and Tiff is seventeen. Maureen and Collette, they're with the state. Maureen is in Sunny Creek Mental Institution because she beats her head into the wall. She has to wear a football helmet and she has to wear Pampers. She's fifteen. They say she's autistic, whatever that is. Collette is in Dogwood, Pennsylvania. She's fifteen. They're the twins. Marisol and Raisa are seven and six and they're with Angel and his mother. I feel guilty sometimes about not taking care of them. Like I said, I'm glad I'm not one of them people that just take them to get money for them. It's a long goal, but I want to get myself together rather than put them on a seesaw and think I can take them and then fall back into dope and have to give them back or lose them to the state.

I only see Marisol and Raisa. I haven't seen Tom and Tiff since July. The two youngest, I have a good relationship with them. I'm not happy with the relationship I have with Tom and Tiff. I'm just hoping that as they get older they'll understand that it wasn't that I didn't love them, you know. Now, especially Tiff, since she has her own baby, maybe she'll see. It was born in August. So it's four months. I don't have a good relationship with them because of my mother. She tells them all kind of shit about me. They're like against me. But sometimes we have talks when we're alone and I can tell they have more feeling for me than a sister.

All of the children were born after my drug addiction. I was using heroin when all of them were born. With Tom I wasn't using heroin yet, but I was using acid. And he was born with three holes in his heart. He was only three pounds, nine ounces 'cause I wasn't eating or anything. My mother wasn't aware I even had the drug problems. I was doing it when I'd go downtown for the weekend. With all the other kids I was either on dope or methadone. When I learned that I was pregnant the first time, I didn't get any special health care. Not the first time. Only the second one. I was on methadone with the first one and with the last one I was on methadone too. There is only one program in this city that will take you if you're on a program and that's Roosevelt. I was a high-risk mother, so I guess they call themselves monitoring you. You know, you keep your appointments and all. Like when you're on a program you're more responsible and they may keep up with it better. The babies stayed in the hospital for a month or so and they gave them medication. For some reason the last kid came home with me. She had shook a little once in a while but . . . you know.

When I found out I was pregnant I was happy. My mother threw a shower, all my girlfriends bought me little things and stuff for him. Then after I had him I realized I wasn't really cut out for this thing. But I didn't believe in getting my tubes tied and I really didn't believe in abortion because of being Catholic at the time. I really wanted the child. After he was born, I guess I was so frightened. Like I had raised kids already. I never got to be a kid, you know. I kind of felt like maybe she owed me now. Let her take care of him. I took care of her kids.

I was the first one to use hard drugs in my family. I don't think I used drugs because of the people I hung with. Sometimes I think it could of started when I was in the home and they had started me on Thorazine. Sometimes I think it was when I met my father and it just turned my whole life around. I just wanted to hurt everybody, forget everything. It was never to be a part of the crowd. And once I did heroin it was clear that I liked it.

I don't think the dealing got me involved in hustling. No, that had nothing to do with it. I used to buy downs off my mother and she'd let me buy them and if I ever get too high she'd put me out after she had sold me the stuff. I started buying downs from her in my twenties, like twenty-three or more.

As for my mother, I begged, nagged her until she gave me money, pills, downs. I robbed her once. Like when she was dealing I took three thousand and something off her. She thought I'd be the good one, but that just went down the tubes, you know. She just didn't trust me. I can't stay in her house. I probably couldn't stay in anyone in my family's house. Maybe I could stay with my favorite sister, but she's with my mother now.

When I was growing up I never even thought about fantasies . . . When I was in the home I was thinking about becoming a nun at one point, but like most kids think they want to be a doctor, I never went through that. I never felt as if I had a childhood because I was basically taking care of the other kids in my family. 'Cause my mother had to work. I would say that my life was very hectic up until the age of sixteen. I changed around and got thrown around a lot. I learned a lot in my adulthood. I'm a whole different person. I'm not withdrawn, you know. I'm not afraid of nothing. I don't feel as though I'm ugly, you know, the way my family brought me up to be. In my mind I believed I was ugly for a long time. You know, my mother told me, "You're the ugliest in the family. Your sisters are pretty." I believed that until 1983, and that's when I went in Pegasus. I learned to fight for myself. I used to be very withdrawn and I'd accept anything. Like I took blame for shit that I didn't do, let her abuse me mentally, tell me how ugly, and that I was flat-chested.

I don't know if my early years influenced me. I think as I got older, I got better. As I got older, I learned more in the streets, and by going to therapists and programs I learned more about myself. I learn not to be ashamed of myself and not to be withdrawn, and if something's wrong, not to take the blame for somebody else's shit. You know, not to be afraid to say no. If I feel something's right, I don't care if everyone else thinks it's wrong. I'm sticking to my guns. In my early years I was unhappy. I was lied to. So I never knew who I was when I was younger.

I left my mother's house because I got sick of the things that were going on in my family. You know, the dealing, the busts, the robberies. You know, it was just too taxing on me and I just lost a lot of what I had for my mother in my younger years. I was about sixteen or fifteen and a half when I left home. I just told her I was rolling. There was nothing she could do. I mean, I had a job. I had two jobs. I was working at a restaurant down on South-bourne Street and I was dancing at a place called Steppin' Out at Eleventh and Mill. It's not there anymore.

When I was dancing I had pasties here and a little G-string. They didn't have a liquor license and people brought their own bottles. Sometimes the place got busted for that. You know, I made good money an hour, plus guys would give me tips. It was a place really for laundering money for the Mafia. That was basically what it was. I worked there for almost a year. Me and two of my sisters all ended up working down there. One was a cashier, and me and my other sister were dancers. We have what you call "sets." You know, you could play three records on the jukebox or bring your own. Three records was one set. And I would do three or four sets a night.

I finally robbed them and that's why I had to leave. It really wasn't my idea. He was sleeping with one of the cashiers, and he started being really shitty with my third sister, my favorite sister. She just told me one Saturday night, 'cause that was a big night, you know. She was allowed in the safe and all. She said, "We're gonna take them off." The sister next to me, we didn't even let her know because we'd know she would "No, no." Because we were making good money down there, me and her, you know. But Phyllis just had it in her mind. So she said, "What? They really can't call the cops. This is Mafia shit." And we knew we could end up getting killed if they found us, but she was determined to do it. She was my favorite sister and I wasn't gonna let her go down alone. It had nothing to do with me getting a split of the money. We got about fifty, sixty thousand dollars. Ah man, we spent it on clothes, hiding out. We couldn't come out for a while, you know. Like we found a hotel that, you know, we paid them enough where we were good to go for a month or two, you know. Clothes and drugs. Oh, my mother, we gave her some of course.

When I left home I was just using acid and IV-crank. I started the crank at sixteen or seventeen, and I was doing pot here and there. I don't like pot. I lived on Southbourne Street. That was my first apartment and I lived there about two years. I stayed in that area until I was about twenty-two. I was doing my waitressing and dancing. I was getting a welfare check too, because the dancing and my waitressing was under the table. I was doing burglaries, stickups, robberies. It got to the point where the neighbors were putting up a petition. They didn't want me in the neighborhood.

When I was sixteen Amy Doyle was one of my friends and Janet Healey— yeah, that's right—was one at eighteen. She's the one that hooked me up with heroin for the first time. After she hooked me up, me and Shawna became best friends, and we were best friends till I was locked up. When I got out we were still best friends for a while, then she went to California or somewhere. Shawna was the best. I should have ended up staying with Amy 'cause she ended up not being in drugs and all, but Shawna was my really best friend.

So when I moved to Sixteenth and Southbourne I was living by myself. Sometimes my favorite sister would come down with Shawna. If it was too rough at home she would come down and stay with me for a couple of weeks or whatever. I was going out with Scott then, the two oldest kids' father. I was working, you know, doing my little burglaries and shit at sixteen. But I never got caught at any crime until I was eighteen. For some reason I've always felt like I'm born in the Falk Corrections Center. Every year since then I've made it there. Every year I've been locked up, even if it was for a month or a couple of weeks, except 1990. I know that's Darrin. I know it.

Like I said, Amy was one of the people at sixteen. We used to go up to the Art Museum. In the summer they used to have the . . . what they called the "Funky Dog." People would come out from all different neighborhoods and they would have bands and shit out there. You know, we would mess around up there. Or go to the movies, go down the ice-skating rink and watch the ice skates. Like Broadway they had a ice-skating rink.

Janet was with a dealer down in East Jefferson named Terry. There was a crowd of us hanging around together at that time. Janet was sent with a couple of bundles a day because Terry would let us do it for free. Then after about two weeks, when, you know, the ones who are going to get into it got hooked, we were told, "Well, you know, Terry can't just keep giving his stuff away. Now you're gonna have to start paying for it." So with our little group Terry had more customers. See what I'm saying? There was about twenty of us in this little group, but not all of us got into it. Amy not being one of them. Shawna being one of them.

The first time I did heroin I did two bags. She tried one bag, I didn't feel nothing. She gave me two, and I felt it. Then I started building up. Like they sold six-packs, half a bundle. It took me two weeks to have a habit. I thought I could control it. I never knew about heroin and getting a habit and all. I knew I had lost control when she had said that she couldn't give me any anymore. I went to her one day, and said, "Janet, could I have a couple of bags?" "I can't give it to you no more." I was like, you know, running nose, my eyes running. I was just jittery. I knew then I needed to do dope. It took me a couple of months before I could hit myself, but I've always preferred someone hitting me 'cause my vision is bad.

One night I got grabbed by the cops, and about six or eight of them beat me real bad. They fractured some of my ribs. I had two black eyes. They busted my nose. They caught me in a burglary. So they said, "You like to do crimes like a man. We're gonna treat you like a man." When I got arrested, the matron told me, "Don't ever say that I told you this, but I am going to say that you asked me take pictures of you. No woman should be beat the way you were beaten." I mean I was bruised . . . I couldn't even . . . I crawl in the Falk Corrections Center.

It turned out that I was going to sue. . . . She told me what to do. She said, "One of two things. You have so many . . ."—I had one armed robbery, two robberies, and three burglaries. . . . She said, "One of two things. You're gonna do a whole lot of time and come out a very rich woman or they'll drop all your cases and you won't do any time in prison." At the time I was about twenty, twenty-one, and I was scared, you know? So I was suing the Eleventh District. That was where I lived. I liked that neighborhood too. I was suing the City of Jefferson. So they came with a deal. My lawyer had to sign it. I mean, I got a copy, the lawyer got a copy, the city got a copy, the Eleventh District and the district attorney and. . . . I was facing forty to sixty years at that time, and that scared me. You know, I mean, goddamn, I was twenty years old, I wouldn't get out until I was sixty or eighty. Well, they said they would drop my armed robbery, my two robberies, and two of my burglaries. The one they caught me on they would charge me, you know. So at that point I was not on probation or anything, you know, so I figured, well, I'll end up getting probation. When I went to court the judge gave me eleven and a half to twenty-three months and you could have knocked me over with a feather. I didn't expect that.

When I was in prison I was there for like seven months. One day the head girls in the jailhouse had planned on robbing the infirmary. I happened to be up there when it went down. And I got in on it. I was a drug addict. I'd been clean for seven months. I just couldn't help myself. It was just such a . . . seeing all the drugs. There's cough syrup, Valiums, methadone tablets. I was like, "Oh, my God. I'm in heaven!" So I got in on it with them. They had to call the men's side police to come over. They threw gas at us, you know, and finally subdued us. There was like thirty of us. I woke up a week later. I didn't remember anything. All I remember, I woke up, I was in lock and I was starving. And I hit my . . . you know I banged myself. One of the jailers came down and said, "What's the matter, Toddy?" I said, "Damn, I'm hungry. What the hell am I in lock for?" And then things started coming back in my mind. She said, "You have thirty-one days. There's about thirty or forty of you." And I said, "Oh, my God!"

The lock is when you're in isolation. You're not out in population. You're in lock twenty-four hours a day. You get to come out one hour and that's like to shower and make a phone call. And you get one hour of exercise. So you get out two hours a day in twenty-four hours. It never dawned on me about my parole. I was due up for parole on my eleven and a half months. When I went for the hearing that was the only thing I had done wrong, but that was enough. When I went in front of the parole officer, the parole board told me, "You have a bad prison record. We're going to max you out." So I had another eleven and a half, you know. It wasn't worth it. That high.

I just had to accept it. When they brought me back, you know, I had to walk in the wing, and the girls would say, "What happened?" You know, I was just . . . I told the CO, I said, "Do me a favor. Just lock me for about five or seven days. Because right now I feel like a volcano and I just want to hurt somebody, anybody, for nothing." You know. I said, "Just please for my . . . so I won't get into any more trouble. Just keep me in lock for seven days at least. I want to come out only for a shower. And then please stay with me." You know. They loved me out there. I was a friendly person. You know, I get along with blacks, whites, and Puerto Ricans. I could talk some Spanish. You know, I just had a lot of friends.

The worst time was only when I was in there the one time I heard that my stepfather had hung himself. And I felt bad for my mother and my two little kids 'cause they called him their dad. But I never had problems far as fighting or being robbed. Prison is basically black girls. Not now though, there's a lot of Puerto Ricans, because most Puerto Ricans sell drugs. And there are more white girls than there used to be too. But it's different than it used to be, you know. There was respect and stuff before. These young kids are a trip. They don't respect older people. They just don't care.

So I was doing a lot of crime before I got arrested. I was doing burglaries at sixteen. I just did them. I would just kick a door down. Back in them days, you could use credit cards to get in doors. It was ridiculous. People would cash personal checks. I mean I would get a personal check and write it out for a certain amount of money, go to a grocery store, purchase about twenty dollars' worth of stuff, and get the rest in cash. You know what I'm saying? And at that time welfare checks were coming out in the mail, SSI checks, Social Security checks, and there were a lot of people you could go to and get like maybe two-thirds of it. You know what I mean? It was great! You know, like you could sell a color TV back then for seventy-five or hundred bucks, a nineteen-inch. At that time I would take major things. I was into coins, guns, money, stamp collections, and . . . you know . . . if . . . that was because they were more easier. You're desperate and they don't have none of this shit in there so you take a TV or a component set. For that kind of stuff you would have to have somebody with a car. With a gun or stamp collection, coin collection, or money, you just walk out with that on your person.

The drug world is a world where we know each other. I had people that I knew that were good fences. Like you might needed somebody that says, "Well, if you give me a couple of dollars, I'll take you to this person." Once you meet them, you've got the connection. You know, it's a whole different world. It's not an ordinary world. You meet them where you go and cop— you know, people that are into burglaries and stuff—and you just take the chance of asking them do they know where you can get rid of something. Then you could have somebody that knows you're a burglar and come up to you and say, "Charlie, I'm looking for a nineteen-inch color TV. Could you get me one? How much would you charge me?" you know. So like they put their little order in and I know what they need.

Then another thing, and I remember back then, I met a telephone man. This was when telephone calls were a dime. You know how long ago that was. For three hundred dollars he sold me a key to open all the telephone coin boxes. I know now where I made my mistake. I was hitting, oh, my God, for the longest . . . I didn't even have to do burglaries . . . I would just, you know, at night carry this nice big heavy bag. I had my "watchy," Shawna. It was great for about two years, you know. This was one of the best things I came into. But the mistake I made . . . I was taking everything. I should of left some of the dimes in them. I didn't think like that. I thought, "Go for broke." And I was just hitting all them downtown, you know. A lot of people make phone calls, and believe it or not, it took like two years before Bell Tel finally realized something was wrong. "What the fuck? Nobody's making phone calls downtown." So I had that for a while.

I did burglaries all the way up till I was twenty-two. Like even after I got out of jail, I was doing them. Sometimes by myself, but usually Shawna worked with me. We became very good friends and I trusted her and she trusted me. Usually I busted in, and she watched, but I was never unfair, you know. I'd split it down the middle 'cause we were really friends. But a lot of times I did it myself, you know, 'cause I know I'm not gonna tell on myself.

But we had this thing going, right? At that time my hair was about down to here. Yeah, almost to my ass. I don't wear much makeup anyway and I could pass as an Italian girl . . . where when I would do a burglary I would put a bush wig on, put makeup on, and I would exactly look like a Spanish girl. People would say it was a black girl or a Spanish girl, and the cops knew it was us, but they couldn't. . . . They'd take us to the person and then I would have my hair back down, my makeup off, and they couldn't finger me.

Then I remember a time. This was unbelievable. My uncle, my sister's father, sent me to get milk and bread at this corner store. Borchert Grocery and Grill. It was at Eighteenth and Carpenter. And I was like five months pregnant with my second kid. I walked into this store and there was two bags of money sitting there. Like they were getting ready to close and forget to lock the front door. So I was like "Oh, my God!" you know. But I was a little heavy, starting to get heavy, and I was afraid to run, you know. So I went outside and I'd seen one of the people I hung with. I said, "Brent, just act normal." I said, "Inside Borchert Grocery—there is two . . ." They had Borchert Grocery and Borchert Grill, that was a beer distributor. So that must have been that night's take. I said, "I want you to go in there and take it and meet me at Gessler's." Which was a deserted lot that we knew. I said, "If you don't meet me there, I'm gonna give you up." He was like six foot two, he could run. I could run too, but I was pregnant. So he met me there and both of us got nineteen hundred dollars each. He had him, his sister, his brother, his girl, his sister's boyfriend, you know. I said, "Don't . . . you know, get a used car, don't come out flashy, you know, with clothes and shit. They know we're addicts and all." They did it anyway. So they all got grabbed and I was scared to death that they were gonna give me up. They didn't for some reason, and they got out of it. Like the man couldn't say for sure they did it. So we were barred out of there, but we didn't give a shit.

Then I had this other thing, this was just ridiculous. This guy was nuts. They ended up killing him at Fifteenth and Wicomico. He killed a cop. The week before his mother died he died, and then in a week later they found his sister OD in an alley up at Tenth and Doyle. His other brother is doing forty to sixty for robbing a gas station down at Fourth and Pendleton. But he just knew I had a lot of heart. I knew with him I didn't have to worry about anything 'cause he really would kill you. He had uniforms and sometimes we'd go to the corner as cops and take all the dope. You know, tell them, "Well, we're willing to just take the money and the drugs and we'll let you walk rather than lock you up, 'cause we're not into the paperwork anyway." You know, stuff like that. We'd like walk into a gallery and just, "Everybody drop! Put your shit down, your drugs, your everything!" When I'm in that relationship with him I take a more passive role, and I just always knew I was safe with him. He used to hold the gun and he'd tell me to go around and pick up all the money and all the drugs.

This other thing I was involved in was a stickup at this corner bar on Bridge Street. The man never told me that three weeks in a row he had done it, or I wouldn't have did it with him. He caught me one night and asked me. I knew the bar, and I was sick. So me and Shawna went. I put my wig on and all. All we got was four hundred and some dollars. That next week, being the fifth week—I was in on it the fourth week—there was a stakeout there. They blew him to bits. He was still alive, but now the girl he was with was also an addict and a friend of mine, she didn't want nothing else to do with him after that 'cause he couldn't hustle anymore. Like he had bedsores all over him, you know. He just faded away and died.

These things took place before I was twenty-three. When I was working with women I played the active person. I would plan what house, how we're gonna get in, and all that kind of stuff. Like one time for instance . . . he was a trick. The landlady knew I'd been to his room before, so she let me in. I was just looking around the room. It wasn't about nothing. I found six hundred and ninety dollars. So I just rolled. So the next time I went around, I got in without the landlady. There was six hundred and seventy in the same place. It was like he was saying, "Take me!" I never knew he was a numbers writer. Now, about a month later, I took my girl with me. At the time it was Sissy, and I said, "Knock on the door." She had a suitcase. I said, "Say you came in from California. You're Alberto's. . . ." 'Cause by this time he had told the landlady, "Don't let her in." He knew it was me. So I told her, "Say you're Alberto's sister. 'Oh, my God! He's not here! Could you please let me in so I can wait for him?'" Once she got in, I told her, "In a few minutes, come down and let me in." There was twenty-three hundred dollars there. Couple of days later—I used to hang this place called Santiago's on South-bourne Street, it's not there anymore—some guy came in and told me,

"Charlie, I've got a message for you from Alberto. The next time you come around in his house he's gonna blow your head off." So I just said, "Well, three's a charm. That's the end of that." I was about twenty-two then, and this is after I got out of prison.

At one point, I was living with a dealer who was implicated in a couple of murders. It was in '75. I was twenty-one, and he was forty-five. That was Julio. He was obsessed with me. He used to keep me locked in the house, but I could have all the drugs I wanted, you know, air conditioner, color TV, but I was just kept in like a birdcage. And then he got busted and went to prison.

I also went to prison for something. While I was in there I met this brother, Travis. To me it was just a thing in jail. I don't know why, but I kept writing to him when I got out, bringing him stuff, which I should have never did. I had no feelings for him. After he got out and he realized that I didn't want him, he raped me. I was dealing with this guy Tico and I don't know if the twins were his or Travis's. And during '75, he had me move into Eleventh and Pendleton.

Travis I was afraid of. I stole one of Julio's guns. He had a twenty-five and a thirty-two, and I stole the thirty-two 'cause he told me he was gonna kill me for not staying with him. So I was with Travis. Next thing I know we were in a cab. This white guy was driving. I don't know where Julio came from, but as soon as I seen him, I knew it was going to be a problem. I said to the cab—we were at a stop sign at Hillside and Doyle—I said, "Please, there is going to be a problem." He jumps out and runs. I don't know how to drive. I was on a methadone program at the time, and I was ripped off my ass. Travis grabbed the gun out of my purse. Julio said, "I got a gun. I'm gonna kill you." Travis shot him once in the shoulder. Then it turned out Julio was bluffing—Julio had turned into a drug addict. When I met him he was an alcoholic but he wanted to be like me so he started doing drugs— they just decided they were going to have . . . you know, whoever won, got me. They didn't even ask me what I wanted. There was a second shot. Julio pushed the gun and he said, "If I'm gonna die you're going with me." I got shot. The impact of the bullet blew my blouse in half. I was bleeding. Travis shot him in his head and his head was like . . . wheee! Travis runs with the gun. I'm left with the body. All these clothes are in the back of the cab.

So I said, "Oh, my God, I got a body." So I ran and I call my mother. She thinks I'm all high. "What part of the game is this?" I said, "Mom, please I'm serious. I'm shot. I think Julio's dead. Travis's on the run with a gun." So she told me to go down by the Art Museum and hide my stuff and my stepfather would come and pick me up. So by the time I got to her house, she said, "I called. Julio is in Rolnick Hospital in intensive care. He's comatose. He's probably gonna die." This was the twenty-first of June. "They got Travis already, but no gun. They want you to turn yourself in. I told them you're six months pregnant and they said go down to Jefferson Hospital," which was across from Sixth and Commerce. "There will be cops down there waiting for you. Let them attend to you and then they want to take you to Homicide for questioning."

Julio died on the twenty-fourth. I buried him on the twenty-eighth. All I could think . . . well, maybe I could just put this basically on Julio 'cause he died anyway and at least try and help Travis 'cause I was feeling guilty, like this is my fault. You know, until a couple of years ago.

It wasn't my fault. I didn't plan that, but my mother said subconsciously I wanted to get rid of them both. Travis was black and Travis got two to five for involuntary manslaughter because Julio was Puerto Rican and was a dealer. They didn't care. He didn't have any family.

From June twenty-first to June twenty-eighth, it rained that whole time. It's not like that in June, you know. But it rained, and as soon as he was buried, the sun came out again. I've gone to one funeral because I had to and that was the one. And for years I felt really guilty, you know, like it's my fault. For real I didn't want to use one of them and you know my mother kept saying, "You like it. You could say you engineered it. You wanted one to die and one to go to jail. This way you'd be rid of both of them." I kept that in my head. I was twenty-one or twenty-two when this happened.

I started prostitution when I was twenty-three. I met a friend of mine, Kathy—her mother lived across the street from my mother—and, you know, she told me that the crimes I was doing carry hard time. I said, "Kathy, I could never do it. I'm flat-chested. I'm not pretty." She said, "Not pretty!" She said, "First, if all girls looked the same, it wouldn't be interesting out here." And she said, "And guys are into different things. Some guys are leg men, which you have great legs. You got a nice ass. You got nice hips." She said, "And there is some guys that like blondes. Some guys like redheads. Some guys like dark-haired girls." And she said, you know, "If you put a little makeup on," she said, ". . . 'cause you're a mix, you got this look, like a different look," you know. And I said, "But I can't do it." I said, "Suck a dick! Ughhh!" You know, she said, "I'm telling you. Just get high before you go out." 'Cause I know when . . . I knew how it is when I do heroin. For one thing I get horny and I am more open and everything. So I tried it. At this time, the cops weren't bothering us. They're "Hi. How are you doing, Char?" And I'll jumped out of one big car and get in another . . . it'll be lined up. I was doing it at Warminster and Winter then.

And prostitution at that time, you know, you're like a revolving door. At that time it was fun. I mean the Avenue was really fun. You know, Warminster Avenue, Dock Street. You know, like there wasn't pimps and all that. You know, not people trying to like. . . . Now, I'd be afraid to be out there. Like they're out there killing. Guys will spot a girl and realize she has money and beat her up. The tricks are cutting girls and doing all kinds of shit. The pipers are selling themselves for five dollars for a blow job that I do twenty dollars.

Back then blow jobs were ten dollars, to fuck was twenty-five. Or depended if you wanted more time. Now, blow jobs are twenty. If you want to fuck, I'm not gonna fuck for no less than thirty-five, you know. And for that thirty-five you might get like a half-hour. That's it. When I'm out there, this is how I do it. I light a cigarette and I tell them when the cigarette is burnt down, your time's up. If you want more time, that's more money. If you want to touch me, that's even more money. You know, if you want more, it's more money. The most I've ever made in a trick, I think, was five hundred. I met famous entertainers and I dealt with judges. I dealt with all kinds of people, firemen, cops, you know.

So Kathy introduced me to the Avenue, and she hipped me to what prices were. I didn't know. I'd always say if you want you can give me a tip, you know. Then later in the years I came up with a gimmick, because more girls and all were coming out. I came up with "Money back guarantee." Money is always first, you know, but if you don't come, I'll give you your money back. And the girls hated me for that.

I was in Pegasus in '83. When I came out, that's when I got my teeth fixed. I start realizing I'm not as ugly as my mother said and I totally changed. I had a Jherri Curl, you know. I really looked nice. And if I would put a little makeup on, I looked nicer. And a girl came to me one day and she said, "Watch your ass, Char, because there's a couple of girls out here that want to cut your face." And I said, "What!" I said, "This is free enterprise." It's not like . . . you know, I don't make guys stop me. "Why would they want to do that?" They were jealous.

Once they had this new thing called the John Squad. They—the cops— come out as prostitutes. They bust the guys and bust girls. They go down the Avenue and pick us up even if we're not doing anything. They call it "Obstruction of the Highway." Then there's been a couple of times where I've been tricked, you know. Like quote the guy a price and he turns out to be a cop. At another time I worked up in a dirty movie for a few months. It's around Grant Street where Warminster turns into Hewitt, and I had a deal with the guy where you buy a ticket to get in. I'd pay him a certain amount of money, me and Kathy. Kathy would sit on one end and I would sit on the other end. The guys knew that and they would come for quick blow jobs. So we'd be in the movie. We had a good three and a half months with that. I mean we were making money and we didn't have to worry about being out on the street. Then one night, two undercover cops got us, and that was the end of that little happy period.

I wasn't on welfare all the time. Like I got to a point I was making enough money. Then I started SSI, but then they were taking me through too much shit. So I said, "Fuck them," you know. "I don't need it anyway."

Right now I'm thinking about getting on a program and working toward getting the girls back. So I'm working on their trust again. I take them out once, either Saturday or Sunday, and I stop through once a week to help them with their homework. Now I'm gonna make it twice a week because they got their first reports. . . . Like they're in first and second grade, and between his drinking and him and his mother being illiterate, the kids need more help with their homework. But I hate going down there when he's drunk. I hate drunks. That's another reason I left him, you know, but he has it in his heart that we'll get back together, but it's dead, wanting to get back together, you know, for the kids. No, not for that. Right now I'm trying to get housing or something where I can get them like overnight sometimes and on the weekends and maybe eventually get them.

I lived at twenty-two forty-six Taylor with Angel for about two years, I guess. 'Cause I was with him all together seven years. Like the last year I started cheating on him with this guy Buddy, which turned out to be my worst mistake. He used to beat me. I mean bad. One day he hit me with this golf club. The golf club broke. I was bleeding so bad, because he thought that . . . sometimes you get into a car with a trick and it turns out that, you know, he just wanted somebody in the car to talk to. So I got out of the car figuring on the way back up the Ave. I'll pick up a trick. I didn't. It was a bad night. He thought that I went and took the twenty dollars, and got a bag and did it without him. He beat the shit out of me.

When I was with Buddy, we lived in abandoned houses for that two- or three-year period of time. We were living in South Jefferson. He was Puerto Rican. I don't know why we didn't go to a shelter. It was just that, you know, the drugs just meant everything to me. We just found abandoned houses. Sometimes other people lived there. We'd just go in and just squat, and sometimes like if we found it first, like people come to get off, we'd charge them a couple of dollars. It was just terrible. Sometimes we leave our things there and like go to the mission and get more clothes. I had to go to a mission to get baths, or go under the fireplug in the summer to stay clean, 'cause I was working in the streets. I couldn't be, you know, all stinking and dirty and stuff. When we were in the abandoned house, we used the mission as a place to eat. After I was done work at six in the morning, we'd always eat a good breakfast. I had money on me. Then we'd go do our morning shot, you know. At that time I wasn't using rubbers and stuff. Which I do use now. You know, I have had a test for AIDS and they've come up negative, and I'll keep taking them for a while because I know the incubation period is five to ten years.

I was never even worried about my safety there. You know, I just figured when my number was up, it's up. That's how I felt then. I didn't worry about other people coming in and invading because I had him. He was supposed to be my protector, and that was the one thing he was good for. Sometimes we found houses where you could tap into somebody else's electricity, but sometimes not even that. If there wasn't any electricity we used candles to get off and everything. There were rats in a lot of these places. Oh, my God! They were there. You had to be real careful. Just hope they didn't bite you. In the winter, sleep under covers and . . . I don't know. We slept on a mattress, most of the time during the day, 'cause I'm working at night.

When I was with Buddy sometimes I'd hold money back. He started shooting my own shit in front of me. I started learning . . . like if I make a sixty dollar trick, tell him I made forty and hold twenty. And then, you know, find a way, some kind of way to get away from him during the day and run into one of the girls and say, "I got twenty. You got anything?" And she might only have ten. So we might get two dimes of dope and one nickel and we still have five dollars to eat or to buy cigarettes or something.

Yeah, Buddy would take all the money and buy the dope and shoot it all up and make me watch him and stuff. Get back at me for something, you know. See, as soon as I get out of the car, I give him the money because of the way the Avenue had become. You know, the next car you get in, the guy might take what you just made. So as soon as I got out of the car I give it to him.

Now it's Darrin. I give him the money. I don't have to worry about him. Once in a while—like I know all the dope and what it cost—once in a while Darrin will tell me he got a twenty dollar bag when I know it was ten dollar bag, but it's no big thing. I figure, you know, like . . . he might have been putting money on a ring. It doesn't happen often. Like in his mind he probably thought he got over on me, but I've been down that neighborhood for years where he's only been down there a couple of years.

So how I finally got rid of Buddy was by calling and telling them he had bench warrants and how . . . you know, they grabbed him. Couple months later, I got busted. It was September of 1988, and I didn't get out of the system until October 1989. So then I met Darrin in November. We didn't hook up then. January twentieth 1990, on my birthday, I finally, you know, got to talk to him. I was real high and bold and I just took the chance.

So when I look back I've had a number of relationships. My first relationship was with Scott. It deteriorated when I was eighteen or nineteen and I was pregnant with . . . it turned out to be my daughter. I caught him in bed getting fucked by a man. I was out working. He was illiterate. A lot of men I've got involved with for some reason are illiterate. Scott used to always go down this guy's house and the guy was deaf, an old guy. Scott would come back with money. I was very naive at that time. And I just asked him, "Why does Al give you money?" And he said, "Oh, I help him with little things around the house and stuff." And I believed it, you know. I got home early from work and Scott was in my bed getting fucked up his ass. I just couldn't deal with that. I took . . . he tried and said, "Charlene." I said, "There's nothing you can say," and I just grabbed my son. I haven't seen him since then. I left everything and rolled. Went back to my mother, and that's when she kept Tom.

It hurt me when I found my man having sex with another man, and I felt, damn, it's not even another woman. Am I that bad? He's with another man, but I believe everybody has their own choice. I mean men enjoy or watch two women have sex, but I don't think I'll enjoy watching two men. I imagine he was gay. Scott wasn't fucking him in his ass. He was getting fucked. So that told me he was not normal.

The next person I got involved with was a female. That was Stephie. I met her in the neighborhood. I hadn't been involved with a man since that happened with Scott. I lived with her for a year or so. We had an understanding. I told her if she wanted to go out with men, as long as it wasn't in my house. . . . I knew she liked men also, and I was very confused. I didn't want to get involved with any man, and I really loved her. It turned out that she had just used me. That's another day I came home early from work, and she was fucking the guy. I picked up a bat and the guy picked up his clothes and just ran out the door naked. She was a black girl and we lived down Fifth and Southbourne and I ended up cutting up her face. I put a "G" in each side and told her she'd remember me for the rest of her life. She laughed at me—that's what got me mad—and she said, "I never loved you. I just used you to keep me high and buy me clothes and I had a place to stay."

It's all right for women to have sex with other women. I've had female trick. I mean, there's women that have paid me to go down on them. They have this thing now. You can even use a piece of Saran Wrap, but there are dental dams, you know. You don't have to worry about AIDS with that. And I've been with a woman and her husband. Her husband's fantasy is to be with two women.

When I was with Buddy, he tried to talk me into going to New York. In New York they have this thing that . . . you perform on stage. He said, "Fuck it. We'll get high. You can't see anyway and you get paid anyway and then men throwing money up on the counter," you know. When me, him, and this guy did it . . . like, you know, when he was talking, he was gung ho for it. I know he would like to be with a girl, me and him, but he said, yeah, he would go for it—a three-way with another man, but not like the man doing anything to him, like me working on both of them. And when it came down to it, he got dead, he couldn't do nothing. I got paid and all for it. Like I told the man I was a drug addict, you know. Walk with us. We went up and got two twenty dollar bags and a dime. I got off before, you know, the session, plus I got fifty more. And he ended up giving me a little more. Buddy fell asleep and I finished the night with him, you know.

Well, I know I'm bisexual, but I mean. . . . In jail, sometimes I get involved with a woman. But I know I prefer men. You know, women know each other, what feels good to each other, and you can talk to a woman. Where sometimes men just want to jump on and get their shit off and fuck you, you know. With women, we're emotional. We can talk to each other about problems and stuff. So what I like most being in a relationship with a woman is that we're compassionate, emotional, and we can talk, and it's not all just sex.

After Stephie I started to go out with just any Puerto Rican guy I could. You know, by that time I was known to always have money and I was real cocky about it. You know, if I do something, I'm a whore, but men can fuck all different women. Well, I'm gonna be that way. I would say to them, "Tonight's your lucky night." Like they'd be waiting, you know. Like I had a good name for sex and I got them high too.

So there were all different guys after her. Then I got involved with Julio, who's the one who ended up dying. I met him buying dope. He was a dealer, and I got involved with him for that reason. He supported my habit. I was with him for about a year and a half, I guess, before he died.

When I was in prison, I met Travis. He'd seen me in the mess hall. I worked in the mess hall and so did he. And men used to have to bring the food into the mess hall, 'cause we shared the mess hall. And he seen me one day and he asked me could he write me. I said, "Sure." I got out of jail first. I should have just ended it there. So when Travis gets out, I start hanging with him out of fear for a couple months. I had told him it was a mistake, and he raped me. I was in the subway at High and Southbourne. He pulled a knife on me and told me that I had misled him and everything and I was gonna fuck him and if I didn't, he's gonna kill me. So I did and he kept me with him with fear.

So much happened because of this rape. Like I said, Julio got shot. He went to jail. I had twins and I ended up putting them with the state, and then me and Tico finally got involved. Like I knew one day we'd get together for real. He got together with me anytime I wanted 'cause I bought him stuff. We had great sex when I met him. He had lied to me about his age. He was fourteen, but he looked a lot older, you know. I was eighteen, his mother was going to charge me with rape, but that never happened and my relationship with Tico finally ended about when I was twenty-three or twenty-four.

So when I got out of prison, I lived with my mother and lived with her for about two months. Then I left there and I went to Fourth and Clarence. That's when I met Angel. We lived together for a couple of years at Fourth and Clarence. Then we moved around his mother's at twenty-two forty-six Taylor. Then in 1983 a law came out, if you did drugs when you were pregnant, it was abuse to the fetus. So my daughter was born an addict. So the state got involved. My sister took responsibility for me and the kid for a year. One weekend I . . . she was working, I was keeping her house clean, watching her one kid—this is Corrie, my youngest sister—and one weekend she said, "You're doing so good, Char. Take . . . go out for the night." Why did she say that? I made a weekend of it. We were due in court the next week. My mother told her, "Fuck her. Tell them to take the kid." They took my daughter.

That's when I went to Pegasus, to try and fight to get my daughter back. 'Cause Pegasus takes mothers and your kids can live there too. My counselor, who is the head of the program, reneged. He told me if I made an improvement that he would let Marisol come live with me by Christmas. Two weeks before Christmas, I asked him. He said he didn't think I was ready. So I left Pegasus. He said, "You'll never get your kid back." Well, it took me about eight months after that, but I got her back and I had another daughter, who is the youngest one. I called him and let him know, you know. For a while I was doing all right on the methadone program. Then I started doing the coke.

So when I left Pegasus, I went back to twenty-two forty-six Taylor and lived with Angel and his mother. So I was in Pegasus for like five months. Then I was on the methadone program 'cause I started doing dope again. I was on seventy milligrams of methadone. So sometimes I'd be so high I started doing coke. Angel got me into it. He was doing it.

God, I didn't do coke until I was in my thirties. Angel's mother ended up throwing me out because I was getting high. She kept him, and I hated him for that. Like "Damn, don't even . . . if I get put out, fight for your kids," you know, but I guess he didn't want the responsibility. And then one day, you know, I left the kids with the trick, didn't let him know, went down to get medicated, and figured I'd call from the program, which I did, and he had already called the cops and said that I had abandoned my kids. I lost the kids.

It was never really a court thing. Angel's mother have them and I'm comfortable with that, because I know they're well taken care of. I see them. I talk to them every day. I'm starting to get their trust back again. Like if I say I'm coming over, I come. Like Christmas, this is the going to be the first Christmas like I'm trying to get every little thing I promised them. I got almost everything. I have a few things left. I don't know if I'm going to make it. But I'm really trying, you know. Then I had a few other little people to buy for. I already got his mother's gift. I gave it to her last night, 'cause she's going to Puerto Rico Friday. I'm going to get him something from the kids. On Father's Day, his birthday, and Christmas I usually do that. Halloween I took the girls out. Like he wouldn't do it. He was drunk. I got their costumes, took them out.

I first met Darrin in November '89 and I was trying to hit on him, but he didn't get it. Finally, January twentieth 1990 is when I just laid it out. You know, took my chance. I still had a little doubt. I was afraid, 'cause to me he was so handsome. "He ain't gonna like me," you know, but I just got all high, as high as I could get just in case the rejection came, you know. I just approached him with some remark that I made to him. He told me now that's what really made him take the chance with me. We're still together. Next month we'll have our one year.

Me and my mother are in a battle right now over Darrin. Because in the beginning he was the greatest. He landscaped her yard, put up her ceiling fans, put on her front storm door shit, was cooking, you know, and all of a sudden—I mean she liked him in the beginning—now all of a sudden. . . . She started getting pressure in the neighborhood about him. A lot of people think he's Hispanic. We were living down the street with my other sister helping her paying her rent, and one day, from the clear blue sky, my mother just came and demanded that we get out. Put us out in the street, you know. She didn't know where we had to go or anything.

We ended up finding this place, because we had all our clothes in a cart and this woman, this Puerto Rican family, just happened to see us. Pulled us in. We pay her one hundred and sixty dollars a month for a room in the house. No cooking or anything, or she wants more money.

So Darrin and I are living on Benjamin Street, down Conshohocken and Benjamin. They call it the Flats. It's Broomtown. It's all white. But this one section we found blacks, Puerto Ricans, and whites. The neighborhood is somewhat maintained, you know. It's all right. But where we live we're not happy with. That's why I'm meeting this lady today. I have to meet her at three-thirty and we're gonna talk. . . . See, tomorrow my rent's due. We're hoping that we can come to a thing with this lady today so we can move.

I think I'm in my ideal relationship right now. Because this is the first person I can actually say I've been happy with. He's trying to pull me off the Avenue. We're gonna get on a methadone program. He has a lot of talent. He's been a painter, he's been self-employed and, you know, like interior decorating, and he went to school for welding. He knows things about cars. He isn't happy with me on the Avenue, but we have habits now. So now we're planning on getting on a program, me getting off the Avenue and applying for SSI—we'll have more money than I get from DPA—and then try to get under-the-table jobs and do little things like this.

The thing I like about him most is that he knows everything about me and he still sticks by me. We share everything, you know. He doesn't hit me. He doesn't abuse me mentally, you know, and he likes me for me. He's younger than me and sometimes I worry 'cause he's real nice-looking. I know a lot of the girls like him. But I trust him.

I think a woman should play an equal role in the relationship. Like I don't think it's "me man, you woman" or Tarzan and Jane type of thing, you know. I guess the man should work, you know. If he sees I got too much to do in the house, help me out, you know. Not cheat on me. That's the one thing I told him, if he ever did it, it's done. The same with me. Just be there for me. You know, we can talk to each other. We don't really argue that much. Our arguments are very minute, over minute things like "you got a couple extra units than me" and stuff like that.

We were even thinking about if this methadone thing works and I can get SSI and I'll try to get a grant for minorities and go to college. I'm a great minority. I'm a female and I'm half Puerto Rican and half white. I'm also disabled. So I might be able to get a grant. When I was in prison I took my SAT and haven't had this eye operation yet and they said that my score was good enough to put me in Jefferson or Community College. But they suggested that I take another one because I could probably do better now that my vision is better in this eye. So if I do that, I would like to major in psychology and eventually help other drug addicts. It's not the highest-paying thing, but it's something that I believe I'd be good at.

When I think about the women out there, there's a big difference between women who do crack and the ones who do heroin. Oh, yes. Definitely! Pipers are petty. They'll do anything for five dollars, and it hurts the girls that are out there that are making. . . . Like my drugs—I need at least fifty dollars to go to the cooker. You know, a guy will come to me and say, "I'll give you five dollars for a blow job" and I'll look at him like he's crazy. "I can get it down the street." "Go. See you. Go down the street." Or, "Do you accept food stamps?" or "Can I pay you later?" I never heard such shit until recently. I mean, these girls . . . and they have the nerve . . . they'll say,

"Well, at least I don't mark my body with needles." "Well, bitch, look at yourself in the mirror. The way you look. You're dirty. You stink. Appearance. They'll give you five dollars, and you'll do anything to them for five dollars." Some of them even for a hit they'll do you all night, you know, and that's bad for me.

And a lot of them are going up with AIDS. We're hearing a lot of girls on the Ave. that have AIDS. That's why I definitely use rubbers. I have a lot of them. I sell some of them on the Avenue, and that helps me too. . . . Like a guy that picks you up has more respect for a girl that has rubbers. You know what I mean? Most guys these days want rubbers because they're scared of AIDS. Even for a blow job. Yeah. They have them. I have these coins, they're non-lubricant. Then I have these Kiss of Mint, that's good for me 'cause it's mint-tasting, you know. Then they have all . . . you know, like different kinds, colors, blue, you know, yellow.

When I'm in the street, nothing attracts me to a man sexually. Purely business. I don't mix it. I try to deal with older guys. I try to deal with white guys 'cause that's where the money is. I try to stay away from young guys because they think if they give you twenty dollars they want you all night, you know. I don't deal with guys on coke or crank, because it takes them too long to come, you know. I rather have a black older man, you know, or a young black guy. Like sometimes, you know, some people kind of look at me as white and other people can tell that I'm mixed. Some people might think I'm Puerto Rican, you know. Some young black guys are really tacky. Like "I want to fuck that white pink pussy." I don't like that. And "You need me for your drugs." No, I don't. I have girls out there that will say, "Charlie, if you turn somebody down, would you send them to me?" I would never do that—"Can I have your leftovers?" "Yeah. Sure, you can have my leftovers."

Sometimes on Friday and Saturday like after hours, after two, . . . like when I'm real ripped sometimes I'll pick drunk guy's pockets. Yeah. Take some money. I got messed up one time, about five year ago. I didn't know he was a numbers writer. I took like five hundred and some dollars. A couple of months later these four guys beat me so bad I wish they had killed me. I was in the hospital for a month.

I usually get done working like six in the morning. Then we go out to breakfast and we come home, you know. Take a bath or shower, and rest from the night. He's already went out and copped the drugs. So we do a morning shot about nine o'clock. So that's to sleep. Then some time during the day we'll wake up and get off again. Now we realize now that it's better for me not to go out sick. So right before I go out, which now is about seven. . . . In the summertime it don't get dark until like eight-thirty, nine, and I don't like to work in the light. I never work in the day. In the summertime more people are out, especially on the weekends and all. In the wintertime sometimes guys don't come around. But then you have regulars. I have this guy every Thursday. I go down his place on Dryer and Fisk and I'm with him two hours, but I get seventy-five dollars, and then every Christmas I get a hundred-dollar bill. I've been dealing with him for eight years.

When it gets dark, I'd do a shot so I'm not sick. It takes time to cop and then get off. That takes a lot of time that I could be making money. So now what we do is, you know, I go out with a shot in me. The next day Darrin cops before we come home and we do it during the day.

I go out maybe five nights a week. Sometimes four. We cop at Second and Benjamin, sometimes Ludlow and Wade. It's like a twenty to twenty-five minute walk from the Avenue, where I'm working, and then we got to find a place, an abandoned house, to get off. To have candles, and you know. . . . I'm pretty easy to hit, you know. He's not, sometimes, 'specially it's cold— you know, your veins are cold. And then we get back down the Avenue. Where like all that time I could have been making some money.

We cop from different people, but most of the time, it's the same person. You know, they have hours. They take turns. Sometimes the way it cooks, you know, you can tell you've been beat, you know. 'Cause when you're there like they're rushing you. "Got to come on. Move. Move. It's hot." So you can't. . . . Dope comes in a cellophane-type of thing, where coke come in plastic bags. You can't open it there and test it, you know. They're pushing you to move. Then down the block, "Oh, we've been beat." You go, "Ray, that's bullshit." You know, what can you do?

I've been in shooting galleries. In a shooting gallery everybody is begging you for a taste. It's bad enough you have to pay somebody, you know, whoever run the place, either a little bit of your stuff or money. But then you got so-called friends, "Please. I'm so sick." After a while you don't . . . you rather go in an abandoned house. And then you have to worry about, you know—especially if you're a girl and you're alone—some guy just taking your stuff. Horrible. I've seen people getting robbed. Some shooting galleries have a room where the girls can take a trick for five or ten dollars and the tricks have been robbed. Some of the shooting galleries were just abandoned houses that someone took over and hooked up the electricity. They have water, you know. Somebody is there to collect something from you. You don't get away with just doing your stuff. If you don't have works, you can buy works or use a set of works. It's just a bunch of leeches, you know, trying to get anything off of you. People just sitting around either nodding or bugging, you know, if they're coke heads.

I find selling drugs terrible. Especially Puerto Ricans, like they're put little kids to sell it. Put it in their baby's Pampers, you know, and I think that's terrible. I don't even buy off of little kids.

The government says that they're doing more to get the drugs off the street, but I know some cop . . . I know for a fact 'cause when they busted my mother, I've seen cops pocket some of the money. I've had cops give me some drugs, friends of mine. They busted some little guy coming down the street and they didn't feel like going through the paperwork so they took the drugs. They know that I do it. You know, I might have ran into them earlier and I'm having a bad night. I'm sick. And they give it to me. So I know that there's cops out there—you know on busts, there's thousand of dollars and all—they pocket it. They probably have some people in their family that do drugs. They might take some of the drugs and make sure their family don't get in crime. They don't want their name, you know, hurt.

The longest I've been clean was about twenty-two months and the shortest was about four months. As far as treatment, I was an in-patient at Pegasus and at Female Offenders at Petersburg. I've been on about six methadone programs. When I got out of prison I'd been clean for two years, almost two years, and I messed up again. I didn't feel great, but I just said, "The hell with it." The money was still flowing good and I just thought I would always be lucky. You know, always have my dope money, which always didn't happen. I was getting older.

I continue because I still like heroin. Yeah. Even if I get on methadone and detox and everything, I always believe that once in a while I'll do dope. I like heroin. Just makes me feel down, you know, and not give a shit about anything. I enjoy the sex too when I'm high.

The Avenue has changed. Tremendously! I hate it out there. That's another reason we're looking towards getting on a program or something. Girls will set each other up. Like girls that make more money, you know, the less fortunate will set us up. Mostly every girl has a guy now to watch our back. I started that trend, you know. Then there're just guys that walk around the Avenue just looking to see when a girl jump out of a car. They know that she has money. A trick will put a knife to you and take you for nothing, you know.

A guy took me up around the prison out on County Road. I was virtually blind. Made me do everything and just dumped me there. And I was like a little kid. I couldn't see. I was scared to death. He made me suck him. Fuck him in every position and then he smacked me around, you know. Another guy cut me. I jumped out in midair and just jumped out, you know. He said, "Did you ever hear of Jack the Ripper?" and I heard the blade. A lot of times I'll . . . sometimes I have a icepick on me. Sometimes you can't get to it quick. Like these pants are . . . rough to get an icepick that's here. Then, if you get stopped by a cop, that's a weapon, you know, if you happen to get busted that night or they pull . . . do a sting right down the Avenue and just lock you up.

The streets are dangerous. You're actually fighting for your life. That's another reason I want to get out of it. These kids are afraid of nothing, and they'll do anything for five dollars. They, you know . . . they have no scruples, no respect, no fear, and they travel in gangs.

The most bizarre thing that somebody has ever asked me to do was to get into leather and get handcuffed and let them beat me. They'll pay me tremendously, but I wasn't into that. And then one time a guy asked me would I let his German shepherd fuck me. "There's no way you could get pregnant." I said, "You must be out of your mind! A German shepherd fuck me? Oh, no!" He said, "He knows how to do it, and he's done it to other women." I said, "Well, I'm not the one," you know.

The street scene is a trip. You either just standing there or you're walking up and down. You know, yelling down the street something to each other. Ducking the cops. You know, you see cops and you try and move around. Sometimes a trick might pull up and you know they want you and somebody else is obviously not making money will try and run and take your trick, you know, and sometimes the trick will just pull away. So everybody lost. Or else he's just nervous and he'll just take her and, you know, you get mad because you know he was there for you. If there's two girls on a corner, guys tend to pass 'cause they don't want to hurt the girl's feeling. He might know them both or something.

It's hard to say where the best place to work is, 'cause it starts from Pendleton all the way up to Ferry Street. But, like my particular block, there's about twelve girls. Just on one block. Some of them are girls. Some are guys dressed like girls. Some are just guys that guys pick up. It's free enterprise.

There are rules on the corner. Like the corner I have if I . . . once I come out there, if anyone's there, they know to leave. You know, that's my corner and people respect that. I just took my corner 'cause for a while I had hardly no vision and it's a little street. If a car pulls around there, I'm sure he's for me and, you know, you come right around and that's the first corner right there. You know, it's rough about the cops too. They can sneak around and before I realize it, and some of the girls won't tell you 'cause they wanted you to be picked up. Then there are less girls out there. It's hard to say how many women are out there. Some of the cops that are our friends tell us, you know, that the John Squad is out.

I wished I hadn't prostituted, you know. It's degrading. I can't go back. I did it. I have to live with it. Simple as that. So I'm not happy about doing prostitution, but like anything I do, I do my best. The worst thing about doing it is that it's just degrading. It's something I don't want to do, but it's something that my addictions make me do. I'm usually high when those really unattractive people approach me or I turn down people. That's one thing about this. You don't have to go with anybody. Like they might walk up to me and want me to go up an alley with them and blow them. No. You have to have at least a car or something. I've gotten in a car and wanted to go down on a guy and gagged because the guy smell so. I say, "Look, I'm sorry. Here's your money back. No hard feeling. I changed my mind." This is business. If they look too grubby, I just tell them to roll. "There's a lot of other people out there and I'm sure there's a lot of girls around that'll take you." I would also turn down a bunch of young kids. You know, just calling me names and making me feel bad. Throwing things at you. Throwing eggs and tomatoes, especially around Halloween and stuff.

"When you recognize you're doing something that ain't doing you

no good and you don't do nothing about it, that hurts the most."

Virginia

My father has used drugs as long as I have known him, and when I realized that he was my father I was six. I always thought that my brother and them father was my father, you know. One day my father came to my elementary school. . . . I was in Horace Mann, and this man came. That's how I knew him. Some man came up to me and was telling me he was my father. When he arrived and I just ran. I ran straight home, you know, straight to my mom's. Telling my mom there's this man telling me he's my father. You know, I was screaming, hollering, crying—you know, scared to death. Couldn't believe that, you know, he was really my father.

He just appeared out of the clear blue, you know. Well, see, from what my mom told me that . . . right. . . . See, I have a sister on my father side and we're like months apart, you know, nine months apart. When my mother was pregnant they weren't together because he didn't want my mom to have me and then the other lady was pregnant too, so that's why that was like that. He was like "Both of y'all," you know, and he wanted to pay for my mom to have a abortion, but my mom chose to have me. Then he wanted to come and play the father role. I don't know. So at age six, he decides he wants to see me and know his daughter, but he could never be a father to me, you know, 'cause he was into his thing.

So as long as I've known him, he's been a drug addict. Far as I know he was a heroin user. I guess he was probably shooting all kinds of things, you know. All I know, he shooted up. That was the phrase that I knew, you know. He died of an overdose when I was eighteen.

When I found out he was dead, it wasn't . . . it didn't affect me as if it was my mom, you know, because I never really knew my dad. I was never close . . . you know, we have never had that family, you know, gathering and nothing like that. There was a time when he wasn't allowed in my grandmother's home. Actually I had lived with my grandmother—my father's people—for quite some time. But at that particular time I wasn't staying with them. So they came and got me and told me about my father.

So I was never really with him, you know. Off and on he might have came to my grandma's and I seen him, but he was never a father. It wasn't something that really affected me. It was not like "Oh God, my dad is gone." I went to the funeral. I didn't even cry, but I felt something 'cause it's a part of me and he is a part of me. It wasn't no damage done. My mother was like "Ha!" Just like that. Yeah. "Ha!"

Both my parents were born in Jefferson. My family is close, but it's a space, you know. There's a distance, you know. I mean, we don't have those little family gatherings to keep the closeness. . . . It's not that tight. I'm semi-close to my mother. Our relationship is fucked! Okay. But what keeps things there is—that's Mom, you know, but as far as when I'm down and I need somebody to talk to, she's not the one.

Me changing my life as far as into drugs, it affected my mom badly. Okay. In other words I'm a disappointment to her, which I'm a disappointment to myself in a sense. Like I tried to tell my mom, you know, it's got to be within me. I'm still your daughter. Don't treat me like I'm somebody outside. She treat the outsider that gets high, you know, she treats them better then me. You know what I'm saying? "Mom, look. I know this thing ain't right. I know what I'm doing to myself. But I'm still your daughter." That's why it's fucked, period. There's a lot of other things, like the relationship that she was in. She took me through changes and I took her through them, you know.

So our relationship was fucked before I started using drugs. She had a friend—he's in jail now—and they used to fight all the time. I mean, physically fight each other. I mean, he would physically do harm to her. You know, like he done stabbed her, and all that. Me coming up, I couldn't deal with it, and that's what set me to stay with my grandmother and them. He was a friend of my mom's, period. My mom and my dad never been in the same household.

I have two brothers from my mom. That's my two brothers, not step. My father only had just me from my mom. The two boys, their father is Duke. I have one half-sister. I don't feel like they're my half-brothers though. They are my real brothers. Duke is the one I thought was my father until my father showed up at school. Duke stayed there for a long period of time. Like he actually raised us. I was in junior high when the other guy moved in. I was about twelve or thirteen. I mean, when they used to fight he might leave, but he's always there.

My relationship with my brothers was cool. They was my little brothers, you know. They were always protective of me. Always! They always protective over me. I'm the only sister, you know what I mean? The one brother is in jail and the other one is working. He's living with his people, his woman. He lives in another building in the projects. We're all in the same complex right over here on Herbert. Yeah, I've got another sister. That's my father's child. I don't have contact with her. She wants no contact with nobody. I don't even know where she lives.

Me and my brothers would fight when we were coming up. Maybe about what I want to watch on TV, you know. "I was watching it first," or "Mom, you said I could have the pickle out the refrigerator." You know, little things like that. Little minor things. "Well, your feet stink" or "Move over" or . . . you know, little stuff like that.

When I was growing up I was closer to my father's people than I was to my mother. I'm saying, they're my aunts and my uncles but they're 'round my age. They talked to me. They treated me like . . . you know, they treated me like I was somebody and they cared about what I did do and what I didn't do. You know, when I was wrong they chastised me. You know what I'm saying? They just didn't let me go 'head and do what I wanted to do.

My father's mother was more like a mother to me than my own mother. It was kind of touching. Okay, see, coming from my mom and her going through those changes, felt like I ain't have nobody . . . nobody cared. That relationship my mom went into tore us apart. 'Cause before it was a meal every day. But she had got to a point where she put him before us. We didn't live in luxury, but we lived comfortably. These things just started falling down, you know. He would steal things from us. And beating on my mom. You know, drove her to drinking. Going to my grandmother's and them I didn't have to go through no changes.

My mom's friend's name was Howard and he's just a total disaster to our household. It was great from the time I was born up until the time he came there. When I was born my mom was in the relationship with Duke . . . 'cause my father was into his own thing. You know what I'm saying? She had . . . they had their little thing or whatever, but it wouldn't work. Like I said, my father offered to pay for her to have an abortion. Duke said—you know, Duke had always likeded my mom—"You don't have to have no abortion," and that's how they got together. Duke was my father. He was more a father to me then my dad. It was great with him in the household. We did things together, you know. My mom was into her family before she met Howard. Then she got into him. Nothing meant nothing but him.

So when she was with Duke she was a family-oriented person. Because we were her life, you know. It was important to her about what we thought or what our opinion or what we wanted to do or what we wanted to eat, you know, and what we wore to school. It wasn't like "Go find something to put on now so you can get out of here." That wasn't my mom. My mom seen that your shoes were tied and that they was clean. Your clothes were laid out for us to put on. Oh, we could go 'head in the bathroom and wash up ourselves, but our clothes was ironed, pressed, and right there and break-fast on the table. She cooked our meals and cleaned the house. We did movies, parties, playground. See, we watched TV together. We had little family gatherings, talked, you know. We laughed and joked. It was none of that anymore when Howard arrived.

The last time that I seen them fight was before Duke had went to Dallas. Before he left to go to Dallas, they had a fight. I'll never forget. It was Christmastime, and he was beating my mom with the baby stroller. I forget how old I was at the time, but he was beating my mother with my baby stroller I had got for Christmas. You know, that's the only fight that I've seen. She wasn't seriously beaten 'cause she would rumble. I mean, she used to fight him back. He left like a month or so afterwards. When she was with Duke they had their little arguments—words or whatever—but it never extended to nothing big. He would go 'head out or whatever.

I don't know why he finally left the house. There were these other men that she was dating when Duke left, and they would stay over occasionally. They were introduced to us as a friend. It's at this point she started seeing Howie. So about a year after Duke left Howie moved in. It took about a year or two. Now, unlike the others, that's one that she didn't let us really know about. She hid him 'cause he was younger, you know. He's much younger then her, you know. My mom is forty-six, which makes Howie probably 'bout thirty-six. So he had to have been in his twenties when my mom started messing with him. Like twenty-five maybe. He could have been my brother.

So it was Duke who was the one, the key to it—to help the family. He was . . . he did his little hustles and had his little jobs and . . . you know. My mom has always had hustling guys, but I couldn't tell you the hustle he did. Some of this was legal and some of it was illegal. My mom always had them kind of men or men that maybe sold drugs. All of them used except one. That was her type of man, I think. She didn't use. Nope. But my mom used to snort monster. She was never a shoot-upper.

Now she's struggling. You know, she's mentally disturbed. When I say that, I mean she letting everything just worry her. My baby brother is in Abingdon. I smoke. He was smoking. Her man that she loved no matter what he did to her physically or mentally is never coming home. Okay, so the pressure on her, you know . . . you know, it's just taking its toll.

But when she was with Duke she was beautiful! Beautiful. Ain't nothing my mom won't do for you if she can do it. That's for you, me, or anybody else. When you get down to it and all, my mom is very, very sweet, a very sweet person. Don't get me wrong. Mom wasn't no wallflower. No, no, never! But that's the kind of men I think she likeded.

Well, when Howie came, he was one of them that couldn't control hisself, you know. The rest of them, they were controllers. These guys were users— day-to-day users—but they were able to control their habits. They wouldn't bring it home, in other words. I never seen them use drugs. I found a needle once with Duke, but when Howie came in the household we found needles all over the place and everything. It was "Just don't care." The one time I found a needle when Duke was there my mom hit the ceiling—I mean, hit the ceiling, you know. And I had never seen . . . found one in there since until Howie arrive. See, when Howie arrived it was like everything there was fucked up. They didn't care about nothing. My mom loved the shit out of him, loved his dirty drawers, couldn't see nothing beyond, and that's plain and simple.

Before Howie I would say my mom was not a real strict mom. We didn't have to sign in or check in or whatever. You know, you tell your mom you're going to be outside on the bench or whatever so she would know where you were in case something happened. At this time the projects were so clean and so coordinated. I mean, the people wasn't like they are now. 'Cause we used to stay at the Recreation Center. You know, they had little things for the children in the basement of the building. So everything that we wanted to do was in the area. So it was like we say, "Mom, we're going outside." "Go 'head on out." She didn't have to worry about us. We knew everybody and we just had a certain time we had to be in. I was in Barnfield Street Projects then, living on Twenty-first and Barnfield. I live in the twenty-one-oh-five building for thirteen years.

When my mom came up here to live in North Jefferson I had to be sixteen or seventeen. As a matter of fact, I was going to North Jefferson High when we moved up here. I was in the eleventh grade then. I was living in the eleven-twelve building at Eleventh and Herbert. Was it different? It's like . . . I take it with strides. Yeah, it different because it was new people. But other than that, no. Because I'm born and raised in the projects and the projects is what I know. In the projects you meet all types of people, conservative, hoodlum . . . you know, it's all in one.

During that first year when Howie moved in, it was nothing. He was a new person. He was just somebody new to us and it was like we were observing him, you know. It was like a trial base in other words because he didn't know us, we didn't know him. So it was day-to-day, you know. . . . He revealed himself the first time I seen my mom and him fight, 'cause it was continuous after that.

I guess the fighting started a year or so. You know, I guess he felt he was in. So I'm gonna say about a year or so. I don't remember the very first fight 'cause I wasn't at home, so I don't know. I just heard of about it. I didn't see it. Their fights were all physical. From the very first time, they were all physical.

I also remember he killed a guy, a friend of my mom. See my mom and my aunt look alike, and my mom and a friend, Harold, and my Aunt Eunice was in a bar. They were sitting at the bar talking and everything. And Howie comes in the bar. I'm briefly telling this from what my mom told me. So him and the guy, Hal, get into a argument and then they get into a physical thing. Howie leaves the bar and comes back and kill him. I think because of the fact he thought my mom . . . matter of fact, he thought my mom and the guy was messing around. When Howie leaves my mom leaves 'cause she know how he is. My mom was kind of high too anyway. So my mom leave. When Howie come back in the bar he thought my aunt was my mother. Right? So he called for my mom to come here, and my aunt had turned around. Howie had pulled the gun out and he shot the guy and killed him right in the bar. Howard went to jail. He's in jail now, but not for that. I'd say about two years if that long for that, and my mom wined him and dined him throughout that. Took care of him. We still lived at Twenty-first and Barnfield when that happened.

The worst fight between them was the time they were fighting up in the hallway. My mom was over a girlfriend's house sitting talking and he knocks on the lady's door and asks for my mom. Starting this shit. We were living at Twenty-first and Barnfield. My mom was on the second floor, but we lived on the tenth. He knocked on the door and told my mom to come out in the hall. Mom came out in the hall and they got into a thing. He pulled a knife out and tried to stab her, but she moved and the knife went in the door. My mom grabbed the knife and stabbed him. And all of this part of his chest was hanging out. Yep. I refused to go get the cops. Somebody else had to go get them. When the cops came they took him to the hospital. He wouldn't say nothing like who did it or what. He refused to press charges.

I remember one time like I went to go in the house and it's a chair up against the door. You can't get in. When I do finally get in my mom is sitting there and her face is way out to here. He had took a slat from a bed and beat her in her face with it. Them the types of fights they would have. Real raunchy, physical.

She was injured a number of times. I mean twenty, thirty . . . I don't know . . . 'cause every time there was a fight she got physically hurt. If it was nothing but a black eye or broken arm, she was hurt—broken arm, black eye, her lung collapsed on her right side, a ligament in her finger. He cut the ligament in her little finger. It's bent over like this. She has little scars. Yeah, she got scars on her body too but she don't look like that rough, you know. My mom is still nice-looking.

I think the longest time she was in the hospital was for a week or two. He did whatever he wanted to do while she was in the hospital. Did he take care of us? Come on! There was no daddy! Okay, the only reason my mom went to the hospital was about her lung 'cause she had no alternative. Any other occasion as far as the rest of that shit, she didn't go to the hospital. She wouldn't go.

When these fights started, most of the time we were outside 'cause that was most of the time he would do it. My mom wouldn't want us to jump into any of the fights. It was nothing we could do. She didn't want to see us get hurt. You know, we were young then, but now once my brothers done got bigger, it was none of that, you know. Like sixteen and seventeen my brothers were like "No, that's dead. We ain't going for that. We'll whip your ass." But, see, he'd wait till we're gone. Then he would go into hiding until it dies down, then my mom and him was right back together.

I felt a lot of hatred. I hated him. I hated him. Because of him doing this to my mom. I thought she was the stupidest bitch in the world to be going through that. I be like "Ain't that much love in the world." She stayed because she loved him. No, she never ran away. All that, "Oh, she tired, and . . ." Drama! Drama, strictly drama! 'Cause soon as, you know, I'm saying in a couple of days they right back together. I was like, "You stupid." I would say to her, "Why you take this stuff? Why you go through that? He ain't nobody. I hate him. You talking about love. How you're gonna love somebody that just beat you all the time?" But she say, "But I love him. That's it."

So once Duke left and she met him, the change in my mother was a gradual change. It had completely changed like around when I was sixteen. Yeah, sixteen, everything is in his hand. The whole ballgame. He had control over my mother. He never touched me 'cause I told him, "If I gotta wait till you're sleep, I'll kill you." I hated him. Still! I hate him. Now the boys, they're guys, you know, they don't care for him to beat on my mom, but they still would shake his hand, you know, so I can't get into why they would do that. But he wouldn't get a piece of bread, the crumb parts, the ends, from me.

When she was with Howie she would drink—just drove her to drinking. Vodka! But when he left she stopped that and now she drinks beer. My mom drink plenty forties. Plenty! So she started drinking when he started. She started drinking vodka. "What is you doing?" You know? She would be really out and he whip her ass. Always! 'Cause, see, one thing about my mom, if she ain't drunk, she's gonna rumble. Oh yeah, she's gonna rumble. See, when she drunk, she ain't got no wind. She ain't got nothing to her. It's like throwing her every which way but loose.

She just stopped doing everything and all she would do was drink and cater to him! That's all she knew. Whatever he says goes. I need some sneakers—uh-uh—but she'll buy. . . . I can't get no sneakers 'cause she ain't have no money. I'm on that check. And he can have hundred dollar shoes and hundred dollar sneakers. Oh, come on! "I know I'm getting out of here." So she was giving the money to him that she was getting free for us.

My mother is a welfare recipient all her life. My mother loves collecting government assistance. She love it! Yeah, free money. That's how she look at it. She used the money to buy food and pay her rent up until she got with Howie. She would. Sure, yeah, don't get me wrong. She would cook here and there. I mean, we were raised on TV dinners, sandwiches, you know. But it wasn't like, you know, we didn't have a full-course meal like we should've. Then when shopping time came . . . when she would shop, it's things we could cook ourselves. Did he work? Never! He was a freeloader.

My mom was never strict, but she became less concerned when Howie came in there. She wouldn't know where we were. For real! When I was . . . at times I might have been at Sears shoplifting, you know. She wouldn't know unless I got caught. She wasn't religious and she didn't go to church.

There were not important rules either. Oh, I mean, my mom brought us up real respectful, in fact. Because, see, my mom didn't really have no problem with us, you know, because she brung us up well. My mother bought us up best to her ability and that was all she could do.

Before Howie we would usually sit down together and eat dinner together. One person might come in later than the other person, you know, just being outside a little longer, but other than that dinner time was at a certain time. Sure. After Howie dinner was whenever. She was concerned about the way we dressed before Howie, and then when Howie got there we was washing our clothes on our hand. Laundromat day wouldn't come for . . . till the clothes got yea high. It wasn't like that before he came. Before Howie we had a certain time to be in the house because she was there, you know. She would request that. But when Howie came it was like . . . she wasn't even probably there. If she was there, she was probably either drunk or sleep.

She required us to help out in the house. Everybody pitched in. When I got home from school I would throw my books down and go outside. Here and there there were chores to do, occasionally, like if I didn't clean my room up before, you know, clean my room up and then go out. I spent my days during the summer in the street. Did I have a curfew? Yeah and no. I mean, when it got dark, yeah, we had to go in. When I got to be a certain age I didn't. There was never a period when I had to go to bed at a certain time. I mean, when we was going to school, you know, we go to bed a certain time. She can't make us go to sleep.

She was concerned who I hung out with before Howie. I mean, you know she would . . . all we did was hung around project people. You know, everybody knew each other. But, see, I only hung with the ones that wanted to shoplift and things like that. You know they were my kind of people. This was when Howie was there. Before Howie I hung out with boys and climb trees and play ball.

These were kids that weren't in a lot of shit. I started hanging with the other kids because I couldn't . . . like if I wanted to take lunch money to school I couldn't get it. She didn't have it or like if I wanted a nice dress or whatever she ain't have it, you know. So I went and took it and got it. Getting the things I wanted. They were the things I needed and wanted. I took things that I needed first. I think I did it because she wasn't there to provide the things I needed. That played a good part.

So I feel that after Howie arrive I raised myself. I was trying to take care of her too in a way, but I couldn't. I asked her what she wanted. I mean, "What's wrong?" you know. I mean, "You got to tell me." She said, "I'm all right." In other words, she was trying to say, "Accept this because this is what I want," and I couldn't.

He finally left because he was doing stickups and he got caught. Well, I don't know if it was during the stickup, but he got caught, and that's why he's in prison now. He got ten to twenty for one case, ten to twenty for another, and five to ten for the third one. My mother acted like her world came to an end. I was like "Hip hip hooray! Put him under the jail cell." He in a federal prison out of state. She writes. She send him money.

In a sense, in some aspect, I would like to be the kind of person my mother was when I was growing up. The part that cared about people, you know, and wanted to help herself. I wouldn't want to be that part when she was going through it with him—Howard—the physical beatings and having the children.

Did she have dreams for me? Naw, come on. If she did, she didn't tell me about it. Yeah, I disappointed her. Only girl, you know. . . . Well, I'm a disappointment to myself, so. . . . In a sense . . . not for real, 'cause I'm only doing what I chose to do. I can do better. That's all. I know that but I chose to do this shit.

She never told us anything about the kind of person we were going to be. She let us live and guided us the best she could. See, when I got to the certain age where I knew right from wrong. So I knew my mom did all she could do. So whatever was done or whatever decision I made, it was up to me.

If I was punished I had to stay in the house. Couldn't go outside. Yeah, I had beatings. Little beatings, yeah. Not brutal. A typical beating was with her hand or she might pick up something and throw it at us, you know— stuff like that. Never was like, you know . . . I ain't had a beating in so long that I've forgotten what I ever got a beating with. You know, my mom wasn't into that beating us. She'll say, "Stay your motherfucking ass in the house." She did curse like a sailor though. She would say "bitch," "motherfucker," you know, stuff like that. So she would say things like "Stupid motherfucker." She talks like that. Just screaming and hollering. . . . I was like "Dag, Mom! You could have waited till I got in the house." She might talk about my girlfriends like they're bums. "Them little bum-bitches you be with" and stuff like that. She used to call me "bum-bitch" too. I run the street a lot, so that's what she says about me now.

When we were younger, she would buy hot stuff from people. But if my mom take your pencil without you knowing it, it'll eat her up, her conscience, you know, 'cause she feel like she's stealing it. You're gonna come back and she's gonna tell you. She has been arrested. A guy stole my color TV and she stabbed him up. I don't know the story behind that. All I know is that the guy had supposed to had stole my TV out my mom's house. My mom found out because it was a friend of hers. She asked him about it. The next thing I knew my mom was locked up. We were living right on Eleventh Street. Yeah, she stabbed him up! Hospitalized stabbed up. She had to be put in jail stabbed up. She had a big bail, high bail. She was in jail twenty-something days. This was two, three years ago. This was the first time for her, you know. My mom ain't never been in jail before this. They threw the case out. He never appeared in court. He didn't want to press charges. He was in the hospital a week, if that long. We were like "Get the fuck out here! She's in jail? No, not Bertha!"

My brother is in jail now for snatching a lady pocketbook, running and robbing people. He got two to five. He's got 'bout three more years. Yeah, that's my baby brother. He had started smoking crack. That's my mother's baby, you know. It bothers her, you know.

I learned my hustling from the streets. She didn't have to try to keep me off the streets when I was younger 'cause I ain't start getting into trouble till I got grown. The first time I got locked up I was nineteen, twenty. I was fifteen, though, when I did my first crime. I was shoplifting. Stole something. I went with my girlfriend and seen it lookeded easy and I just did it. I just did what she did. I was like "Yeah!" After that I was rolling. You know, everybody got their own different way. I mean, somebody might say you could do it this way. Like throw it all in one bag. You know, stuff like that. But no, nobody. . . . See, I'm just. . . . All you got to do is show me something and I'll put my touch to it real fast. You know, I like to do it my way.

The worst thing that happened to me when I was a child was being locked up when I was fifteen. Well, I wasn't really locked up. I was detained. Locked up, you know—who wants to be confined though for real? I didn't think I would be able to steal no more. I thought my mom would pitch a bitch and thinking they wasn't gonna let me go home—that's what came to my mind. When my mom came to jail, she said, "You the best bitch! You the best bitch!" That's what she said, "You're a motherfucking best." She said that 'cause I ain't right. She's hot 'cause she had to come all the way down there to get me. When she came and got me the first time from jail, she didn't put me on any kind of restriction or nothing. No, and I came right back out that next day and went downtown in Blair's and stole. It didn't scare me. . . . You know, I said, "Damn!" You know, I thought about not being able to come home, but I was like "Damn, they ain't put that much fear in my heart 'cause here I am again."

Oh, I learned things like taking it and putting all in one bag. Sticking it under your shirt. How to look out, you know. Make sure you look around before you stick something somewhere. That's about it. Shoplifting is nothing. It's only but a few basic things you got to worry about. Matter of fact it's only one thing you got to worry about and that's somebody seeing you. Anything other than that . . . hey, you're safe.

I met this guy—I knew the basics of this con thing—I met this guy when I got up here to North Jefferson. We became close friends and this is what he was into. I always wanted to get some money. So I said "Con! Well, tell me about it." And what it was is that what you say out your mouth to try to make somebody give you. . . . Put your money in this handkerchief and tie this money up, right? He used to talk in a foreign language. All I had to do was stand there and say what he was telling the people—whatever he was telling the people—was true. But he'll be telling them little stuff that he gave his money to these people and they were supposed to find him a hotel. He had gave them two hundred dollars and they never came back. He had a knot full of money, but it'll be money on top. . . . It's a mitch, they call it, but it don't be nothing but a green dollar bill or something on top of this mitch. You just got to convince somebody to put their money with your money. Supposed to be your money, but it ain't no real money there, and that's how you con them out they money. They end up giving us all they money 'cause whatever he be saying, he be saying to convince them. Like he might say somebody tried to rob him and he don't want to go to the bus station to get his clothes or something because the same people might be there and try to rob him again. So he ask you to hold all his money and you would say, Yeah," and he'll say, "Well, wait a minute. What if you go and put my money in one place and yours in another, and I come back and you tell me somebody robbed you up, but only my money? So why don't you put your money and my money together so that way when they steal my money, they'll steal yours too?" And they'll put it together and he'll tie it in a handkerchief and switch it on them. Instead of giving them the one with their money in it, it'll be the handkerchief with some newspaper. That's all I knew. I just knew the basics. . . . All I really was was a yes'm—meaning all I said was, "Yeah, he telling you the truth." That's all.

When I was growing up at Twenty-first and Barnfield, there was plenty of crime there. I may not have been much aware of how much 'cause I was younger, but now that I'm into it, you know, it's like more. By the time I got over to Herbert Street at like sixteen or seventeen, I was bumping then. There is a lot of crime and stuff in the project. Sticking people up, snatching people's pocketbooks.

Drugs and money are the things that's important to the people in this neighborhood. Fast money. When I was living at Twenty-first and Barnfield, it was the same things. . . . Well, okay, I'll put it like this. Yes and no, because I wasn't into that life then. So I couldn't say how much value they took in that, but from what I basically see . . . yeah. I knew what the deal was when I moved here. So immediately that's where I placed myself, because that's where I wanted to be, you know. I mean, 'cause quite naturally other people has other values. My group of people. . . . Drugs and fast money, that's the only thing I can round it off to.

When I think about the project, I see all kinds of people. This is what I'm saying. See, I don't even try to deal with the ones that ain't into what I'm

into. They value their children, I guess. Clothes. Jewelry. I mean, 'cause this is what I'm surrounded by. Fast lifestyle, you know. Basically the only important thing to them is either cars, having a car, having jewelry 'round they neck, some nice clothes, some drugs, and some money. Maybe they value fighting and toughness, but I'm telling you, selling they drugs. 'Cause they all that! 'Cause they getting the money, you know. I mean, in the projects it's . . . that's all that goes on. Either you get . . . they either a seller, a buyer, and that's it. You know what I mean? They all of that 'cause they selling it, you know.

I ain't trying to know any of them that don't sell or use drugs. You know? I'm serious. I don't get into them. The people I hang with ain't got time to fight. Yeah. And if they do get into a little thing it's about a cap of crack, you know. So it ain't about how tough you is. They really don't want a fight. They really want a hit of crack. So it's like "Come on, do what we gonna do here, so I can still go and get my blast" and that's the truth. That exploitation and taking advantage of people . . . that's all within the drug game, that's all in one. So they're more concerned with manipulation than with toughness. They ain't about to get in no fight unless it has something to do with protecting their drugs or getting drugs from somebody or there's money to get, you know. Their image is that they're getting theirs, plain and simple.

Hell, yeah, there are people who are more skilled than others. Sure it is. If they are highly skilled, I respect you. You get the respect 'cause you spending your money. Look, if I can spend eight hundred dollars or two hundred dollars or three hundred dollars with you a day, damn right I'm gone respect you 'cause you bringing that money to me. You know, I got to respect you for what you do 'cause you're good 'cause I don't understand how you be doing it. So people who are not as skilled try to get skilled or try to get close to them to learn sometimes so they can get on top of things. They learn so they can get what they can get—those skills to get theirs and to impress other people.

When I was about twelve or thirteen years old my best friends was whoever was shoplifting. So there was no one in particular. I hung out with them all. But later I did have a good friend. Her name is Karen. I was going to Columbus then. I guess I was sixteen or seventeen. I mean, we did a lot of things together. We talked, you know. I told her all my secrets. And she was real! She was down to earth. I don't got to see her for three or four years from now and we'll still be the same when we see each other. We went to movies. We schemed, you know . . . or guys, see who we could get. You know, we had fun together. We laughed. We joked. That's what I likeded. Karen was down to earth. Plain and simple. She was real.

I didn't experience a lot of pressure from my friends to hang out. I just wanted the money. It started out money for the things I wanted. The other stealing was for the 'caine. So it started with, yeah, like if my girlfriends come to school with all this new fly stuff on. Man! I wanted it too. You know what I mean? I've always likeded nice things too, you know.

I lived with my grandmother and them when I was fifteen. Something like that. I stayed with them a couple of years or whatever off and on. I went to get away from my mom. Get away from that nonsense. Living with them it felt like I was home. I was in a house. I feel like I was with a family. It was my people, you know. They was concerned about me. I didn't think about the fast life when I was living with them. I came back to my mom's 'cause things got a little hectic there. Meaning I couldn't do like I wanted, you know. . . .

Well, all right. It was like I used to go . . . to come to South Jefferson to be with my South Jefferson friends and I was still being involved in things. You know, things started getting, looking gooder and gooder, you know. It drifted me away from my grandma and them. That got to be a bore, you know. I was becoming a L7, you know, and I stepped off from there. Went on back home to Mom. Plus I felt like my mom needed somebody there. I didn't want to leave my mom from the beginning, 'cause I knew she needed me. I was getting into the fast life. It was just me going to South Jefferson on weekends and stuff like that. I was getting into what I was into and it got exciting. More exciting than just sitting there. I was stealing! I would steal and go to parties.

Getting involved in the fast life didn't have nothing to do with sex, though. No, that wasn't important to me. Sex ain't never been that important to me. You know, never. I would be partying and hanging out. Having all that fly shit on. Yeah! That kind of thing, yep. I could go when I was at my grandmother's, but no long hour, night thing. She had a curfew for anybody. My grandmother don't play that door flying open all times of night and all that. All that screaming and hollering and jumping up. Uh-uh.

My mother never talked about the birds and the bees and all that old stuff. No. But that's how fast I was. That's how fast I had become. I got my period at sixteen. It didn't freak me out. . . . Didn't nothing come to me as surprising 'cause that's how fast I was. I was into the street life, you know. I wanted to know everything. It's from being in the projects. So I knew things that most kids don't find out till late. Hell, I knew where babies came from at a young age. Yeah, how it was done and all of that. Yeah, and it was not like "Oooh!" and all that. I didn't go through that.

When I had my period, my mother didn't try to keep track of me. No. No, 'cause I was always hollering I ain't having none—having no children. And this is like the honest truth—I have always sat around and said I will not have any children. I don't want no children. I don't want the aggravation. I don't want the responsibility. I love children and I'll take your child from now till doomsday only because I can give them back. I have enough responsibility myself. I have to keep myself.

So when I got my period I was outside playing. My period came on and that was that. It just came on and I just went and told my mom my period came on. I knew. I was aware. She had never talked about it, but I knew from girlfriends that already had them. That kind of stuff. My mom talked about that kind of stuff through open conversations, not direct—through conversations she was having with a girlfriend or whatever. I learned about babies from the streets and TV. A girlfriend might have said that she was with somebody already, you know. Sort of like that, you know. Some of them are always faster than others.

I was eighteen when I had my first sexual experience. Nothing really happened. It was not . . . it ain't like I bled or nothing like that. You know how they say you bleed. No. I went in it open-minded. He was a friend, a guy who was supposed to been my boyfriend. It came as simple as pulling teeth. Serious! 'Cause I was aware of whatever, you know. We just did it. Up and did it. We were at his house. We was going together—it had been like four months. Well, we had planned it the day before that we was gonna do it. Well, see, I was . . . when I went over there I knew what I was going for because we had talked about it the day before. I'm saying it wasn't like I was a little kid. I mean, it was plain and simple, like "You know, Ginny, you know we gonna do that thing. It's about time now. We been together like four months and you ain't gave me nothing yet." And I said, "Yeah, sure, it is about that time." When I went over there, that's what we did. We went straight to the bed.

Okay. It didn't make a difference to me at all. It didn't make a difference. I mean, it was like. . . . you know how some people can't wait for it. I wasn't in it. You know what I mean? I wasn't looking at it like I couldn't wait. You know, acting like I'm really missing something. I ain't look at it like that. Yeah, whatever is clever. It won't no thang at all. There was no peer pressure or anything like that. I had sex with him 'cause he was a friend of mine.

Hell, I'm not excited about sex at all! I mean, you know what I'm saying? For real! 'Cause that don't excite me. Always been like that. I wanted to get a feeling. You know, all this . . . you talking about it's all that and you missing it and what I'm missing. . . . Pressure. I was curious of what these people keep saying I be missing. After I finished I said it was cute. That's all I could say. It was cute. I had missed something because I hadn't had it. Other than that it wasn't like . . . goddamn, they made it seem like . . . like God! You be in heaven, you know. Drugs is my sex partner.

I stopped school. My senior year really. So I completed the eleventh. I dropped out in the twelfth. I was a C student. When a test came I half-ass cheated. For real! I'm telling you the truth. I didn't skip a lot of school until I got up there to like the eleventh grade. We used to cut classes then. I thought I was all that! So I skipped whenever I felt like it. I skipped 'cause I didn't feel like going to a certain class or I didn't feel like school today. I wanted to go down to the arcade or hang out at McDonald's with all the rest of the people. Little bullshit! I got in fights at school a couple times, nothing serious. 'Cause she punched me. Little bullshit, you know, 'cause she don't like me 'cause I was maybe the first one with a pair of sneakers on. Stuff like that.

If I did something wrong at school my mother would ask me what was wrong with me. She wouldn't go to school unless it was required for her to. She'd see my grades when my report card come. That's how it was. For real! Seriously! If I got bad grades she would tell me I got to do better or I was gonna get left down. That's it. School was fun. The people were fun. Yeah, when you're in class, ain't no cutting out. I was never with that. I'm in class, I'm gonna do what I got to do and I'm gonna step off.

Some of my teachers were bitches 'cause some. . . . Well, they're bitches because they ain't play that. You know what I mean? They were strictly straight up. You couldn't even laugh or nothing like that. Them the ones that is bitches and them the ones I cutted out on.

I respect everybody though. I wouldn't give the teachers a hard time because I know they ain't doing nothing but telling me something, right? If I took that type of attitude, I wouldn't . . . if I had that type of attitude I wouldn't take it and subject somebody else to that when they only doing their job or whatever the case might be.

School wasn't important to me 'cause I ain't . . . It was like this. I went to school because I know I needed it. I'm saying, you know, it was mandatory. That's why I went. But I felt the streets was more important to me than what school was. If I had that guidance, you know, straight guidance, I think I might have gone. If things hadn't got hectic the way they got as far as my mom and things like that, you know, 'cause I drifted when that happened. I may have, but I didn't because, see, it's things I wanted then and my mom couldn't give it. I know I really ain't have no job, have no money, and I wanted to go have sneakers and things like that. So I didn't go to school so I could go to steal, you know, or cut out of class early to go steal and have lunch money. The materialistic things and the street life became more important than school.

I already knew I had a good mind. That's the bad part about it. See, that's one thing I found out in getting high. When you recognize what you doing, that's what hurts the most, you know. You know? When you recognize you're doing something that ain't doing you no good and you don't do nothing about it, that hurts the most. I knew within myself I had the potential to do it. The fast life stopped me from doing it. Plain and simple.

'Cause I ain't want to go to school without no money in my pocket if I wanted to buy a sandwich or I wanted to go to McDonald's where everybody else gonna be. You know? That's how it was.

It's within yourself. All you see is what you want to see and want. That's just like . . . it's mind over matter plain and simple because, see, I can sit and tell you that I want to hit this pipe and know what this pipe is doing to me and to see that I can go over there and things will be a straight path and eventually at the top of that hill everything will be all right. So what! You know 'cause this is what I want and that's the pull. It's within yourself and what you want.

Choosing between the streets and school was clear. It's just like . . . it's this clear to me. What I'm doing now I can see the harm and see how it has affected my life and my family's, you know. I done did my things. You know what I mean? I done did my dirt. I done hurted people mentally, you know, where it affected my family mentally and done damage to myself. But, nevertheless! . . . ain't gonna stop me, you know. The only way I'm gonna stop . . . like I tell everybody, it ain't gonna be no plan or something I done dream—you know, like I done thought about and thought about and say I'm tired. It's gonna be up in one day. It's gonna be up in one day and it's gonna be over 'cause it's gonna be a shock to me too, you know.

It gonna take something big. That's how it gonna hit. It gonna be like the way they say people get the Holy Ghost. Huh-huh. That's how it's gonna be. You don't know it's coming and that's how it's gonna be for me. Where would I go if I was to go now? Ain't nowhere I'm going but jail. But that's where I'm going if I don't straighten up my act. That ain't gonna happen. Not right now, anyway. So I know where I'm going. I'm gonna go to jail. I been in jail twice. My longest stay was three months.

I had a choice. 'Cause when I went to live with my grandma and them it couldn't have been no better place. You know what I'm saying? So I had the choice, you know, but I chose finger popping, bullshitting, conning, and all the bullshit. That's what it was. I looked up to Grandma and them. Because they was, you know, they were always on time. They talkeded to me too because my mom was into her own little world. My mom wasn't approachable. No. No. And then my aunt and them used to talk to me about how guys would be and . . . you know, all kinds of things . . . and what they used to do—all of that. So shock . . . it wasn't no shock. When they used to have their little parties, I used to be at their parties in the basement.

When I look back now I still ain't there. I still ain't there 'cause I done got involved in something else that's even worser. That straight life is not into my interest. Now, I see it and I know what's ahead for it, but I ain't trying to get there yet. Still on a roll. When I get there all them things like school and all that's natural, it's gonna be there 'cause that's all in the straight life. So all of them things come in coordination to hit me. I'm gonna do all of that. I got to get there first, though. I ain't . . . can't see . . . I ain't making it yet, you know.

Did I dream about being famous? Famous, yeah, all right famous! Oh no, I didn't. I always said to myself, "Look at me, I'm messing with these drugs, I could be a goddamn lawyer, doctor, or something." I would say that. Or a private investigator. Dreaming about being rich—that's fabrication. I don't do that. I don't fabricate about stuff like that. If I was to be rich I wouldn't know what to do with the money. You know what? My mom has a comfortable . . . you know what I'm saying? . . . she don't play that drug thing in her house or none of that, right? If I was rich and live like them rich people live I wouldn't be happy. I'd be uncomfortable. You know what I'm saying? They're saying, "Three bathrooms. Ah, get the fuck out of here with that shit." You know what I'm saying? Gimme some, gimme some . . . let me sit on a couch with some crates underneath.

You know, I ain't no fabulous this and that, wall to wall carpet this and that, and mirrors go all over. You know, these thousand dollar mirrors all on the wall. That ain't me. I'm a ordinary person. It ain't like "Them motherfucking projects, I would never live in there. Boy, I be glad to get out of them motherfucking projects." No. Born and raised in them! Love them! So I see myself living with my mother. At this present point. Long as Bertha got a roof, I got a roof. So if I came into a lot of money I'd buy my mom a home. I wouldn't want to be rich, see what I'm saying? I would buy every little fucking thing I see, you know, and forgotten all about the things I had needed. Yeah, that's crazy.

I don't want to be in no fucking place where all of the bitches are in there like putting on airs. No! I mean, I'm not no dog either. I know how to, you know . . . and if I drop my fork they won't, "Ooooh, did you see that! Oooh!" 'Cause I'm damn sure gonna pick him up and wipe him off, you know. "Oh no, she should have took that in the bathroom and rinsed it off with some water!" I don't need that. 'Cause see what I do is cuss them out.

So I would associate with people who didn't live in the projects as long as they're real and down to earth. That's the only thing that matters. Them the only kind of people I . . . I don't care where you come from. Real people is who I like to deal with. If Bryant Gumble came in here right now, I wouldn't open my mouth. I would say, "Hi." I wouldn't say nothing until I was spoken to. I just deal with people as them being them. You know, straight up from there. You know, "Fuck what they told you to say." You know what I'm saying? Just be you, 'cause I'm gonna be me, you know. Accept me for who I am or don't accept me at all. Get away from me, you know.

When I was growing up I wanted to be me, that's it. I didn't have no . . . you know how you . . . when you young you say, "I want to be a doctor or I'm gonna be this or I'm gonna be that"? I did not have none of that. I just wanted to be what I was gonna be when I got there. I'm just being me. I have no plan of what I want to be.

I've always lived with a guardian, and I've never been in a live-in relationship either. So I've never had my own responsibilities with bills and . . . no, never. I've lived at Eleventh and Herbert for eleven years. I had to have been seventeen when I got there. During those eleven years the projects changed gradually, you know, 'cause they started fixing up things. As far as the apartments, they put new bathrooms with showers, you know, and now they got the security . . . security to the building. You got to go through the security guards now. They got little booths. . . . You just have to be on someone's list in order to come in the building. But the building still is not well maintained. They're trying to get it well maintained, but it's just like something just running loose. Gradually they're trying to get things in perspective.

I love living in the projects. Born and raised! You know. So doesn't nothing surprise me. You know what I mean? You know, like people say, "I ain't going in them projects." But I know that it's not the projects, it's the people. So, I mean, it's nothing wrong with the projects. I love them. It's the people that makes the projects.

But I can understand. If you don't live there, it would scare you off. I would say it's a tall building that's raggedy and dirty. It got holes in the walls. Trash all in the stairways. It's nothing but what the people done, you know, 'cause the people don't clean it up. That's how I would describe it. A dirty building with a bunch of trash and a bunch of people. There's graffiti downstairs, you see trash sometimes . . . yeah, and they even got a garbage disposal on the other side, you know, where you put all your trash and everything. Of course, you got to go through seeing the security guard, and people hitting, smoking in the lobby part. You see a bunch of people standing smoking crack. The security guards do the best they can. You know, they run them away. You know, they call up the police or whatever. See, they can't see over in the opposite side of the building. That's where everybody's dumpster is at, where everybody is standing around in the stairway smoking.

And, yeah, you have the children that run up and down the steps. They smoke through the stairways. You got the trash, Pampers, all that kind of crazy stuff in the hallway, stairway, wherever. Some people don't empty they trash in the incinerators. They don't put it down. That's mostly basically what go on. I mean, you got the little graffiti. But they done painted. They painted the whole buildings, the hallways, the stairways, you know. They're coming along from when I first moved there, but it's still odds and ends that has to be done.

There are hit houses in the projects. There are four in my building. These are the houses that you can go to hit. There is just one place in my building where you can go and buy crack. You know, people don't like selling from their house because it be a lot going on. People don't want to get their house busted and stuff like that. Most people just sell on the outside. The only thing you can buy in a building is beer. People are selling forties in my building and other buildings in the projects.

As for the project, the building that I live in is the worst one. They call my building Saigon. They call it Saigon because most of the times when people come on that side there . . . if your face is not familiar you're bound to get robbed or, you know, something is going to happen. You either get your stuff tooken or you'll get slummed, meaning they give you fake 'caine. In my building just about every day somebody get robbed in some kind of way. You know, if it's just verbally, you know, or physically somebody gets robbed. Plenty gunshots go off in all the buildings. It's more action in my building than any of the others. Not too many knives. . . . I mean, they got a thing about guns now. Mostly drug-related most times, and that is coming from the drug dealers.

I like living there. It's like fitting right in. I fit in 'cause that's the life I live. Fast life, right? All this activity that's going on doesn't surprise me at all. I'm like a pig in shit. I'm okay. I got established there by staying to myself. You know, I know everybody. I speak. I might conversate, but I play single-oh. Meaning by myself. You know, I do a lot of observing, you know, and that's just me.

If I weren't the person I am and I walked in the project I would say, "These some dirty motherfuckers." I'd say, "Damn!" you know, but see I don't. . . . Even though I live in the projects and I mean I'm comfortable, you know, I don't approve of them standing in the hallway. I don't think that's cute. Them standing out in the hallway smoking crack and all the trash— all of that is ugly. It's nasty because children got to play. They're standing up there smoking and all of that. If a child run past and see them doing that. I don't approve of none of that. I don't think it's right. I mean, I do get high, but I am discreet. I respect everybody and I think the projects are the slum.

The people who live there are all different. Okay, you got people like me that's in the fast life. So we all mingle together, basically. Then you got people . . . you got, you know, nice, considerate, respectful people. You got all types of different people there, but my type is more than any other type. Right? Then you got over here, you may have the hoodlums. Then you got all the drug dealers and then you got all the pipe smokers. So you would look up and say, "Damn, we got all kinds of people." All the pipers is over there somewhere and that's how it be. It's bunched. If you notice when you come to the projects, you got bunches. You see all the smokers in one place, all the drug dealers hang out with each other basically, and all the girls that think they all that, Miss This and That, with a bunch of babies, they in one group. So it's like groups.

I think young people value older people in the projects. The violence is from the drugs. Yeah, and it's all . . . it's like it's too close . . . it's too much . . . because, see, you got . . . say you got one hundred and you got ninety-nine of them selling dope, drugs. So it's the competition that plays a part. You know what I'm saying? You want to make just as much money as that one is. Then you got the group that smokes that certain people they won't buy from. That creates a problem with the dealers, but these the ones that make the money. The dealers is the ones that make the problem more so than the ones that smoke. Drugs, that's basically what it is.

It's more now being sold than when I first moved in. When I first moved in they were selling powder. Powder was the most thing that was bought, you know. Then when they came up with the lazy thing about these crack caps—yeah, these little vials—it just got. . . . Then the little ones that started selling powder got a little big. Now they got the little children selling them. You know, they might have like six young boys that sell for them. The youngest person I've ever seen sell was twelve. The youngest I've ever seen smoking in the projects was fourteen. His mother turned him out.

To survive in the projects you have to accept facts—to be to yourself and to accept things and to reject. I mean, you know, you got to be yourself and you have to have enough sense to analyze things. You have to have enough sense to stay away from something that you know or stay away from somebody that you know that don't mean you totally no good. When I say learning the facts, I'm saying dealing with people, period. I mean, when you deal with somebody, you got to get into them. You've got to have your head on your shoulders. You've got to be more cautious because you're surrounded by all types of different people and things.

So it's always something happening. It's sort of like a little city into itself. There's nothing going on out there, because the project has it all. Has it all in it. It has police. It has your drugs. It even has stores. It even has your beer. All in the projects. Right there in the buildings. Stores because people are going out to shoplift. You got little candy stores where they sell candy and cigarettes. You know what I'm saying? In some cases they sell hotdogs, you know. All that . . . you got a city inside a city. There is no need to go out 'cause you can hustle right there. Most of the times when people go out to hustle they . . . or when people just come into the projects . . . they come from all over, like 'cross High Street and everything, to come to the projects. To cop! You know what I mean? So everything is right there in the projects. Somebody selling clothes. Come in the projects. You'll find somebody selling them. You know what I'm saying? Guns or whatever the case may be.

The worst thing I've seen happen there was somebody getting. . . . You know, shooting scared us. It scared everybody. It was a shooting. A guy just rode up in a car and he started shooting with a machine gun. He was shooting at some other guy or something. He just started shooting so he didn't care who he hit. We was all by the bulletin board. You should've seen everybody dodging. I hit the floor and they were tramping all over me. Do you know what I did do? I couldn't get up at first. I seen my girlfriend picking up all these caps. Popped up!

A innocent person got shot, though. The guy he was shooting at didn't. A innocent person got shot. He didn't get killed. He got shot up in his legs, and they had to skin this leg for this leg. He got a big, big . . . he got a big old chumpy like from right here to right here on his leg. A gash all the way down there. So they had to take this one here and put it there. He could have lost his legs. So that's the projects.

My first real relationship was with a woman. I met her. . . . Okay, she come home from Irwin, right? And it was a girlfriend of mine that she knew and she came over my house to see my girlfriend. She's in Irwin for . . . she maxed out at Irwin. She was in Irwin for robbing something. Okay, she seen me, you know. It was like the eyes . . . you know, gave me the eyes. But I ain't pay it no mind. So two days later I go to the bar—Herman's Bar, at Eleventh and Hubbard—and I'm sitting in the bar, me and another friend of mine. We've talking, lollygagging, drinking beer, and all that, and here this girl come that just came home from Irwin. So she got on these corduroys. I'll never forget this. She got on corduroys. They is tight as I don't know what. So—you know how you just look at somebody?—so I looked. So she said, "Can you see?" Right? So I said, "No, I can't." So she walked from the front door of the bar . . . no, she walked . . . yeah, the front door of the bar to the back where I was sitting by the jukebox. She said, "Now, see." And she pulled her shirt up. She said, "No, better yet," and she walked up back to the front of the door and bent over and said, "Now, can you see?" while everybody was in the bar, right? And I just bust out laughing and from that day we started talking to each other. We became buddies.

That wasn't my first sexual relationship with a woman, but that's the first real sexual relationship 'cause she turned me out! That was my first intimate sexual relationship. I knew I was gay at the time. I knew I was gay when I was fourteen, but that was the first intimate relationship. I met Maria when I was twenty-one or twenty, something like that. But at fourteen, fifteen I knew something was shaky. I had my first sexual relationship with a man at seventeen. From seventeen to twenty-one, I was with him, right? But I knew my interest was in a woman. That's why I think he ain't do nothing for me, you know, 'cause my mind was there. I likeded him. I fell for him, but as far as the sexual part, it was like "Yeah, whatever is clever. Come on." You know. All right, then we got cute, step off. You know like that. We had fun together. We laughed.

My ideal partner is a female. I would want her to be real and understanding—that's all I ask for. I don't ask for nothing more, nothing less. There is no role I would want her to play. . . . In my relationship there is no role. . . . Equal rights. We do this thing together.

I just got this thing about people being real. No matter what it is. I feel like this. Look, the truth is the truth. Fact is fact. You know, truth hurts. I may go cry in this mirror, but the bottom line is that I got to deal and that's how I feel. I don't care what it is. You know, some people say you don't tell nobody 'cause it will hurt. But the bottom line is I got to deal with it. So that's how that is.

She's nice. See, two women know what another woman wants, you know . . . they know what each other like and how they like to feel. When two women . . . so sensitive . . . oh, it's just . . . all that and some. It's touching. Everything is soft. It ain't that old rough hardness men give out, you know.

When I met Maria we were 'round the same age. She was like twenty-one. She came with a reputation, yeah, and I was told . . . and I always heard about this girl named Ria. I call her Maria, that's her real name. Everybody else call her Ria. I used to hear about her, you know, this girl Ria. She's rough. She will fight you. She's a rumbling motherfucker. That how they used to say, and all of that. But who I know is Maria, and she is a whole different person than Ria. Ria is that little rough person. You know what I mean? Maria is nice, sensitive, respectful, and cares about others. But the Ria they know don't give a fuck about nothing. I wasn't introduced to her as Ria. I was introduced to her as Maria, but I done seen Ria in her—you know what I'm saying?—that hoodlum, you know, that two parts.

It lasted two years. It ended 'cause I just ain't no good. I'm known not to be no good, you know, that cheating, running around, messing, whatever, with other women. She ain't never caught me. See, she started smoking before I did. That did it too.

She started using cocaine first, smoking out the pipe first. I started using about six months later. She didn't introduce me though. I had already been aware of the pipe, but I hadn't used it.

See, I'm a turbo—that means lace it up in a cigarette, right? She was smoking and I would go and find her. She would be in these smoke houses and used to go through changes. I said, "Damn! If you got to smoke or something, you know, you ain't got to be in these hit houses." You know, we used to go through things like that, and that took its toll too.

I didn't want her in no hit house because them places ain't. . . . And then they ain't clean. You got caps and matches all throwed all over the . . . you know, that . . . I just ain't . . . you know, where you're with somebody who you know and all they want to do is sit around and talk about caps and. . . . You know I get high, but there's more to life than. . . . In places like that most people, all they talk about is the 'caine. Nothing about like . . . even "Remember when we used to go to school?" and such and such. It's never that. And I don't like that. It's dirty, the environment, the people, you know. I didn't like it, and I don't like it still now.

She didn't know that I was having these relationships with other women, but that's what they said. I'm saying that's how they was saying that I was— you know, being bad and messing with all these other people and. . . . She was saying that I was doing that, you know, from all these rumors. That's like if I stand there and talk to you and you're a woman, you know, what people think right off the top that we're doing something. I wasn't then when she was accusing me, but then afterwards . . . I might have been like drooling in they faces, but, you know, not like the way they tried to make it seem.

Those two years we were together were all right. You know, we enjoyed each other. We went to movies. We used to do crimes together. We used to go for walks. We used to play racquet ball, tennis, ride bikes. You know, we used to do a lot of active things together. She lived in my mom's house when we were together. See, Maria just started staying nights. Plus my mom and Maria was all right, you know. That's the type of person my mom is. If you don't have nowhere to go and y'all all right, you can sure come there. My mom don't approve of it, but she had to accept it. She likeded her and she respected her. It ain't like we laid up, you know . . . like that. My mom's down to earth.

The relationship ended because Maria went back to jail for credit cards. That's not the reason why the relationship ended, but that's how it completely ended. The drugs was the thing that was wrong with the relationship. Two lovers can't get high together. No! It won't work 'cause you be so worried one person will get mad if you got more then the other or you want to take your money and you want to do this but, no, they want a cap and all that old kind of crazy shit.

We didn't argue about drugs that much. Not much. Maybe like . . . well, not really, we didn't really argue. Maybe once a week, argue . . . well, you know, have different opinions, you know. Basically that's every day 'cause everybody have their own opinion about something. When the drug came, we got to rumbling. We got the fighting. They became more frequent. Very frequent. Like every day. They would more likely turn into rumbles then. Well, her rumbling me, 'cause I wouldn't hit her.

Other things cause these fights too. Things like she wanted to do something or like she had stayed out too long, too late, you know, things like that. Or she was supposed to cook something and didn't do it. Something we supposed had did or I didn't do what she asked me to do, you know. Stuff like that. Sometimes we started fighting because I be acting like I ain't trying to hear it. She would push and shove me and tell me, "You think I'm playing," and all that old kind of crazy stuff. "I'll punch you in your mouth. You think I'm playing?" I start saying, "You better stop playing. You better keep them fucking hands off of me." She be like "I'm gonna fuck you up." She might try to hit me and then I might push her and then she just start swinging on me. I be like "Go 'head." It would be a little catfight.

It would usually end by. . . . Sometimes we just go in the house. Sometimes she'll go to her sister's and I'll go on 'bout my business and then later on I be like "Come here, Maria." I don't believe we had what I would call a serious fight. I believe if we got to get into that that deep, then we got to leave each other alone.

We supported each other drug use by doing crime. We did whatever to support ourselves. . . . I mean, I did crime. Her crime was pickpocketing. We used to go around Kroger and you know how them ladies leave their pocketbooks in the cart and go all way over there to bend over to pick up something. Yeah. And we used to take their pocketbooks like that. We'd shoplift, steal out of automobiles, whatever.

Drugs don't take my nature and it don't make me hot. What makes me hot, it got to be the person. The person got to make me feel special. But not all that romance and trying to touch on them to make me hot 'cause we smoking. Come on! You know. I don't especially enjoy sex after smoking like crack. It take too long to come. Once you smoke enough of that shit you can't. For real!

I ain't into exchanging sex for drugs either. I ain't into that. For money, but not drugs. I only got one friend like that I do. Yeah, he old as dirt. Yeah, he is. That was before my drug use. He was like a sugar daddy. I met him when I was in junior high school. He has always been there regardless of who I had and they're gonna have to always respect that. Whoever I deal with gonna have to respect the fact that this man is always gonna be in my life. He's a lifesaver. He's older than old—I would say about sixty-six, in that age bracket. I met him one day coming home from school. I was going to Columbus. I got to be around sixteen then. Yeah, I was sixteen, and I still see him up till this day. I've been intimate with him irregardless to who I was intimate with. When I met him, though, we didn't do anything. I didn't start having sex with him until I was eighteen.

He always took care of me, in other words. Always. Well, I would use that phrase as saying that he's always been a father, friend. You know what I mean? Like, you know, I don't love him like that as far as . . . I love him as him being there for me as a friend and as a father and all that. He was into real estate and he lives in Laurel Hill. I may see him once a week or twice a week. He comes down here to see me. He's the only man that if I was to have sex, it would be him. We don't have sex. We used to, but we don't, 'cause I ain't got the patience for that. You know what I'm saying? I'm not into be sucking and all that, and I ain't with all that, you know what I'm saying? And that's how much he feel about me . . . that, you know, we don't even get into it. He comes down in his car. Gives me money. Talks to me, you know, see what I've been doing and what's going on. He lectures me, you know, about when I get myself together and blasé this and blasé that. Get my money, kiss him on the cheek, see him later. He calls on the phone and all that. The visits are no more then a half an hour, twenty minutes sometimes, and that's it. He parks right out front of my building. I see him once or twice a week and then sometimes a month might pass.

Female attracts me. I want somebody that I can just enjoy myself around. They can't be real ugly. They have to have some kind of looks. Yeah, kind of cute. And they teeth has to be clean and right, straight, not all lapped up on top of one another. That plays a big part.

The type of person they are is also important. It got to be somebody that can keep up with me. I don't want nobody who think they all slick and all they about is a bunch of that old hip-talking stuff. You know, I mean, plain English. I need a plain English-talking person. I don't need nobody "And dig this and dig that." I don't need that. I can't relate. I would want somebody in the fast life as long as they ain't faster than me. I would get involved with someone who's not in the fast life too, 'cause I'm versatile. I could get involved with somebody who don't get high. Sure. I'm very versatile. I can relate to practically any type of person, but I don't really be around the ones that don't get high. I go into my own little world.

Yeah, I'm a gay woman 'cause I desire a woman more then I ever desired a man and that's the term they use. I ain't using no excuses for being gay. That was in me. That's an excuse to me. That was just something that was in me when I was born. I believe that I was born this way. I don't think about how gay black people are treated. I've never got into that because I think whoever that treats a person other than the way they are, you know, treating them as bad, then something is wrong with them. So I don't get deep into that.

I don't think about gay liberation. I don't think about none of that. You know, I mean, I just live. I'm just gonna do my thing. I wouldn't care. But I do have discretion. You know, I got to respect everybody. Everyone knows I'm gay. I ain't in a closet. I'm not in a closet, and the ones that can't accept me for who I am I stay away from. I don't tolerate that ignorancy and I don't. . . . Some people might say, "Oh, that old bulldagger" or "That old gay bitch." I don't feed into that. I laugh at them and keep on stepping 'cause I'm gonna do what I do. I'm gonna do what makes me happy, not for what society say is right.

I didn't tell my mother I was gay. She told me. See, she didn't ask me, you understand. She just told me. All right, well, I never tried to hide from my mom or nobody. You know, I was never really what you called a closet case. You know what I'm saying? You would know that I was attracted to women, but I was never like just didn't give a fuck. . . . You know, like I'm out there in center public and I'm feeling all over this girl. No, I don't do that. You know, my mom is crazy. She just said . . . she got mad one day about something I did. She goes, "You be messing with all them old dizzy bitches," and that's how she . . . and I said, "So what? I'm gonna do what I want to do." She wanted to ask me, but didn't know how. So I answered it for her when she said it that way. I gave her my answer, "So what? I'm gonna do what I want to." And it was no big thing. . . . That's how she really found out. It killed her curiosity.

I don't deal with my mom too much. I mean, not . . . more so now because of, you know, I get high. I don't deal with my family too much at all, period. I don't even ask my mom for money. The relationship with Howard really sort of just cut the ties. It killed things, and me and my mom didn't relate for real, so there was no reason for us to get into that.

I have never stolen from my mom . . . not from my mom, but out of my mom's household. It was somebody's else's, like a girlfriend of my brother's or something like that. But never . . . I would never steal from my mom or a family member. 'Cause, see, I'm a straightforward person. I don't lie about nothing I do 'cause, see, I got too many talents in criminal things. If it got that hard up, I would just say, "Look, Mom, I need five dollars." Straight out! All she could say is no.

When she found out I was using drugs, it hurt her to her heart. You know, she didn't say anything. See, my mom . . . see, I think being that my mom and me never had a type of relationship where we talked. She don't say anything to me like as far as asking me what I'm doing or what's wrong. She'll wait until something goes wrong and she gets hot-headed and she'll be like "I know you smoking that motherfucking pipe," and I always answer her. 'Cause that's her way of asking.

It really hurted her. She cried. I mean, I knew how she felt before, but she wouldn't say nothing, so I wouldn't say it. So, I mean, it bothered me that she cried, and I told her I know how she feel, and she said, "You need help." "Stop telling me I need it, and help me! Help me get help"—I'm saying—like "whenever I'm ready to get it." You know, that's the only way she can help. When I decide, then just be there for me, you know, that's all. I don't need you on me, talking about what I need to do. I know what I need to do. I don't need that from you and nobody else.

I puffed a joint. That was the first drug I ever used and then from there to 'caine, crack, I didn't use nothing until I was twenty-one. Didn't drink, didn't smoke joints, didn't do nothing. That's why, when my aunt seen me, her first words was, "What! I couldn't even get you to smoke a joint." You know? Yeah, surprised a lot of people.

Actually what happen was that I had took twenty-three hundred dollars. I did a sting for twenty-three hundred dollars. I call myself . . . plain and simple, I called myself tricking with this girl. So I'm over her house because I'm on the run and I got twenty-three hundred dollars. I got this cocaine. I got a ounce of 'caine and I'm snorting like a Navaho Indian. My nose began to get fucked up, but they smoked it. So my nose got so bad I said, "Yeah, cook up the 'caine." I got all this money. I'm steady spending and splurging and I decided to pick the pipe up and take a try.

So up until the time I was twenty-one I wasn't doing anything and then I started smoking cigarettes. . . . I didn't really smoke J's. I might have took a puff. . . . Say, like I'll took a puff today, I probably won't take another puff of joint till six, seven months from now, you know—just to be doing it—and I ain't gonna take no more than two puffs. I don't even consider that smoking joint. You know, I would take a cigarette and put some 'caine in it and smoke it, you know, or rolling it. I don't know how often I did that . . . maybe about two days out of a week.

When I took that first hit of crack. . . . Well, from my knowledge, if that's what they call a blast, I felt good. I didn't feel hyped. I felt real content, you know. I mean, my body was just totally relaxed and I felt good. I knew I was an addict when I kept buying it. It didn't take long after smoking all of that. I blew all the money and the 'caine—like a five-day period. I was smoking and getting high for like five days straight. That first time was my best experience. I didn't schitz. I ain't into none of that shit. Now all this is a chase. Now all I do is chase. I'm running back and forth, back and forth.

That first time they held my match. You know, they hold my match for me and all I did was just. . . . It didn't take me long to learn to hold the match, not long at all, the same day. I ain't slow. It ain't gonna take me long to catch on to nothing.

I've only stopped using when I was incarcerated. That was for two months . . . three months. A month after I got out I picked up again. It just came into my head that I wanted a hit. It just popped up in my head. I wasn't like under no pressure or anything. I don't use no excuse for this thing. It's no excuses. It just be within me. You know, mind over matter. I was sitting on the bench and I had money after I had got up. Went and bought a cap and we light the girl pipe and started smoking.

I keep using because I like it. It don't do shit for me. I like just giving my money away, I guess. Just throwing my money away. It don't help me cope. Problems gonna be there. See, they're excuses. Ain't no excuse. I tell you, ain't no excuse to this. I ain't trying to use that to substitute nothing. Depressed at the end, at the end you're depressed. You just want more. It makes you chase, plain and simple. How it actually makes somebody else feel I don't know, but it makes me chase.

In the beginning of my habit I workeded at this little Burger King. Fast food. I always was a shoplifter, pickpocketer, con artist, whatever you want to call it. A yes'm. Anything that's criminal I did. Always. Always, always hustling. Once I started smoking I did more hustling and stuff. Wow! Plenty of hustling, baby! I hustle every day. Every single day! If ain't nothing but going to the store for people, Ginny gonna go. I wash cars, somebody's car, clean somebody house up, anything somebody gonna pay me to do, I'm gone do it within limits.

I get up in the morning . . . like ten o'clock. . . . It depends if I go to sleep. Sometimes I don't go to sleep. I get up, I comes and goes to my mom's, right? Eat sometimes. Sometimes I don't. Come out, get a blast about ten-thirty in the morning. I got people I can go to and just get caps. Sometimes on credit. . . . Look, that's how much business I bring to them. 'Cause, see, at one time I would help somebody . . . I was helping somebody sell caps and I used to get paid for that. See, I know everybody. People know I'm a good people and a lot of people just come up . . . most people look for me to find out who got the best stuff. I bring them people good money. I'll campaign for them. Yeah, I campaign, charity, whatever. So in the morning I get up, eat sometimes, wash up, take a shower, go outside, and then when my day begins, smoking. Sometimes I wake up and I'm still sleep, you know. I mean, beat tired. My body feel beat because I done been up like two, three, four day.

When I wake up it's not like the first thing I want is a hit . . . 'cause I know eventually I'm gonna get me a hit when I get outside anyway. See, as long as you got a tool for a person to use you're gonna always get one. I smoke like thirty, forty caps a day. That's average. Good days I'm busting loose. Oh, my goodness, fifty, sixty, seventy caps. Yeah, I'm busting. I'm constantly on a clock tip if it ain't nothing but a dollar. Yeah, on a clocking. Meaning getting mines. The afternoons is the same thing. My day is consistent. The same thing every day. Hustle. Hustle. Hustle. 'Cause I got to have it. You know, I got to have it.

I don't have a usual place to go. I ain't prejudice. Well, I used to go . . . most of these places is burnt out now, meaning they done dogged it. You got to go to Saint Elsewhere, so that's where I'm at—Saint Elsewhere. I mean, I will go to Dryer and Northway. I would go to Cumberland and something, you know. Hey! I prefer white people neighborhoods, things like that, because I think they have more. They more clumsy more or less.

Not as careful as us. See, we gonna make sure ain't nothing change there. Ain't nothing in there to steal.

I cop right there at the building. It's not even necessary to go outside the building to cop. Never been given dummies. No, nope. I gag . . . I do it. I don't burn nobody but whities. They come to the block. They come to the neighborhood, especially on weekends. 'Cause Northway Avenue is right there. Boom! Ain't got to even walk to Northway Avenue in some cases. If it gets slow on Herbert Street, I walk onto Northway, but they come straight down Herbert Street and be looking for reefer and vials. I got regulars. I give them real caps and real weed. I sell them weed for ten dollars a bag. It be five dollars. I got vials, they pay ten dollars a vial. Huh-huh, every single day faithfully. Faithfully! They don't have no special times—day, night. I got a white boy that comes through every single day. He come eveningtime 'cause he be working, so he comes during the evening every single day to buy caps. I had one dude to buy twenty at one time and I've had blacks that buy that many.

I'll gag folks. I'll issue them. Sometimes they'll come back after I've gagged them. They come back. They just say to me, "Look, come on. You didn't have to do that. Just give me some real stuff." "Oh, okay." Now, I just made them a regular.

I ain't never begged or panhandled. I ain't with that. I ain't got to do all that. I tell you I'll steal some newspapers first and sell newspapers. I got that hustling thing in me, you know. I'll sweep the front. . . . I'll wash a window for something I want. If I can't get enough money from that I'm gonna do what I do best—pickpocketing, rob a car, whatever, shoplift. So I'll do the legal stuff first—try to do something legal—or I'll gag somebody 'fore I'll break into somebody's car. I do that, but, see, then if it's getting too loose I'll get impatient waiting on somebody to come up and buy them and I'll say, "Look, I'm going to step on off, and I'm gonna try to do something else."

When I socialize I socialize with my lover or mostly the dope dealers. I'm semi in a relationship right now. It's been three or four years. We have not been intimate like that, and we just getting into each other on that intimate base. We've been intimate about a month. Give it a month. Give or take. She works. She got a son. She uses, but not like I use. She's a real every-now-and-then person.

I don't smoke in my mother's house. Hell no! My girlfriend house. She don't be home anyway. She be at work. So I be there by myself. I don't like smoke houses. If I smoke in the building, I go up to the eleventh floor or jump on the elevator. My mom don't play that smoking in her house, no way. I either go anywhere where Bertha won't find me. Seriously. I will go into a abandoned house first before I let my mom see me get high. She has never seen me high. Oh, no! Never! She know I be high, but she ain't never seen me get high.

Sometimes when I'm out there, baby, sometimes I don't make it. I mean, ain't no time, ain't no curfew to my hours. I'm in and out, you know. Sometimes I'm up two to three days without sleep. Yeah, 'cause I be delirious, you know. I get delirious, and then my body just, "Ginny, lay your ass down." Boom! I'll sleep for a day or two. In some cases I'll sleep for twenty-four hours like and then . . . or I might wake up, get a meal. If I'm at home or I'm at my friend house, they're gonna wake me up to eat, but I be sleepy. If I stay up too long my body will not tolerate it. I'll usually have two marathons a week. Some people stay up six, seven days. Some people can. I ain't with it. No, no, no, hell no.

I don't drink. I'm serious. I don't drink. If I'm geeked, I'm saying it's time to go to bed, plain and simple. You know, I'm not a alcoholic drinker. If I'm geeked, I might drink some milk, you know, or something like that, but other than that I don't use no other drug but crack.

I carry my straight shooter with me. I mean, I don't leave home without it! It's like luggage. You know what I'm saying? It's like got to have it with me. I get high by myself. I keep my own chumpy. I'll get high with my girlfriend, but she won't go on one of those marathons. She don't. Noooo! She got to have limits. She got a son and she got to work. She be trying to tell me, "Won't you go to bed? Won't you . . . I'm gonna cut you loose soon."

When I'm campaigning or cheerleading I just tell them where and who got what. They ain't got to come up to you. One smoker knows another. You just say, "Yo! You looking for something? So and so got it." When I was working for this one person, and I'll go out there from twelve to four and I was making forty-five dollars. Not counting my caps in between . . . in between, you know, I might get them to throw me one now. But automatically

I get forty-five when I stop out of two-fifty pack. Out of a two hundred and fifty dollar pack of caps I get forty-five dollars, which doesn't including what I make when somebody. . . . I'm still gonna have my chumpy. Somebody always want to use my thing, and that's a hit, plus them dollars. Then you got some people that don't want to pay you nothing but two caps. I don't fuck with them kind, 'cause you ain't gonna have me campaigning for no hours and hours and give me ten dollars and here you selling a whole five hundred dollar pack of caps or two hundred and fifty dollar bunch of caps. I ain't the one. Forty-five dollars don't seem like much for four hours of work, but I'm saying . . . I mean, I ain't doing nothing but sitting right there plus hitting. I'm safe!

There ain't nothing I wish I hadn't done to my mother because of my drug use. To my friends in some cases, yeah. You know, like tell a lie. I might tell a lie or I might have stole something from somebody, whatever the case may be.

My regrets? I don't have no regrets. You don't supposed to do nothing you regret. If it got that deep into thinking about it, the only thing I regret is that I even started smoking. I've lost twelve pounds. I weight one-thirty. I stay grubbing, but I keep the pipe in my mouth more than I eat food. I stay showered, clean clothes, iron, and I goes to the laundry. I do all that. My health hasn't suffered. I got tested for HIV in jail. I ain't got no AIDS. One time I did get kind of sick. I overdid myself. I got asthma and I smoke the pipe and cigarettes. Ain't I crazy?

I don't worry about stuff . . . because I done been through the changes as far as being slimy and conniving, and I done been through all that. You know what I'm saying? I ain't gonna use the pipe as an excuse for my wrong-doings anymore. I don't worry about picking up infections 'cause I ain't doing a whole lot of fucking, but I think about my health sometimes. As long as I'm spending money on what I like, I don't worry about money. I don't worry about getting arrested because I know the consequences of what I'm doing and being sent to jail doesn't bother me. Sometimes I worry about the types of relationships I have with people because of drugs, but it depends. Like when you got a relationship with another user, you often go through the change of wondering why you're going through so many changes and why can't your relationship be this way or that way when all the time you know why. It always boils down to the fucking drugs. I don't care what it be. Somewhere along the line it'll be drugs.

People schitz all kinds of ways when they'll sitting up in hit houses. Trying to find the rocks on the floor. What you call it—hallucinating. That's about it. That's all I seen. They be seeing things that ain't there. I just get quiet. I don't schitz. I didn't even believe in schitzing until I saw a lot of people schitz.

The only thing I don't like is to be around a lot of people. I don't like a lot of people around me and I can't be nowhere where it's dirty 'cause I get a buggy feeling, like, shit, things crawling on me. I just be like, "Huh-huh, it's time to go. I feel shit crawling," and I get up and go. The funniest thing I've seen is dude do this . . . he be acting like he be playing a piano. We call him Orchestra.

When I'm getting high, I can't stand the noise. I don't want to hear a lot of noise. So no television. Don't like a lot of activity. That blows my high. You know what I mean? I have to be watching out, and. . . . Naw, I want to get a hit and be content, be relaxed, and go 'head and get my blast.

The only way I say crack changed me—I'm gonna speak of me—it don't change . . . it took a toll physically. Other than that, mentally it hasn't done anything. I'm saying, you know, like some people just ain't got it all. They ain't as sharp as they used to be. They used to be all that. Ain't did nothing to me.

Smoking this taught me a whole lot about people. I'm saying, you know, just people, period. Okay, be like the people I came up with, we used to could talk about anything. You can't do that no more. Everybody life is just surrounded and based on crack. I was like that, but I was like "Damn!" you know. When I was in violation—meaning doing something wrong—I used to have my buddy and she'll say, "Ginny, dig yourself." Ain't none of that no more. Just gone and do what you're gone do. What the fuck I care?

Don't nobody care about nothing. They don't have no morals, ain't no principles and no respect for each other. They lose all they morals, principles, and respect. And I had did it one time too. You know, thing like I seen somebody take some residue from the pipe or take five dollars for a hit one time. You know, buff somebody, buff the dude—suck somebody dick. Buffing up them guns. People have said they children are in the hospital, all that kind of shit . . . they mother died. People do that shit for hits.

Shoplifting was my first crime. I've stolen out of cars, pickpocketing, robbery, burglary. When I do a robbery, I'll do whatever it takes. Sometimes I work with a partner. Sometimes I work alone because—you know what?—it doesn't always have to be physical to rob somebody. You can use your mouth. The most robberies I have done was when I had a partner and they hemmed the person up and I just go in their pocket. Most of the time they be spur of the moments. When I do burglaries, I always be the watchout. When I worked with a partner, everything go straight down the middle. In these serious crime I do the support. That's why I like working with men 'cause I really don't have to do nothing. He carries me along as a watchout. When I do shoplifting I go with a partner. It could be a man, but it don't matter. With robbery and burglary I would do it only with a man. Because a man is a man, and . . . just in case, you know, we might be burglarizing somebody and get caught or the person might come home or whatever, I need the man to fight. I need the strength. But breaking into cars, pickpocketing, and gagging people I can do by myself. I don't like working with women 'cause there ain't too many women that are real hustlers. You know, men, they can do it all! I might need this nigger to climb up to the top of this roof, you know.

I learned how to do these thing by going with somebody and seeing them do it. To get into a car I use a screwdriver and put it up the top of the window and just pull the window back and I just put my arm down there. Don't have to break the window. Some windows you just have to break. Like the Hyundais—you see how they made? The window made like over . . . like, you know, they don't have that piece . . . you know, like a curve, so they like flexible, so I just bend it back. Hyundais are the best ones to get 'cause they got the trunk release in the bottom of the floor. Sometimes I might use a hanger, or I just break the windows.

I learned how to pickpocket by watching. I always watched. Anything I learned as far as that I seen somebody else do it. The only skill to that is don't get caught and don't touch the person. Don't let them feel you. I developed the touch by constant practice at home. My little brother or my cousin or I had my girlfriend hold her pocketbook and I would just practice, constantly practice, practice. And I'm still not excellent. You know what I'm saying? Still not.

Sometimes I might use a partner to pickpocket, use somebody to block. Like a lady might be at the counter. My partner would block out the view. So somebody would be at the checkout counter and their purse would just be hanging. I'll be behind and the other person would be like on the side on a slant from where they could block the pocketbook out. You know what I'm saying? Like the other people in line can't see my hand or the pocket-book. Or use them to bump—bump the next person—'cause in some cases it be that hectic. Like if I know they're gonna feel me going in their pocket-book then I'll have the partner ran into them or something like that. On a bus we might bump into somebody and grab the wallet and pass the wallet to my partner. I'm saying, pass the wallet off. 'Cause really the person is gonna look at the person that's next to them. So in case, if they call the cops, you get searched, "What? I ain't did nothing." The bus be so crowded and because I'm standing there. "Why me?" Pass it off. The only way they could find the wallet would be to search the whole bus.

When I do a crime I don't think about nothing. I go straight at it. Boom! The only time I get to thinking about what might happen possibly this or this and that is when I'm high. That's why I don't do nothing when I'm high as far as crime. I always get that second thought when I'm high. You're paranoid, period, so I don't do nothing when I'm high.

So not getting caught and the large amount of money is what's important to me in doing a crime. But getting the money out of the vic is more important. I wouldn't even think about getting caught. Getting it first and then worry about caught last . . . the last thing I would think about. I don't like to do nothing that ain't worth it. You know, I ain't gonna go steal a bag of potato chips. See, let's say if I rob you. I'm going to make sure you ain't got nothing left. I ain't leaving you with nothing 'cause it's the same consequences, in other words. You know, I'm gonna get the same charges. So I got to do it all.

I don't stand there and contemplate on nothing. Naw, naw, I don't do it. If I can go 'head and do it, I do it. If I can't, I just step off. I don't plan nothing. If you're an opportunist, you're not going to sit around and worry about what the risks are. You know, you'll look at it and say, "I'll get away with this." Plain and simple.

And it's not important to have my vics very close to where I cop. I don't look for vics close to home or close to where I cop. I would like to catch somebody closer to home. That way I can go home quicker and safer. I don't think about no hit or none of that or no drugs when I'm out on my missions. That's a distraction. I like just to be in the white neighborhoods where the majority of the white people are. I like Penrose Square, Melbourne Park, places like that. More opportunities up there. If I go pickpocketing I would go more or less to malls, Metro Center, you know, where it's plenty traffic of people.

The first time I went to jail I went for retail theft. I was there for a week or two. The second time was three months, two and a half months. The second time I went to Riggs. I was in Falk Corrections Center the first time. The second time I went to Riggs. Riggs was like home. It didn't feel like I was in jail. I didn't feel real confined. I just come home. I was twenty-six. I was just surrounded by a bunch of women where I just fit in. You know, they had their little fights or whatever, jealousy thing. They rumble. But you don't really have time to really fight 'cause they ain't gonna let you. You know, somebody might pass a couple of hits.

The second time I went to jail it was because I was going into the van. 'Cause I was with a partner and he went up into this van. He pass me the radio out the van. By the time he . . . but I had told him not to go in there, I just felt . . . and he went in anyway. By the time he gave me the radio, here was the cops. Came out of nowhere. Someone called. Had to. They arrested me. I had bench warrants. Took me down to the Police Headquarters and fingerprinted me and pictured me and they locked me up. They kept him too. He's still in jail. He had other open cases.

So when I was in Riggs I didn't see no bad things. I was comfortable, content. I mean, I had more peace of mind there than I do out here. We didn't sit around and talk about that. Most people don't like to talk about what they locked up for 'cause they mad about the fact that they there. So basically what we . . . what was going on in there was, damn, what they had for lunch, they boyfriends and who they messing with now on B side and A side, you know, the gym, and things like that. It's plenty gay women in Riggs. Basically that's all that's in there.

I know doing crime is wrong. It's no justifications to it. It's wrong, period. Do I feel guilty about it? No! Feel guilty about it, then I shouldn't do it. I'm not sympathetic to it. I do crimes for drugs, period. If I wasn't doing drugs I still would be doing crime to get the things that I like. Used to be primarily for the money, but now for the drugs. Drugs is the root to all evil.

Why don't I earn money some other way? 'Cause I don't have time to go sit around and try to find no job when I can go get it quicker. 'Cause, see, first of all I ain't gonna hold the job. So ain't no need of me kidding myself. I ain't gonna take myself through all that. I ain't gonna hold a job, and plus the money ain't fast enough. I want a hit. I ain't trying to wait until Friday.

It's possible that I might get a job. My potential is there. Drugs keep me from doing anything positive. I was designed for fast money. I want free money. I will accept free money and still hustle. You never get enough. You never get enough. Never.

I wouldn't say people who do crimes are deadbeats and lazy. No. I wouldn't say people that get free checks are lazy. See, downright lazy is downright lazy. You know, you don't do nothing but sit there and wait on a check. That's lazy! Just constantly sitting home and waiting every two weeks. . . . Yeah, but that's just some people. I couldn't say everybody on DPA is lazy. I couldn't say everybody that do crime is lazy. Hustling takes a lot of thinking. So how can that be lazy? Because it's all these other kinds of skills and things that they have. Hustling requires people to get out there.

So I don't think drugs should be legalized because it's harmful. Why do you want to legalize something that's harmful? That's like saying do you think we should legalize robberies, bank robbers, and all of that. The world wouldn't be nothing. It would be a total disaster. How do I feel about what the government is doing to get drugs off the street? What are they doing? What I feel about it I don't get into because—you know why?—as long as there's drugs out here, I'm happy. That's the honesty of the thing. I don't even get into it.

I'm still trying to find out what I like about being high. For real! 'Cause I can't get that blast that I got the very first day and I'm gonna find it. That's what I like about it. I'm gonna find it. 'Cause I'm searching. I'm still racing for it. I know I'm not going to find it. That's why that one day when I just wake up and just come to my senses, I mean, just jump up from here and say, "I'm done," it's gonna be on its own. It ain't gonna be nothing planned or it ain't gonna be resolution this and I promise you, Mom, or I promised her. It's gonna be "I'm done." So it's gonna take my body and my mind to be tired. My mind gonna have to be tired. It's like up pop the weasel, that's how it's gonna be. I can't plan it. I don't know how much longer I'm gonna be smoking this. It might be tomorrow. I might come in here and tell you, "I'm done!" You understand what I'm saying? I ain't putting no time on it.

Drugs have physically changed me, that's all. You know what I'm saying? I lack a lot of things, but if you had seen me a little while longer—a little while back—I came a long way. I was like one of them ones that didn't care a fuck about nothing. I mean, really didn't care about nobody! I didn't care what another person thought or whatever. Said what I wanted to say. Did what I wanted to do.

A little boy changed all of that. A little boy that's close to me. He didn't do anything. Just him. I was real close to him. He was two years old. He's three now. I seen him born and all that. It was a friend of mine. I used to spend so much time with him, and I got into smoking and I said, "No." I had to pull away from him 'cause I didn't want to subject him to this. So I pulled away from him. But every time I would see him he would say, "Ginny, where you been? I love you. I love you. Can I go? Can I go?" All I could do was cry and say, "No!" and then I was like "Ginny" . . . one day I was like "Ginny"—he was crying and stuff—I said like "Ginny, you got to do something. You know, your appearance, you know. Go 'head and do your thing, but your appearance, it plays a hellified part, you know. If nobody don't cares about you, here's somebody that care about you," you know. And I said, "Ginny, you got to get a grip of things." You know, "You don't care about nothing." I didn't even care about him, you know. So I was like, "Ginny, you got to do a little better than this."

I'm not saying I thought nobody cared about me. No. I'm not saying that 'cause it don't make a difference for real. But by him being this way it showed the interest or whatever. You know what I'm saying? Somebody reaching out to me. And it just did something to me, you know. It made me sort of straighten up and be a whole lot different from what I used to be. So in the old days before this happened I was constantly smoking. Smoke, smoke, smoke, smoke. Ah, man! I was . . . every minute I was trying to find something to do, you know, to get a couple of dollars. That lasted for about five, six, seven months. I don't know. It could have been longer than that. I had to go, "Ginny, this ain't gonna get it!" I could buy a brand new pair of sneakers. Two minutes later I was selling them. "Oh no, I can't go on like this."

Now it's limitations to what I will do and what I will not do. Now I'll take my money and I will buy me something to put on my feet and my body. And then look at it like "Now, whatever I got left, Ginny, this is what you play with." In other words, take on your responsibility first and then whatever you got to play with, then you play with it. Just don't go and play with everything. Before I recognized him . . . yeah, that's how it was. Hey. It may be him that takes me out of it.

"I never thought about a world. I couldn't see the world. There wasn't the world outside that project. That was my world."

Tracy

Both of my parents were in the home when I was born. My mother was born in Jefferson and she's fifty-four. My pop is like five years older than her, but I don't have no idea where he was born. I guess I must have been maybe seven to eight when my father left. He moved to Brooklyn, New York. That was a sad day for me 'cause I really don't know why he left. I had a real fine relationship with my father.

I never could express love. Still can't. Never could express my feelings. It wasn't in the home or anything like that. But for some reason I had this strong feeling for my father. Even though my mom raised us and everything, I still have those feelings today. I really loved him, and it really hurted when he left. I is my father's oldest child and I was the closest . . . me and him was, you know . . . were real tight. He was a intravenous user, and the rest of the family didn't want no bother out of him. Embarrassed, you know. They didn't claim him and stuff like that. But I was always there for him.

After my pop left, we used to go to New York to visit him every summer. My mom would send us up to New York. I can remember when I was ten years old and I got busted for shoplifting. I was in the house, and all of a sudden my father, his sister, and my cousin had came from New York. My mom had called him and told him what had happened. So he had came over then. Maybe after eight years or more he came back into our life. I was living on the thirteenth floor of the projects, and he came to visit.

My mother was in her thirties when my father left and was having an affair with another man. It wasn't long after my father left that Joe came and moved in. When I look back, I think Joe has been in our life just as long as my father had, because my two brothers, right, they prefer him rather than my father, you know. They say that today. After my father left, Joe raised us. He stayed for a long, long time. All through my childhood up until my teens. I'd say well over ten years.

He finally left 'cause my mother, she was a alcoholic, and she stayed in the street, you know. Plus she had other friends and stuff. That's why he left. She wouldn't come home for days. Weeks. So when she was staying out Joe took care of us, the two boys and two girls. My sister Myra is the oldest. So she's three years older, my brother is two years older, and my last brother is three years under me.

Joe despised us girls. He despised us girls 'cause he would say, "Y'all know where y'all mother is at." He wouldn't feed us. "Go find your mother. Tell me where your mother at." He would lock us out the house and do all kinds of stuff. He would sit there and buy food just for him and my two brothers and they would sit there and eat. Take them out and all that stuff. We had no idea where she was at. At this time, she was working in a bar.

I would prefer for her to be out because they would just fight and my nerves was so bad. They would fight all the time, and I would run upstairs and go down my godmother's to tell her to ask them to stop fighting. He would always hit her and fight 'cause I guess she was always going out. My godmother would sort of help out and feed and take care of us. Sometime we would go to the bar and my mother would give us food. I didn't wanna tell my mother sometime what was going on because she would come in and argue and they would get to fighting. So it wasn't peaceful.

All these fights were about her going out. I guess he was probably afraid she was fucking somebody. Yep. I was so scared. Scared. Scared to death. Sometime I didn't even want her come home 'cause I knew they was gonna fight. They would fist fight and she would pick up stuff or try to grab knives and whatever was available, you know. I just couldn't stand it. I would run out when they fought. First I would go take all the sharp utensils out so nobody wouldn't cut each other. Then I would just go upstairs and just sit with my godmother.

Whenever I got scared, I would start crying and stuff, begging them not to fight. They didn't care, shit. That didn't matter. Was nothing the other children could do. They didn't cry, scream, holler, jump up and down. I'm the emotional one. No one jumped in. Hell no! Joe would fuck us up! We were more scared of him than her. And he had my brothers believing that was the right thing to do. 'Cause she had no business leaving us. So they would be more on his side.

One fight that clearly stands out is when he knocked her down and her head hit the radiator and he was just punching her. And I just begged him to stop, but too scared to jump in it, right? Cops came up that day. My godmother called the cops and they got him outta there. He stayed away for a while. Maybe a week.

They didn't show any kind of affection toward each other. As far as I can remember, she couldn't stand him. I swear, as far as I can remember, she always wanted to get rid of him. "I be glad when he leave. I be glad when he get away from me." Stuff like that. He was a provider, though. He was a provider. Bought her the clothes, you know. Everything she ever wanted, everything she ever needed or wanted. Furnish her apartment. He did reupholstery. He still does that now. Has his own company at Forty-fifth and Pennington. I saw him about two years, maybe three years ago. I went to visit him.

I believe the whole ten years they lived together they were fighting. Sometimes he would be away for a month, but he would always come back. Then finally he left and that was it. That's when he got his place down Fortieth Street. His own, you know, shop. And that was the last of us being a family. But we would go down to his house sometime and stay.

I hated him for hitting her. For whatever reason it was and whatever she did, still don't hit her. And I hated him for taking things out on us 'cause she wasn't around or she went out and didn't come in. I hated him for that.

As for the children, he would just beat the boys. But I know one time he hit my older sister and her father came down. Now that was a big brawl. She called him. This time I was scared for Joe and was trying to get him out the house. He wouldn't leave. Her father came in and they immediately started fighting. No fucking talking! They immediately started fighting. Joe was hurt. We was living on the thirteenth floor and he picked Joe up and was trying to throw him out the window. Part of his body hanging out the window, and he got a cut right here on his neck from the broken glass. He was almost gone out the fucking window. Myra's father hand had got cut some way, 'cause I remember it being wrapped up. I remember Myra running out with her father. There was blood everywhere. Yeah, Joe got hurt very badly that day. He had to get stitches.

My mother was always dating. That's what most of the fights was for. She brought them to the house, and we went through holy hell. When she had got Joe out of the apartment and brought Donny in the apartment, we could not go to school. We had lookouts 'cause of Joe. He had come trying to set the door on fire. So we had to put reinforcements up to the door. I mean, he harassed my mother for months. Then again, that was hate.

I didn't like Donny. "Be glad when Donny get the fuck outta here, 'cause if he wasn't here we wouldn't be scared." But as long as he was there, she was there, and we had to cook dinner and everything, but I did not like him. So Donny came after Joe left. Guess I was maybe thirteen when Donny moved in. I really can't remember the age. I know all this stuff that was going on, I was under fifteen.

And it was holy hell. Joe found out and was harassing my mother, threatening to kill him, threatening to kill her. We was like shut up in the house for like maybe a week 'cause we didn't know when he was coming, where he was lurking, and everything like that. Then a couple of her friends would look out, you know, look around the neighborhood to make sure Joe's car wasn't in sight. That's when everybody made a dash for wherever they wanted to go.

Yeah, I was miserable when my father left, but if I had the choice between living with my father and my mother, I would still wanna be with her. I just thought that I had to be there to protect her. To help her out. 'Cause I would be the one to go sneak her clothes out the house. Go get her wigs out the house for her, you know. I was always somewhere around where she knew where to find me. And then one point when, you know, she'd go get her check and sign it, I would take it to the rent office and pay the bills and do shopping. I couldn't leave her. I couldn't leave her. I was twelve or thirteen when I was doing these kinds of things for her.

I just didn't care about what she was doing. I guess she could have curbed her drinking habit and her hotness to make sure we was okay. I was mad. I wished she hadda stayed with my pop. I'm a ask her too one day. Now she said that my father was a great man. He was loving. Caring. He never hit her. Never hit us. I feel as though she is the cause of him leaving.

I started doing drugs at the age of twelve. First off, my mother was never there, so I was in the street. I had the option to do whatever I wanted to do. So I started taking pills. I stayed out all night long. Had boyfriends. I was always high. Always high or drunk.

I don't know why I started using drugs. You know something, I can't, from this day, I can't dig deep enough to find out why I started other than it was the thing to do. Everybody was doing it. My environment was doing it. My older sister did it. Her friends did it. So I was always around them. Always around drugs. Used to go steal they syrup and they dope and all that shit. Yeah. Always, always. Right after Joe left and Donny left and it was just us, my mom ain't have nobody living at the house, I was doing drugs. She never knew 'cause she wasn't there.

So everybody I was dealing with or hanging around with was into some type of drug. I was on my own. I had the option whether to go to school or not go to school. So I didn't go to school. If I came home from school with bad grades my mother wouldn't do nothing. Business as usual. If I was misbehaving in school she wouldn't do nothing either. I tell you, it was like we was sisters. She didn't give a. . . . I did what I wanna do. She did what she wanna do. Wasn't no sit down and talk. She took care of us and everything and, you know, we had the best of everything—shoes, clothes, and everything—but that's it.

Even when she was with us and around, man, I smoke cigarettes. She ain't give a shit. I probably started smoking at eleven or twelve. It was great. Now, I feel she should have been more of a mother, you know, not so lenient, you know. She should have been a lot more stricter. Sometime I feel that some of the parts of my life would have never happen if she was there or if she was a little bit stricter. She didn't have no important rules or anything like that. She allowed me to go in town and shoplift. She knew I was shoplifting. She knew I wasn't in school. She knew I had boyfriends. But she tried to act like she didn't know I was getting high. She knew.

My mother wasn't religious. Hell no. Shit. No way. She wasn't religious. I wasn't religious. So church? Hell no! I ain't go to no goddamn church. Church woulda burnt down if I brought my ass in there. Shit woulda caught on fire! Only time we went to church was when we was in Catholic school. I was in Catholic school up until the fifth grade. All four of us were in Catholic school. I was better when I was in Catholic school. Well, we had rules then. Goddamn right. From first to the fifth grade, yeah. Had to go to bed on time and . . . you know. We had rules then. Eat on time and everything. Make sure your homework was done, right?

She couldn't afford to pay the bill for the Catholic school, so she pulled us out and we went to public school, school right across the street there, Alcott. It's a old folks home now. Right in the next block. But I doubt staying in Catholic school would have made a difference in my life. Not nary one of us graduated from high school. So that's why my mother pushing on my nephew. She just want one person to graduate. I did get a GED.

Brad was her favorite. He was the youngest. He would just always get when we couldn't get. He would always get everything. You know sometimes my grandmom used to help sometimes. My brother, my youngest brother is the lightest one in the whole bunch, and she showed favoritism. My gradmom would come with big bags of stuff and it was just for him. Or he would get first pick and everybody had to wait until he was satisfied with what he wanted. Everything was for him. He's not high yellow, but he's light brown skin. Everybody else in the family is much darker.

My sister Missy, she would get all the love and attention 'cause she was the kind who would talk to people. Talk to my mother's friends. Me, I wouldn't say shit to nobody. I didn't talk to nobody. Like she had a friend used to work in the restaurant and she would send Missy and them over to get money from him and ask me to go over there too. He was an old man. I refused. I just would do without. I don't ask nobody for nothing. I was always to myself. I said, "I'm not going over there to ask that man for nothing." Missy, my sister . . . shit. Go over there, come back with five dollars or ten dollars.

We had the sharpest house in the projects. Like back in that time my mother and my godmother was the only two people in the projects that had color TVs. The only ones. I'm telling you, from Joe we had the best of every-thing. Pole lamps and fish tanks and stuff. She cooked and cleaned. She didn't like taking care of the home, 'cause my older sister was there. She wasn't . . . she was there and then again she wasn't there. I could say most of the time she wasn't there. She took care of the house. Like she would go out and come like every check day, you know, make sure the bills was paid and stacked the freezers up and all that. Stuff like that. But she wasn't there. She was gone. My older sister cleaned up. She did the cooking. She did the cleaning and all that.

Shit, my sister's friends stayed in the house. I used to . . . I was a little child, 'cause me and my two sisters, we shared a room and my brothers had a room. My mother had her room door locked when she wasn't there. I used to be right in the bed—they didn't know I wasn't asleep—and they would have sex right there in front of me. This was even before I started having sex. I'd be right there watching. My sister always had friends in the house. Always kept company. 'Cause, again, my mom wasn't there, so that was the house to be in. Wasn't no parent there. Boyfriends. Her friends. Everybody stayed at the house. That was the house to be in, the "Do Drop Inn."

My godmother was very concerned about me and how I looked. She lived on the fifteenth floor and I lived on the thirteenth floor. At one point my godmother took me from that house 'cause she said I was too dirty. I *was* dirty. I was very dirty. She cleaned me up. I think that was when Joe was still there and I went up to live with her. Oh, I was with her for a long time. Maybe a year. And that's the best I was. I was a little lady. I wasn't used to that, but I became used to it, 'cause, you know, I was clean. I had a time to go to bed, right? And she kept my hair done. Then I had to take a bath every night. I mean, all those things. She had a whole lot of goddamn rules. A whole lot. It was new to me. I loved it. I would tease my brothers and them, tell them about the clean sheets and all that. Food every day. The house was spotless. No roaches. No mice, you know. I know I wasn't there to stay, but maybe she was trying to mold me so when I got back down there, that, you know, I would know the things she had taught me and the stuff. I would still be a neat little girl.

When I was twelve a typical day . . . I guess I would just get up, put my clothes on, do whatever I wanted to do. First go in town, go see what I could steal up, come back, eat, get dressed, then later on that night, 'round nighttime, get high. When I was twelve that was the day. So in seventh grade I started saying, "I think I'm gonna stay home today." Or "I feel like going to school today? No. I might go today. Yeah." Like that. Nobody said anything, and hell, they weren't concerned about the people I hung with. I did what I wanted to do. Be who I wanted to be. If my mother asked me to do something or if Joe asked me to do something or Don, I would do it, but hey, I never had, "Don't do that." Nobody ever said, "You can't do that." I was on my own.

When I was growing up I wanted to be the kind of person my mother was. Her life was fun. The bars. The drinking. The going out. The wearing the glamorous clothes and all that. Oh, honey, I just couldn't wait till I got of age where I could really . . . you know, you know. I knew I had to report in sometime and come in, everything like that, you know. Yes, I wanted to be just like my mother. She was a free spirit. It was glamorous to me. My friend's mothers, they had rules. Dinner on the table every day and, you know, moms was always there and everything. They used to say, "Wow! Dag, I wish your mom was my mom. Oh, she so sharp. Oh, y'all mother let y'all stay up this time of night? You ain't gotta go to school? Damn, I wish I was living with y'all." Like that. I didn't want to be like my godmother. She was strict.

When I look back on it now, I wouldn't want to be like my mother, but I am. She'd always liked finer things. She had to have the best of everything. Of clothes. Of furniture, you know. Her kids. Everything was, you know. . . . Outside of the family, you know, she wanted everything to appear beautiful, but it wasn't. But I'm just like her.

I didn't learn anything growing up in my family. We hated each other. We fought. All I learned how to be is fast. How to go in town and shoplift. I didn't learn nothing from them. We didn't talk. We wasn't a unit family. No nothing. No togetherness whatsoever. No values. I don't treat people like dirt, but I didn't learn anything from them. I've always been very open and caring. I've just been very soft and weak. Very weak. I see myself as being very sensitive.

Did she love me? I suppose so. She would take up for us. So to me, I guess she loved me. I'm really not too sure. I guess she loved me in her own way. I said like "Damn near the roles is the same." Like me, I'm a cocaine addict. I had my two children. I wasn't treating them fair. I would buy cocaine instead feeding them, knowing that somebody else would feed them, you know. I wouldn't wash them up properly and feed them right. I remember at one point all they had to eat the whole day was some potato chips or something like that. But I love them. I did. But my lifestyle came first.

We rarely got beatings. She would like talk. We got beatings though. When she first learned I had done a crime, she just came and got me and that was it. I don't remember no chastising, "No! Don't do that," or nothing like that. I went stealing. It used to be this guy who used to live next door—this gay guy—and he was the runner of this whole group of us. It was maybe six of us and we used to be together, and he taught us to steal. And he said, "Come on. Let's go." He showed us who to look for. Who not to look for. Where to hide stuff. And then how to get the coats with the, you know, holes in the pockets so you can just dump stuff. Like you throw your stuff in the coat like that. So he would take us downtown and show us how to steal. You know, go to Blair's, Bonwit Teller, and Freen-Chamberlain. I hit them all, you know.

I was ten when I first started, and that's when I first got caught. We went to Blair's to get these records and we was stealing the records and the guy say . . . came up to me and he say, "Shhhh. I'm gonna steal these records. Don't tell nobody. Look out." We said, "All right." So when he stole his records we stole ours and was on our way out the door and—boom!—he was the detective all along. And that's what happen. They took me to Sixth and Commerce. Took my mug shot and fingerprinted me. I wasn't even scared when she came 'cause I knew she wasn't gonna do nothing but come and get me. Come and get her child. She didn't say anything. I did it again and again and again and again.

The guy who taught me to shoplift was my next door neighbor. He was a leader. We was scared to death of him. 'Cause he had a great big family and they all could fight. All you gotta do is say you're gonna whup my ass and you got me. That's it. He maybe was three, four years older than us. He was like fifteen and he recruited all of us. Plus he used to have us . . . he also had this UNICEF thing to knock on the doors and ask people for money. Child, he gave us all boxes. We went 'round to them white . . . you know, back there where the white people lived at. Went round there. We went round there and, honey, we came back from there, we was loaded up with money. Pocket full of change. All you gotta do is say you for them sick people and shit. Then they used to take us around the white people neighborhood again early in the morning, seven in the morning, at that time they put the milk out. People used to get their chocolate milk and shit. Orange juice. Doughnuts. Man, we had it all.

It was like maybe 'bout six of us in this circle. He was oldest, then I came next. All of us like in the seventh grade. I worked for this guy all my life, from ten on. He taught me how to steal better and better. We used to go to Sixty-seventh and Main. Down there to Sears and the stores out there to steal.

It was the thing to do in the projects. Go steal. Even my older sister was a shoplifter. She bring home clothes and my mother would tell her what to go in town and get. My sister was the biggest booster up Eleventh Street. Steal vacuum cleaners and shit. So it wasn't no thing, no thing to go steal. Just the fuck don't get caught. It was a way of life. Damn right. That's another part of the reason why we dressed so well 'cause my sister and her friends were shoplifters. So shoplifting wasn't . . . that wasn't nothing. She was the type like "You gonna do something, do it and don't get caught. Learn how to do something well." Like that.

So sometimes my mother would beat me. Like if the house was dirty when she came home. Just about her house not being fucking clean. I didn't get no beatings for staying out all night. I know that. She would use the ironing cord. Her routine was to say, "Line up. Line up. Line up." Missy would get it first 'cause she was the wildest. "Line up. Come on, Tracy." "I don't have no . . . I don't feel good. I don't feel good. I'm getting sick." She say, "Don't play that sick shit." And my father said, "Don't beat her 'cause you know she got a bad heart." I had a weak heart. She knew I was scared to fucking death of a beating. She would whup Missy's ass. And I knew by time Missy get her. . . . "Let Missy go first. Let her go first." 'Cause by time she finish with Missy, she be wore out, too tired to get to me. I stayed in that bathroom, and Brad, he was always little and she didn't whup him too long, but that goddamn Missy, they would run up and down that house. One damn day I thought she forgot. I said, "Shit." I come out that fucking bathroom. Whap! She ain't forget. That's how it was.

Oh, she would embarrass me too in front of other people. "You bitch. You stinking bitch. You ain't shit. Talking with a bunch of bitches and shit. Trifling. Filthy." Like that, yes. She always embarrassed me now. I was under fifteen. Shit, yeah, she embarrassed me. I don't fucking know why. She would always call us bitches. "I ain't got nothing. I got . . . I bring five bunch of nothings. Ain't none of y'all shit."

Like her men friends—Donny, Joe, and stuff—was around. "Don't fuck with my girls." We wasn't allowed to like . . . you know how girls play sit on they laps. We couldn't even sit on laps or nothing like that. She always said that. "I don't give a fuck, that go for your fathers too." We bouncing up and down on his legs and shit like that. No! She would tell me today about letting my daughter be playing on her father's lap. "He's a man, goddamnit." Like, you know, how I might have walked around the house maybe at the age of twelve or something, and I might have a slip on . . . that's what I got fucked up for. If I get a sudden smack or pop, it was from not having clothes on. She didn't play that. That was one rule. Don't put your hands on the girls. She'd have a fit about that.

She drank mostly weekends, and she would drink in front of us. There wasn't really any change in her when she drank. She just get soft. She was already soft, but softer. I mean as far as letting us have the benefit of the doubt. Like that. Fuck no, she wasn't no soft. She was very bold—her views about different things—and don't get in her fucking business about how to raise her children. She was hard like that. People would say things to her about the way she was raising the children, and she would kick off. They would be saying things like we be out in the hallways all night long and she said don't worry about it, you know. She . . . they heard us cursing. Knew we went in town stealing. "I done seen Tracy come back with a bag full of shit." Like that. She would defend us to the end. I don't care what wrong we had done, she would back us.

If someone in the neighborhood had disciplined me because I had done something I wasn't supposed to do, she would have cussed them out. Don't fuck with her children! And we were allowed to kick off. Yes. "Get your fucking hands off me. Don't be touching . . . don't be saying shit to me." We was allowed to say what we wanted to say to adults, and she would back us up. Goddamn right. I would cuss them out, and she would cuss them out too. Damn right. They would get a double bubble.

She would give us alcohol. Child, she give you sips. She don't mind giving up that liquor. She give it to all the kids now. She don't now 'cause she's a Witness. But, shit, all the kids, all my sister kids coming up, they all had a taste of her liquor. Take them in the bar. Got my little nephew, he's sixteen now, he was drunk as shit. He wasn't no more than two years old. Drinking her little cream de cocoa milk. Yeah.

She earned money by being a barmaid. Before that quartermasters. She start calming down in that life. She started selling drugs, and she got busted. She did ten months, and she came home this April. This was like maybe two years ago. They sent her to Riggs. I never went out to visit her. When she came out she was a Jehovah Witness. She was changed when she got out, and she didn't approve of us, you know. Now she feeling that her lifestyle was the cause, you know, that's why we are the way we are today. She didn't spend enough time with us. She said had she known the things that I was going through when I was young, you know, getting high. She said, "I never knew you was getting high at twelve. I never knew you shot drugs at sixteen. I never knew you was raped," and all that stuff like that. She ain't had no idea 'cause she wasn't there and I did not communicate with my mother. Not at all.

Now she like trying to make amends through the grandchildren, right? She took my two children away from me till I get my life and stuff together. Now she's trying to make amends. I go, "Look, Mom, I need my shot. I can't take care of the kids. I'm getting ready to leave them in the fucking house." She would go and give me money. "Go up there and get it." Send somebody go cop for me if she didn't have it.

I've been raped. God! Jesus Christ! Some things, I swear, I will try to forget 'cause it's painful. I swear, I try to forget. Oh, Jesus! I think I was thirteen or fourteen when I got raped. I didn't tell anyone. I was home. It was three guys. They was in my house. My house was the "Do Drop Inn." I was taking care of the family then, 'cause Myra had left and she moved in with her boyfriend. So that's the worst thing. I never uttered a word about it again.

We all have the same father except my oldest sister. Me and my sisters and brothers didn't have no relationship. We weren't friends, just was brothers and sisters. We used to get along . . . I mean, you know, we was there. We had to be together, but we didn't, you know, really get along with each other. I knew they was my brothers and sisters and that was it. They weren't fucking supportive. Fuck no!

I let somebody whup my sister's ass. I got in trouble for that. I let these girls beat her 'cause I was always scary. Scared. Scared of fights and all that shit. I don't know if it was from my mom fighting, but I had a thing about fighting, getting hit. I let these girls jump my sister. I had the nerve! I ran home and told my mother. "Mom, these girls beat Missy up." And Mom said, "What did you do?" I said, "I just stood there, and I just ran home and told you Missy out there getting beat up." She wore my ass out. "Goddamn. Both of y'all better come in here fucked up. Don't ever leave your sister again." So I had to say, "Look, Missy, stay the fuck outta trouble." Fuck! So I had to keep her . . . I get, "Please don't hit her." I'd be, "Please, let her slide this time. God knows, don't hit her. Lord." A peacemaker, that's what I was. "I'll pay you. Don't fuck with her."

My oldest sister is a Jehovah Witness. She work in Hi! Fashion in the Marketplace. She been a Witness for years. She been stopped stealing. My other sister is a recovering addict. She's not working. She lives with my mother.

One of my brothers, he's a undercover addict. I don't give a fuck what nobody say. I know the signs. What you keep the fuck asking for cigarettes for if you ain't high? You know you always want to damn smoke a cigarette. And the way his mouth . . . his mouth moves a certain way, and he be going to the NA meetings with my sister on Sunday. I don't give a shit. He undercover. He getting high.

And my youngest brother, he sell drugs. But he never in his life took a drug, but he always take care of his family. He's family-orientated, very family-orientated. He sells drugs 'cause that's a means of making a living. He live with his girlfriend. He got a thousand girlfriends, though. He was everybody's fucking favorite. Missy and Brad. He was the favorite 'cause he was cute, but he has always been family-orientated.

Yeah, him and Missy. Missy was the favorite too 'cause she was always boisterous. She would show out to get what she wanted. She know she couldn't carry a note in a goddamn pail, but she went to that talent show, honey, and she sung her heart out, honey. I can't think of that record, but, honey, she sung her goddamn heart out. She was not like me. I would be embarrassed to show my talent that I could sing. But not her. Even if she couldn't do it, she up there. The first one up in line. That was her. But me, I'm always in the shadow. Back. Back. Always in the shadows. Always in the shadows. Always. Always.

All my girlfriends' mothers loved me, though. "Why can't you be like Tracy?" But I was damn near the worst one. Nobody knew. Nobody knew. My girlfriend Crystal used to laugh, and say, "If you only knew." "Why don't you be like Tracy? You don't see her doing this. You don't see her hanging and. . . ." But she said, "Mom!" Nobody never saw me. Never suspected me of nothing, and I be the ringleader. I was the organizer. I didn't want no publicity. Didn't never have none. They all praised me. The whole neighborhood loved Tracy. 'Cause she's caring. Children. Love children. Had everybody's child. Go to store for you in a minute. Not knowing that this fifty cents was going to my drugs. It was always a ulterior motive of why I was around somebody or with somebody. Something they could do for me. Something that was gonna benefit me. But I would do anything you asked me. And that's today. Go out my way, but very sneaky. Very.

When I think about my life and where I live, oh my God! 'Cause we are lost. I'm serious, 'cause I know what it's like being around here. My life is damn near everybody life I know. Mother not being there. Mother getting beat up. Either their mother's a junky . . . it's like that. So we feel as though that's the right thing to do. Everybody shoplifts. It's a few good people in the projects, but we need to tear the whole project down. Number one is to tear that whole motherfucker down. Tear it down! 'Cause you never going get rid of the drugs. I mean, I don't . . . I can't see them straightening up any blacks in the near ten years. Honestly, it's just that bad. Especially from my point of view, where I come up at, it's no hope.

I've lived in the projects all my life. Left for a few years, but came back. When I was living there as a young girl it was hell. Always been like that. My life has been hell. Hell, hell, hell, hell, hell, hell. That's it. Hell. Good spots, but hell. Shit. Then you have to say, when you grow up in the projects, man, you gotta stay away from the boys raping you. You got to duck gunshots and somebody getting stabbed and then the drugs is there staring at you. And it was a survival for your life every goddamn day you woke up. You was always going to somebody's funeral. It's just living hell. There was never a time when the project were calm. When we first moved there maybe. When all the white people were living in there. I was in diapers when all the whites left and the blacks moved in. Started defacing the walls. All that shit. So when I was like ten, it was done then. It was done.

Cocaine? We didn't have drugs like that then. You had to venture out for drugs and stuff like that. You would. It's open and out now. You ain't had pushers on every corner. Pushers everywhere you look. Mothers pushing. Grandmothers pushing. It's just everybody selling drugs, everybody selling cocaine. So it's worse. Brothers cussing . . . you cussing your mother out. Beating your mother up if she don't give you money to get your hit and all that shit. You disrespecting your mom and all kind of shit. It never was like that. You still had a sense of, you know, you do respect your mother. Now . . . shit. A little boy—my girlfriend, her son—"Get the fuck outta my face." He sell drugs . . . he's fifteen. It was a shock to me. Much as I've seen and been through, shit still got the nerve to shock me.

Like my nephew would never act like that. My brother Bradley, I told you he's family-orientated. "I don't give a fuck what you see your aunt do. This is family. You respect your aunt." 'Cause my nephew said something out the way to me. Maybe he called me a addict. Brad is the kind that will whup ass. "You respect your elders. You respect them." So my nephew always says yes and is respectful even at the age of sixteen. Won't even damn near suck his teeth and stuff like that. But, honey, these kids they come, "Get the fuck . . . you never did a fucking thing for me." Even though my mom and shit was fucked up like that, we would never say it. We better not had never said it.

The worst thing that probably happened to my family when I was a child was when my sister, she was going with a guy and his girlfriend was very jealous and wanted him back. She stepped out to go to this bar on Eleventh Street, Martin's. Honey. We was all sitting up there at home, me and my mother. All of us was there this particular day. They say, "Your daughter got cut." So my mom didn't know how bad. When she came in this house, her whole face was open. All this meat was hanging down. As she walked out of the bar the girl just sliced her. My mother pressed charges, and the girl did time in jail for that. My sister recovered fine, but she got a long scar right there. She has one, a scar, her father had one too, and her grandmother. All three of them got the same scars in the same place, damn near the same length.

Now it's the amount of crime in the projects. It was ninety percent crime. I would say shootings and beating and stabbings and things like that, about ninety percent. Common. Common! Used to run for cover when you hear shots and shit. Now you just sit the fuck there right on the bench. 'Cause it's a drug war now in the projects about this one person is selling three dollar caps, and since you got three dollar caps, our five dollar caps ain't selling. And you got these three guys sticking up everybody. They're running 'round putting pistols in they faces, sticking up everybody. One of them got a guy the other day for fourteen thousand dollars. Fourteen grand! So that's going on.

The place I'm at, right, they're selling drugs, right? It's not so much that it's the best cocaine. It's just that it's consistent. It's always there. So you got the other dude, right?—Matt. He getting jealous. "I want my building back."

So when I was growing up, there was crime, but it was not like this. Back then you respected your neighbors. Yeah. It was a whole lot of respect. People stole only if they were junkies. People in the project valued their attire. The way they looked and the way they house looked. That was it. They don't give a damn about their relationships with other people. Just the way your house looked and if somebody got something you had to get it too. So like that type of thing. It's material things. They're very materialistic in the projects even now.

My girlfriends were the same mode as me. Hanging out. Getting high. Not at ten though. At ten, I didn't have no friends. I was still playing with doll babies. At twelve that's when I was getting high at my girlfriend's. Crystal was my best friend when I was twelve. I did everything with her. Everything. Get high. Steal. Fuck. Everything. Oh boy! We just could talk. She was one that I could talk to. Pour my whole heart and soul out to her. And I never had to hear it from anyone else. It was very confidential.

My mother never talked to me about sex or birth control. When my period came, I thought I was dying. I was 'bout thirteen. I went to Crystal, my girlfriend, and she told me why was I bleeding. She gave me a pad. Her mother had told her about what was going on.

I guess I was maybe thirteen when I had my first sexual experience. I guess I saw this dude I likeded and we just started having sex. He was from the projects. He was maybe five years older than me. I always known him. We all went to school together. It just happen. One day he was in my house, then we got to talking. My friends kept telling me, "You better . . ." 'Cause all my friends had already had sex for years and I, you know, was the only one who was still a virgin. And they kept saying, "You better go ahead now, 'cause the older you get the bigger the dicks get and you ain't gonna be able to take it, and, oh gosh, you gotta hurry up. You better hurry up soon." I was scared the fuck to death about from having sex. I did not wanna have sex with no one. No one. I just didn't wanna have sex. That it was gonna kill me if I didn't hurry up and get it over with 'cause they dicks get bigger and bigger. There was a lot of pressure from my friends.

So we were sitting there and we got to talking, you know . . . it happened. It was at night, and my mother was probably at the bar working. I mean, what can you talk about that age? And then when I first had sex I talked to my sister's girlfriend and I told her. She said, "Girl, you ain't had no sex. You ain't fucking." I said, "I did. I did. Last night." She said, "You just . . . he just laid it on the top, and y'all grind. Did he stick it in the hole?" I said, "He stuck it in the hole." She talking 'bout "the hole with . . . you mean to tell me . . . ?" I said, "I'm telling you." I showed it to her. "The part where your finger stick up there, that's where he put it at."

All I know, I wanted to have it to get it over with. That's all. After I had sex that first time I wasn't active. Not active at all. I was twenty when I got pregnant the first time, but I had an abortion before then, though. I just didn't wanna keep it. I was five months pregnant, over five months, twenty-two weeks, and I got a abortion. That's another thing that makes me cry. Wasn't my decision alone.

I had planned to keep the child, but my friend, the girl I was going with, she was saying . . . I had lied and told her that I was raped, which I wasn't raped, and got pregnant. So she kept saying, "Well, if the guy raped you and all. . . ." She went and stepped to the guy and all this. "Well, why you still pregnant and stuff?" And I always kept saying, "Well, I missed appointments" and shit. So I guess my back was up against the wall, and she said, "Well, shit, you don't want to keep no baby, somebody baby. Why don't you. . . ." So I made a appointment and that's how I got a abortion 'cause she, you know, really . . . if she hadn't been in my life I'd kept it.

He was just a friend. I was high off of reds. I got in his car and we had sex. I don't know what I was afraid of and why I didn't just tell her the truth. I don't know. She had took care of me. I guess I owed her so much. I was living with her. She took care of me. Her and her mother and family, you know, clothed me and fed me. I really didn't want no children too, so that was part of my decision. And I figured if I had a baby that would have been it for my funds. All that shit would have been cut off.

When I was growing up, I wanted to be a teacher 'cause I love children. People always told me that. "You should do something with people 'cause you can. . . ." Somebody will always come and talk to me. I always was a very, very good listener. Everybody would come tell me about they problems. Whole damn projects. And also everybody want me to be a model. I was tall. I was dark. Plus I had nice features, they said. Nice features. Nice legs. A model.

But I was looking forward to that fast life. I didn't wanna get away from it. I wanted to be a part of it. So when I was growing up I wanted to work in the bars, to be in the street. Hang in the bars, work in the bars, the night life, the pretty clothes. The fine . . . that's all I ever wanted to be. No more, no less. I never thought about the future. . . . My thoughts was always what's happening today. Never think about nothing tomorrow, 'cause if I did, shit, if I did, I would like sort of kept money. Tomorrow was another day.

Fuck school! That's how I felt. I never thought about a world. I couldn't see the world. There wasn't the world outside that project. That was my world. I couldn't function outside the projects. That was my life. I swear, I had a complex like "This bitch thinks she's better than everybody else." Every time somebody look nice and did nice things, I always found something wrong with them or, you know, "This bitch thinks she cute" or something like that. "What the fuck? You think you're better than me?" Like that. That's the kind of mood I had towards other people that was living a nice life, I guess.

I didn't belong there, out there in the outside world. There's no way I could be a part of that outside world. My mother wasn't a part of it. Nobody I cared for was a part of it. Nobody, you know, I knew was a part of that. That was a whole different hookup. If I saw a black doctor, right— you know something, this is fucking strange—if I saw a black doctor or something, I figure, I wouldn't want him. I would prefer a white doctor to work on me. Now, I swear! I don't think they're qualified enough to be in that position. I don't know. That they don't belong in that type of profession. Even today went to . . . not today, but couple weeks ago, there was a black female doctor, and I just felt so uncomfortable. I figure white people put one hundred percent into everything they do, and you ain't put no one hundred percent. So something gonna go wrong. You ain't supposed to be up here. Not a doctor. Not nobody working on life and death. You just not qualified enough.

But, see, I don't know if it's because of the way I was brought up that had something to do with it. I know better. That this black man is damn near more qualified, probably worked even harder, did have to work harder to achieve what they got, had to, you know, than that white person there. But my heart know this, but my mind will say, "I don't trust him. Still snuck and cheated on his test to get passed, you know." That's the way I think. But I know better. I know in my heart. I know. Goddamn! It's about time I see a black face. But don't work on my ass.

I have a very miserable life. It's nothing good about it. That's all. I guess it really only became miserable after I had my children. I don't want them to see me like I saw my mother. I'm concerned about my daughter. I grew up to be just like mine, and that's something that gave me misery. Although I did have fun, I'm still miserable. The shit I had to endure, it was a whole chumpy of misery, but it was where I wanted to be. And only reason that I now don't want to be a part of that life is because of my two kids. I'm giving it a try. I'm trying to do the right thing. Eventually my long-range goal is to say no to drugs and do something for these two guys. I'm pregnant right now. I'm saying I'm fucked up. I'm fucked up. I'll deliver in November. I'm fucked up. I'm fucked up. I am fucked up. Growing up was hell. Living hell. Fun, but hell. I had fun living in hell. I'll put it that way. That's all I can say. I had fun.

I was twenty-nine when I had my first child. I never was on my own. Never. Never. Oh, I moved out of my mother's. I was sixteen when I left home the first time. I moved in with a friend, but I moved back maybe 'bout two years after that. I moved again when I had my son. So I guess I was thirty and I had a place of my own in the projects. After a year, I was evicted out of there. But from fifteen until I was about thirty I was with my mother or whoever I was going with. Wasn't never on my own. I lived mostly with my mother and my sisters.

My friends was either pushers or addicts. They were my friends. Wasn't no girls that went to school, you know. So I started using drugs at twelve. I started taking pills and stuff at twelve. I started snorting heroin at thirteen. I didn't start using intravenously till I was sixteen.

Oh, honey, I have lived maybe fifteen, twenty different places from fifteen on up to eighteen on. I lived in the project the longest. Always lived in the same building. I was in Saigon for that year when I had my own place. Well, living in the project is hell. Holy hell. Filthy. I mean the hallways are filthy. There's trash all over the steps. Dirty Pampers. Dirty feminine stuff. Napkins all over the place. The incinerator—you know, we got fifteen stories, right?—the incinerator is backed up from the first floor to the . . . you can't even put no trash in it. That's how backed up the trash is. 'Cause it used to have this fire system where everything was always burning. Like years ago, you always seen fire where the trash was all constantly burning. Now something's up there where it's backed up all the time. Them filthy people. Now they got the hookup out here where you can take your trash outside in front, right? And then you put it in your plastic bags and take it outside in the front. They're too lazy. After they tie they trash up, they just take it and sit it right there in front of the incinerator. So you gotta walk over that trash and there's maggots and there's mice. It's filthy! It's a terrible place to live! Terrible, terrible, terrible, terrible! It stinks! Smells of piss and shit.

Yeah, people piss and shit in the hall. Now like say if you want a hit, right? Say like if I'm contemplating the thought of getting a hit, right? My body goes the same as any other addict. You get that feeling you gotta shit. It gots to come out. You might be just standing in the hall. You can't go in nobody house. It has to come out. I'm on the bus coming from the hospital, right? "Damn, I get a few dollars to get a hit. I need a hit." All the while I was sitting in the hospital I knew I couldn't get none, so I was cool. Once I got on that damn bus—boom! I say, "Oh, God. I gotta shit." That's the way. . . . Somehow, it messes with that bowel system. Me and Laurie, like we get ready to hit, we race to the bathroom. She gotta shit and I gotta shit. I said, "Bitch, you get the fuck up. I'm pregnant." I said, "Go get me a bucket." 'Cause you know, it's like that.

You see rats and mice. Roaches? Honey, they your family! Roaches is a part of your damn family. Shit! They a part of the family and that's no joke. My fucking son will pick a roach up in a minute like it's a pet. "Put that fucking roach down." He will.

I can say one percent of the people are clean, keep their area clean. Fortunately, my floor I'm on now, we have a floor captain and, you know, she's like "Come on. We gonna clean this hall up." A few floors stay pretty clean and neat 'cause of the floor captains. They be smoking, shooting, drinking, cursing in the stairwell. I have seen everything but sex.

I guess like now, the manager they have in there now, he's a little bit more focused. Think it's now they trying to clean it up once a week, you know. 'Cause before the floor and the halls was so filthy. They haven't been cleaned for two or three years. And this no bullshit. Floor as black as them cabinets and they're supposed to be green. So now they got the new manager and he do cleans up. Oh, he's starting to paint the walls and stuff.

There used to be a lot of hit houses in the building. That's how come people hit in the hall now. You got them on the third floor, fourth floor, and seventh floor. There a few houses where you can go and buy crack in the projects, but mainly the people are outside. Each building has its own people, own customers and stuff. 'Cause like ten-twelve is the most peaceful hookup. You get more cleaner people there. They're more conservative people. It's more older people in that building. They more aware of who they sell to. They not all just for the dollar. Don't want everybody to know they're using drugs.

Like Saigon, they don't give a fuck who come. They sell to anybody. White, black, Puerto Rican, they don't care. You got the people in my building, eleven-twelve, right, they don't give a fuck how much you spending. In Saigon, they take you all. The people in Saigon is just like they name. Saigon. From the children to the mothers. It's like that. Terrible building. I don't go, and I'm a veteran. I don't fuck with Saigon. It's just too much. Even though I'm used to the neighborhood. I got two big brothers. I got friends that I came up with and all that. And still it's just so . . . everybody . . . all the riffraff . . . all the people that just don't know how to earn they own dollar. They know to stand in that building and a sucker gonna come in there. They gonna rob somebody. I haven't been in that building all summer.

The worst thing living in Saigon is the pushers and the addicts and the filth and just the not caring. Violence is every day. It's always been like that. People getting beat up. Getting they money taken from them. People getting shot at. People get stabbed. Fights every day. Now Saigon will sell to any and everybody that come along. They don't care as long as it's a dollar. Which ten-twelve won't. You gotta know them. Even like say if I had a white guy on my hip, I might know him from, you know, some other stomping ground I might have been, like on Twenty-second Street. But they don't know him. They don't fuck with him. I can't even cop from them like that.

Shootings. Stabbings. Fightings. That's a part of everyday life for the projects. They shoot off the balconies just to see if they guns working. That's a part of everyday life. We used to duck. We don't duck no damn more. Business as usual! Don't even move unless you see a body being dragged around or something and then you only move to see who got shot. "Is that my son? Is that my nephew?" Or something like that. You just sit there. Even old Miss Dee just sit there. She don't even duck no more. They used to scramble her ass up in the buildings. The worst thing that I've ever witnessed was my girlfriend coming out in a body bag. She had smoked a little bit too much and a blood vessel burst in her brain.

I've lived in a shelter. The last one was at Thirty-first and Sussex, Community Emergency Center. I was there for a while. Maybe 'bout six or seven months, I guess. The story about my shelter is, every time I stay there, no sooner I get a check, food stamps, I'm gone. I can't even get a POS, 'cause they always gimme permanent home in the shelters and I roll soon as I can get . . . I just can't . . . I have to have a hit and I just keep forgetting that you just can't say I'm gonna get a hit and go back. You gonna stay till you ain't got no more dollars. Then you gonna find some dollars. So that's the way that shelter system went for me.

They really care in the Community Emergency Center. They work with me. And, honey, they really was in my corner. Went with me to pick my check up. Then I started going to get my check on my own. I had my drug counselor coming to see me every Wednesday. They even watched the kids when I made my NA meetings. I was clean for the first time in my life. I been a addict for twenty-three years. It was the first time in twenty-three years that I was clean for twenty-seven days. I just couldn't take it no more. I said, "I'm going. I'll be back." And never came back. They was really upset.

I hated to disappoint them and I knew I didn't wanna face them 'cause I just say, "I let these people down." They had more faith and hope in me than I had in myself. It wasn't that long ago. Was about six or seven months ago. Eight, okay? The last day I left was Easter. They take all your money and your food stamps for savings. So you get yourself together. I was gonna pay Jefferson Housing Commission the money I owe them, and they give you money for help . . . like a thousand dollars, for when you need to furnish your apartment after you finish your time out. Everything was happening for me.

Anyway, they had all that hooked up for me. They gave me money. They had got the kids Easter clothes and stuff. They say, "Well, how much you think you need?" Had the free tickets to go to the zoo. I said, "Well, Ethan needs a haircut. Venita needs some shoes." 'Cause I don't like the shoes she had. So they gave me fifty in stamps and fifty in cash outta my savings. That's Easter Saturday. . . . They said, "Don't go up the projects. You can go anywhere to get. . . ." "But I like the way he cuts his hair up the project." Now that I think of it, this was all an excuse just to get the fuck up here to get high. I had twenty-eight days clean. I was going crazy. I told them, "Please." They say, "Girl, fight it." "I don't know how." . . . Then I just found out I was pregnant too.

I gets the fuck up here anyway. I don't give a hell. I'm strong. First time I been clean! Shit! Because this was not the first time I've had money or stamps on my own. I came back and did the right thing. This wasn't the first time. I said, "Shit. Give me a break. Go and get my son hair cut." Did that. Saw my sister, gave her some food stamp and some tokens. On my way up Thirty-seventh Street, I ran into my girlfriend and that was the last I saw of the shelter. And I was in the shelter like maybe four months prior to that. That was the last I saw of the shelter. Up until the time I went back in there when I knew nobody was there that I knew cared about us.

I had about maybe three hundred dollars, four hundred dollars, rest in savings. And my two hundred or something in stamps. I went and picked that up. Fucked that whole thing up! I even sold the kids' Easter clothes. I went back to the shelter that Saturday 'cause they hadn't known I left, 'cause I had a weekend pass. So I went back there Sunday and got the clothes, all the new clothes and Easter clothes and sold every stitch. From that one fucking cap that I bought. So I buy one. Keep on going. Go over my children's father house. Gonna spend the night there. We gonna go Easter shopping. I had stamps to buy boil eggs and shit like that. And from buying that one cap, I'm still here.

I'll never forget that day. That's how powerful the shit is. I knew it, though. I knew it. I knew it. I fought. I made all kind of excuses. I was starting to snap out. Take it out . . . snap out on my kids.

From sixteen on up to a year ago, I was shooting drugs constantly. Then I started with the coke maybe five or six years ago. And then a year ago somebody introduced me to the deadly pipe. That was it. When I was shooting I had a better chance of sort of controlling my addiction. Yes! Yes! Yes! Kept money in my pocket. Kept my place. Everything was fine till I smoked that fucking pipe. I took that hit. My life. . . . I lost my place. I lost every . . . my titties, my ass. I lost it all. I had titties and they just shriveled up to nothing. I was only weighing ninety-something pounds.

There's a lot of hooking going on in the projects, every day, for a fucking blast if needed, yeah. I know I . . . there's people, beautiful girls, girls that I done grew up with. I know one particular guy and his girlfriend, they go together, you know. He be like in somewhere behind waiting for her to finish. Then these people they got kids together and all. He waits for her to finish doing her thing and they go and get high. But lately they been going on High Street. But then she been like robbing white men and shit. So as far as the respect, men don't respect they women. They send them out there. A man will lay on his ass and let his woman go out there and make the dollars.

So the men don't respect they women. Fuck no! They call them all kinds of bitches. Whores. "Bitch, you suck a dick . . . you'll suck a dick for a cap?" I say, "For a cap? You suck it for a blast." That's a hit. That's why I say they done fucked my shit up. 'Cause see, I'm the type of person, I like to get high. Love to get high. That's what's wrong with me. I fell in love with the drug. Fell in love with that motherfucker. Now, I got two greedy-ass kids. I'm greedy. I'm pregnant. Plus I have a habit to support. What the fuck I'm a do with five dollars? See, y'all done fucked me up. When a bitch will take a fuck and give up her ass, pussy, mouth, all for five dollars. Whereas if I ask for twenty dollars, a nigger look at me like I'm crazy. "Twenty dollars! Is you crazy? You nothing."

That ain't my thing, man. They done knocked the prostitutes out. You know them hookers. Them real hookers who used to hook can't make no money. How can they go make money when these project whores is taking five dollars? See, understand what I'm saying? Shit, you know, they maybe would make a hundred, two hundred dollars a night. Not no more. Shit, that cocaine done just knocked everybody out of the box.

I don't have no idea what role a woman should play in a relationship. I don't know nothing about normal. I can only assume. I've never had normal. So I can only go by maybe what I read or seen or what I think. I believe a woman should be home with the kids, right? Man come home, long as he's taking care of the bills, the house. That's, to me, that's what I think normal is. Being with your kids. Being with your kids in the home.

An ideal relationship? It had to be a person that's not on drugs. I'll take anybody, but he can't be on drugs. That sums it all. That's it. I think he can be a goddamn bum, but just don't use drugs.

I had my first significant relationship with my children's father. I met him in a bar. The seven years I was with him, it was holy hell too. He's the type that knew my background. Knew I was a addict. Knew I was gay for eight years. He came from a nice background. He went to college. His family went to college. And everybody said, "Y'all come from two different worlds." Then again, like I said, opposites attract, right? So he figured if he kept me in the house away from all this stuff, then, you know, that would do it. Or if he found that I was around those type of people I used to be with and stuff, he would, you know . . . always fight me. Beat my ass, beat my ass.

But that still didn't work. I'm still like I am. He is the father of my two children and the one I'm carrying now. That's what happened. I was going up his house Easter Saturday and never made it. And I haven't talk to him since, 'cause scared to death 'cause that bitch will kill me. I don't give a fuck what nobody say. He manic depressive too. He will kill my ass dead.

He knows I'm pregnant again. We always talk about all this. He knows all this, honey. He came looking for me. I could have died. I heard something say, "Yo, Tray!" Looked out the window. I say, "Laurie." Oh, I just freaked. I said, "Clarence is out there, oh God!" She say, "Well, what do you want me to do?" I said, "I . . . oh my God! See my mother? I'm a get her. When I see her I . . . swear 'fore God."

See, he fights. Cops told him once to get out. He said, "You mine. You belong to me. Till the day I die or till the day you die." And then one day this bitch said, "Know what? You gonna stop getting high?" and all this shit like that. Then he went so far as to—'cause I was sneaking getting high—he went so far as to get high with me. Long as I was in his sight. I let him get him high. That was the worst thing I ever did done to him. 'Bout three years in the relationship he began to use drugs. Three years outta seven.

Honey, I don't know what attracted me to him. I guess I was hot in the ass and wanted some dick. 'Cause I hadn't had none going with this girl. I wasn't on this crack. I was shooting drugs and shit. I tell you one thing. I was faithful to whomever I was with. I didn't have to go trick or nothing like that. Bonita supplied me with everything I ever needed or wanted. So it was no thing like tricking and all that stuff. So I was faithful to whomever I was with. I just was hot in my ass and it just looked nice or whatever. He was different, you know. I was still riffraff, and he was nice. Calm, cool, collected, you know. And it fucked me up that he had took a interest in me anyway.

So I was sitting in a bar, and he would always look at me, talk to me, buy me a drink. And he would lend his ear if I was depressed or something like that. Then it just happened, and we've been together ever since. It was a physical attraction and that's all. I told him I just want a shot and that's it, 'cause I told him what type of person I was. I've never had no high outlook on me or nothing like that. I ain't cute. That's what I told him, 'cause his girlfriend, you know, was Puerto Rican. Long hair down to here. Cute. Radiation technologist. I wasn't none of that. Somebody had told me, though, you always down-rate yourself and stuff. That's the way I felt. That's still the way I feel.

He knew I was a drug addict, all right. I had told him that I had stopped shooting, which I had lied. You know, we would drink beer and smoke reefer. That's what he would do, but that wasn't getting it for me. So he found out I was sneaking. So some kinda way he figured, if he got high with me, I wouldn't be in the street as much, and he would have to stop kicking my ass. When I would go and come back, he would wore my ass out. So one day I'm shooting or whatever. So he did it. Well, he cried like a baby. But he tried it and that's it. One stick and you hooked. That's the way it was for me. Child, yes.

He was a chipper then. 'Cause he could do without it. He could take money and shit and I wanna get a fucking hit and he wanna do something else with the money. Shit like that. It was all right if like, say, days he didn't have the money, and no work came in, it was fine with him, cool. Watch TV and read. And I'm sitting there patting my feet, "Where the fuck I'm a gonna get a hit from?" All this shit. He was like, he wanted it and stuff, but he could do without it. I couldn't do without it.

When we were living together and it was miserable really 'cause he stayed from his people. 'Cause he was so conscious about a mark on his arm and, you know, his family gonna find out he was using and stuff. So then his ass was under me twenty-four hours a fucking day. It was just a miserable period for me.

I was in my twenties when I started living with him. Twenty-five. Something like that. Yep. See, there's so much shit in my life, I forgets about that. . . .

Remember I said I ain't had to live with nobody or nothing like that? See, I forgets. I lived with him for seven years. And I did live on my own, come to think of it, for five years, at nineteen-twenty-one Lansing. Me, him, and my children. All that is coming back. I was on my own. Pay my own bills. My own rent. He did too. We rented the room. We moved out of the room and moved into the project. I had my own apartment in the projects after I had my second child and the room got too small for me and him, my son and my daughter. Man, I forgets so much shit.

We got our own place. We moved and had the use of a whole beautiful house. The best thing about living with him, he wanted more stuff from me. I went to JSOT, ABS trade schools. Did the whole term at JSOT up until the last two months. I just started getting high on drugs again and I quit. I was doing like forty words a minute with three error. Typing, filing, and working on the computer. I was doing it all. I was doing all kinds of stuff, you know. Going to the movies. Maybe go to the bar. I tried to live that life. I tried. I tried to live the straight life. But it would work for like three, four, five months, then I just couldn't take it.

See, that's the type of relationship. He was very, what you call it, too affectionate. I didn't show affection. It was so hard for me to tell that man I loved him. And you had to tell him that 'cause that's what he wanted to hear. But actually, to this day, I don't believe I loved him 'cause why couldn't I say it? How come I can't look you in your eyes and, you know, hold your hand and all that and feel that and say it and mean it? Only fucking time I say it is when I was high. After I get a hit I tell you anything you wanna hear. You know what I mean? And he accepted that. If that's what it took, he go get me the fucking drugs just to hear these type things. Just to get me going sexually and all this stuff, right, you know. It was like that. My world is built up on I can't do nothing unless I'm high. So I can't say that I loved him. I've never loved. Never. Never! He would buy dope for me to try to keep me with him, but it still wasn't enough. I needed more than that.

As for my children, my babies, goddamn! My mother say, "I'm a tell you. . . ." She talk to my Department of Human Service's worker. They was talking. She said, "My daughter, she's a addict. She gonna take time." I let my mom keep my children rather than have the state come to get them. I go see them anytime. Don't want them until I get myself together, which maybe will come soon. I could curb my habit. That's why they say, "Tracy is something." When I was with Clarence, like I went four months at a time without drugs and sneak back. It's just hard to say no completely. I can't even see it in the future for me to ever say no, you know. I can sit down and say, "Damn. I remember five years ago, I used to be a addict"—I can't see that.

So I was what was wrong with our relationship. Me! Being a addict. That's the whole thing. A drug addict got to go out. Got to go get that fucking high. Got to lie. Lie. Lie, lie, lie.Lies on top of lies on top of lies. He said, "Tracy, did you go pay your rent?" Project rent, right? Three bedrooms. Beautiful! You know, the projects they set up with the modern kitchens and everything is beautiful once you get inside. I had the whole chumpy 'cause it was brand new. He and my mom would go, "Tray, you go pay your rent?" "Yeah." My mom figured, you know, I had Clarence and I was gonna do the right thing. I wouldn't go. Then it's only ninety-one dollars. Take that rent receipt, tear it off, and bring them back the half that said Jefferson Housing Commission on it. They would see that, you know, and figure the rent had been paid up until the time they was coming to get me the fuck outta there. So, you know, just lies and deceit. The whole goddamn time. The whole time.

I just left. He thought I was dead. I went to somebody's house. He couldn't find me. I stayed there a long time, some months. When he found me, he just cussed me out real bad, and he was just glad I was alive. He said he was scared to answer the phone thinking it was somebody calling and said I had died, got killed or something. He just didn't want the kids around it.

He worked all the time. He worked for railroad companies and he worked as a bartender. We had fun together besides getting high. We went to the movies, but it wasn't fun for me. It was boring. Shit. "Let's do something without getting high." Shit. Oh, he would read. Read, read, read. That's how I knew he was crazy 'cause he read too fucking much. He would read from sunup to sundown, but he always wanted me there. Right there. Right beside him. He sit down and watch TV, "Come on, get on Daddy's lap." I couldn't stand it. Here I go wanting a hit or something. He wants me to sit on Daddy's lap.

He would cook for me. Things like that. The house would be clean. Yeah. One day, when we had the place over there, my mother gave me a two hundred dollar package of cocaine. Ten dollar bags. I shot that whole motherfucker. Stupid. He was sleep. I was trying to bust the bars out the window. I was gonna jump out the window. I knew when he got up he was gonna kill me for shooting up that shit. 'Cause we were gonna sell it, gonna make money for furniture, house and all. I figured I was just really into heroin. Heroin was my first choice. So I wasn't gonna fuck up this cocaine. And my mom gave me the chance, shit. I said, "Now it's time to kill myself 'cause that's all that's gonna get me out of this." I was too scared to kill myself. "What can I do? I'm a jump out this fucking window. I got to go."

So I just wrote a note and I started walking. I'm walking and walking. Next thing I know I end up at the Roosevelt Hospital. And from there they took me to Saint Elizabeth's, where I stayed for seven days and they detox me. The first time I did detox for seven days. And when I got back home, damn, I mean, he had that house immaculate clean. Kids was . . . head to toe . . . he did hair. Everything. He's a beautiful housekeeper. My mom said, "Goddamn, he take care of this house, the kids, better than you can." And so as far as him being a great housekeeper, he can do that shit. Pain in my fucking ass, though. That wasn't me!

We argued all the time. That bitch would kick my ass all the time. 'Cause he was very, very, very possessive and jealous. And he knew my background. Knew that I have tricked, and, you know, anybody, any old friend that I never even thought about tricking with would like say something to me, he would whup my ass for that. "That used to be one of your dates. You setting up something with him." Things like that. I would get my ass kicked a lot. That's the only thing my mom hated about the relationship. He whup my ass. He was very selfish. He even got selfish with the kids. Me spending time with them and shit like that.

I would never fight him back. That bitch would do all the fighting. In the course of a week—I maybe say four days out the week—he would be hitting me or smacking me for some shit. I might have said something he didn't like. I got popped. Just like I was a little kid. He just had treated me just like I was his some kind of possession or child. I would get popped for saying the wrong thing. Popped for bringing the wrong stuff back from the store or something like that. I remember one day I had brought some beef liver back and it wasn't calves' liver, which was like two dollars more. "And you didn't read this motherfucking label?" I got smacked for that.

But the worse one was when he tried to stab me. Goddamn. Tried to stab me. I was so fucking scared. I was petrified. I begged for my life. I started the fight. He had came in. . . . I had put him out, managed to get him out of living over there. Somehow he convinced me to open the door and I opened the door and his kids were dirty. He said they looked like they hadn't ate. Plus it was a junky sitting in the chair nodding and there were works all over the house. So he pulled out his fucking knife and said, "I'm gonna put my kids out they misery." And they ran and got my mother. I really can't remember how I convinced him not to kill me 'cause it was just so scary. All I know I kept putting up that fucking Pamper box. And just begging him just to let me explain and shit like that.

I would get black eyes. Swollen lips. I couldn't see out my eye. My toe was broke. I went in the hospital twice for like a sprained arm. Yeah, he put me in the hospital twice. Two days was my longest hospital stay. He took care of the kids while I was there. I never called the police.

Some of the fights, I felt responsible for some of them. Yes, I do. 'Cause I was always lying and cheating on him. He said, "You deserve this, don't you?" I said, "Yeah." I never fought back. Not once. Now, I would run away though. One day my mother said, "He knows you scared of him." I would keep my family off of him. My brother and them would come back there and beat that motherfucker with a bat. I would keep them off of him. I know I got a warped way of thinking. She said, "He knows you're scared of him. Just fight back. Fuck him. You see he don't say shit to nobody. Fight him back." I tried that. That bitch beat my ass worse than I did if I'd just stood there. That don't work. So after that one time, I didn't fight him back.

Sometimes I would stay in the house so there wouldn't be a fight. Stay in the house where he could keep his eye on me twenty-four hours a day. As long as he could keep his eyes on me it was safe and calm. He felt secure. I think it was insecurity. Yes, it was. That has a lot to do with it. So I'd say, "Ah, fuck it!" 'Cause I say, "Damn if I do, damn if I don't." After the fights he would make up all the time. All the time. He'll say he's sorry or cry and always trying to explain his actions and stuff like that. Always promising he'll never do it again and all kind of shit. Then try to go out and maybe get me what I want. "You want some dope?"

Heroin makes me feel sexy. Yes. Yes. Baby, hush! I couldn't even get into that. That's why that bitch wouldn't mind getting me no dope. Now coke, get the fuck away from me. I don't wanna be bothered after no fucking coke. Coke don't make me . . . it does some people, but not me. All it bring out in me is trying to get me another blast. I don't have time to think 'bout fucking sex. Heroin is different. Get the fuck up, get busy, get out. I initiate everything. I want it. I'm the doer. I just get freaky, freaky, horny, every-thing. My children's father used to love it. That bitch would find me some dope. He would borrow money.

I've exchanged sex for drugs. Of course. I used to have a date. Same bat time, same bat channel. Every damn Thursday, two hundred dollars, three hundred dollars. "Let's get busy. Come on, let's go." I do it up there on the third floor. Got his little money and I'd say, "Look, man, you got all this old shit. I'm pregnant. Just get. . . ." Then he say, "Here. Go get eight caps." I be running. "Go get eight caps." I go get eight. "Go get eight more caps." And I say, "Wait. Hold up now. Hold up. Goddamn, we gotta eat too. Gimme some money. Got to pay house lady. Laurie. Got to give her twenty-five to shut her up for a hour or two." And honey, shit.

That's why I think I was going crazy yesterday, Thursday. I'm in the hospital. I knew that bitch came up there. I knew it. It's not every Thursday he come, but I'm a say, you know . . . I was like, "Shit! Motherfucker! You know today's Thursday. I gotta get out this hospital. I'm a call Mom." I said, "Can somebody come sit with Ethan, please?" She knew I was blast fiending. She said, "Girl, you gonna fight this shit out." I said, "Don't you got custody of him?" I'm pacing up and down the hallway. I was like, "What the fuck am I gonna do? Oh, goddamn, it's eight o'clock. I know he there now. Oh shit." So I said, "Oh, fuck it." I had a token. I told my son, "Listen. Mommy got to go. I'm a go up Laurie house and I be up there. I be back around eleven." And he looked at me, he said, "Mom, uh-uh." Got to balling his little lip up and stuff, like that. So I said, "Look, somebody come and sit with him." And he followed me all around that fucking hospital. "Mommy sick now." "No, Mommy not." "Get away from me now." He wouldn't leave me, so I said fuck it. Mad now, though. We gonna go to bed, shit. We just going to bed. He don't give a fuck long as his mother was there. I fought that shit that day and my mother and them wouldn't come and relieve me. "Y'all can come up here. Y'all know y'all can bring your asses up here."

Nothing attracts me to someone sexually. No. No. I haven't had a sexual attraction just for somebody, just to be with somebody, you know. Everything is money. Money or a cap. Well, not a cap, some caps. That's it. That's the bottom line. 'Cause I don't even think of myself as that pretty enough to even . . . I know he ain't . . . who gonna look at me like that? Now if they gonna look at me, it's for this trick and that's about it. I don't even carry myself like . . . I used to keep myself nice and neat. My hair comb. I don't do that. I don't do that. Motherfuckers take me like this. They love me like this. I say they fucked up too. They must be fucked up if they take me. . . . My girlfriend said, "I don't know how the fuck you do it. What the fuck they see in your ass?" I said, "Well, whatever. They gonna keep coming." I told a motherfucker, I said, "Boy, I told you, don't you know I . . . you see these suppositories in there? I'm on suppositories. I have a infection." They don't care. Told you this whole motherfucking projects had to go to the clinic. I tell them I had a infection. I mess with this one and he got a girlfriend. I done fucked up that whole building. I'm telling you. I fucked up that whole building.

The men I exchange sex for drugs with be like people I know, 'cause I don't go out. I'm scared to *death* to go out. Somebody might cut my throat and something like that. I don't know what the fuck I'm a catch and I'm pregnant. These is everyday people that I know. Ain't no new shit coming my way. A friend of mine said, "Well, you know, I know you cool, Tray, and everything. You ain't gonna burn me." I got a date. Number one, he has to have a Trojan. Like that. 'Cause I don't fuck nobody I don't know 'bout, you know.   I think women need more sex. Yeah, horny-ass women. It's the root to all evil. Trust me. Horny-ass women. Look at Eve. That bitch bit that apple and it's been fucked up ever since. Look, it started from her ass. So you know them women. They're something. They start it at five and six.

They get to closing them legs up and stuff. Get them legs open. I know what's up. Wanting to feel that tingle.

Men having sex with other men, that's their prerogative. I'm down. I was gay for eight years. Whatever's clever. That's what I say. I don't have nothing against that. I met her when I came from up here, the projects, and moved down here to Twenty-first Street. She had all the drugs that I ever wanted or needed. So we hooked up and we stayed hooked up for eight years and that was beautiful. Nice and pleasant. I didn't have any relationships with men during that period, but I must have been hot in my ass for dick when Clarence came along after those eight years. Clarence ended that motherfucker. So that's how that went. Oh, child, she threatened to kill him. "He ain't gonna take you from me." Went to his house with knives and all this shit. I had to go get her mother. Oh, she harassed us for months. And I had to keep him in the house and it was so much shit. I said, "For this old funky-ass pussy."

I was seventeen or eighteen when I met her. I met her down on Twenty-first Street. She was selling drugs and I was copping, so we started talking. And from that, one thing led to another. It was the drugs. She didn't have to do too much talking. All she had to do was give me the fucking drugs. That was the whole hookup. She had what I wanted, what I needed. So anything I've done or did that was faulty, the motive was drugs and that's it. That was it. Had she not had no drugs, she would never got a . . . "Fuck, bitch. Get the fuck away from me" . . . been like that. I wouldn't have came out like that, but I'd a said, "Man, I ain't into that." Just one fucking thing that was more important than drugs, and that's my kids. Right? Me staying in the house when it come to my kids or me staying in the hospital with my son when he has an episode of sickle cell, right?

You know, my son has sickle cell. He has had a lot of attacks. He would have three or four episodes a year. The most serious was one when he was six months and his hands and feet were swollen. Clarence has the trait. I had to fight my habit on those occasions, fight my feeling, to be with him. So it was a few, a very few. There's so few, you see, I don't even think about them.

I identified myself as a gay person during that time, but my motive for becoming gay was drugs, but I enjoyed it after I got in it. I even was messing with another girl that didn't have nothing—wasn't a addict at all, you know, just drinking. We had fun together, but my motive that got me there with her was drugs, but I stayed there because I enjoyed it. When we started the relationship I didn't see it as being unnatural. My whole family, everybody fought me against that. They didn't like it one damn bit. And then one day my sister, she's a Witness, she say, here she go, after finding out how horrible Clarence was, she said, "You know what? I rather for you to have been with Tina. You wasn't as miserable as you was shooting drugs with Tina than you is being with Clarence. She didn't fight you and all that shit."

Yeah, my family, shit, they took me through holy hell about that. They were saying it was unnatural. It was against God's whatever. You gonna burn in hell. All kinds of shit. Child, I just went through one extreme to the next extreme. I had gay friends and went to gay clubs. That's all we had. So I really identified myself as a gay person. Then I met Clarence and it all ended just as quick as it started. I had cut off all ties with all my gay friends. They wasn't calling and didn't come and all that stuff.

I tell you, one extreme to the next. That's the way I am. I can adapt to any goddamn thing. That's what's wrong with me again. I can adapt to any situation whether I like it or not. I will just stand the heat. Whatever. Fucked up! Fucked up! I tell you I need a psychiatrist to analyze some of this shit. Why would I hang in a relationship with a man who whup my ass all the time? I didn't love him, didn't wanna be there. Could have got out, but the threats . . . he had threatened me about my whole family would die and all this kind of stuff. But that's it, but I stayed there and endured this for seven years, you know.

I got two children. I was twenty-nine when the first one was born, and the second one came right behind the first one. I was using drugs when the first one and second one was born. I was using both heroin and cocaine at the time. The kids didn't experience any difficulties. Surprisingly. Thank God! From the whole term of my two pregnancies, I shot drugs. And every time I shot drugs my water broke and that's when I had my children. I carried Ethan full term. Venita, five weeks early. Ethan weighed seven pounds, fourteen ounces. Venita weighed five pounds, two ounces. That's not underweight. Five pounds is the minimum weight . . . minimum weight for kids. When I was carrying them that's one thing I did. I kept my fucking clinic appointments. Kept them. Clarence was with me then, so I kept my appointments. This baby, I don't know. Only God knows, only God knows.

When I found out I was pregnant this time, I was clean and was living in the shelter. Then I came up to the projects on Easter Saturday, and that was the ballgame. When I got up here I was two months pregnant, and I'm supposed to deliver November the fourteenth. When I learned I was pregnant, I don't know why I didn't get an abortion. That's what my children's father said. I don't know.

Being pregnant and on crack. . . . See. See, that's something . . . that's another tear jerker. I don't like to talk about that. I don't like to talk about nothing that makes me feel something. I don't. And that makes me feel like crying. My children, this baby. I hate to talk about it 'cause it's not fair. I hate to think about shit. It's just not fair. It's not fair. I should have had an abortion, but I didn't. It's not fair to the child. It's not fair. I know my ass is going to jail or either they gonna take my child. I know all this, but it's not enough to make me stop. I got the chance to stop now and do the right thing, but I can't. And my social worker told me to my face, "When you go to the hospital, we're going to the hospital, and if anything wrong with that baby, if the baby's a addict, we're automatically snatching it. If it's deformed or brain something, you going to jail." I know this, but it's still not enough to make me say no. Even for these few months that is left. You know what I mean? I tell you, you all fucking know I got a problem. Can't stop long enough. Won't go get no prenatal care. They calls me and everything. Send a car to come get me. I gots all kind of social workers working with me, but the cocaine is stronger than that.

It's not that I was against having an abortion 'cause I damn sure had one before when I was twenty-two weeks pregnant. I had that abortion, so I'm not against that. Maybe this baby coming. . . . I hope it do. It must be a reason. Some type reason. Everything is for a reason. That's all I can say.

I do plan on getting some prenatal care before the baby is born. Yes, I do. I don't know when. Only God knows when. I know all the consequences. I know all this. But ask me, Do I care? I'm just powerless. I can't. My mother . . . here go my mom. She say, "I'm tired of this fucking drug shit now. Fuck that. I'm tired of you blaming it on that. That's the truth." I say, "Mom, if you just think about it, Mom. Would I actually do this shit to a unborn child? Would I? You keep telling me . . . you . . . everybody keep saying. . . ." I said, "This is how powerful this thing is, Mom." Then she have to sit back and think. "I know this bitch ain't crazy, so it got to be like that. Shit!"

With my other two children, oh, we close now. We just too damn close. That's why I had to get rid of them. They was down with me on everything. We go collect cans together and shit . . . you know. Collect cans and shit like that. . . . We was just too damn close and they knew too much of my fucking business. Go get the pusher and shit. Go get my straight shooter. They knew too much. Ain't no world for no fucking kids. My mother came and got them one day and that's where they stayed. That was 'bout two months ago. They know too fucking much. They curse. All that shit. And they're three and four. Go get up in the morning and feed theyself and all that. Peanut butter. Bread. Wasn't no fucking life for them. Clarence couldn't take them. He got a little room by hisself. He barely making it through. He ain't got no means to take my damn kids.

I don't discipline them. Fuck no! My mother does. Damn straight. They tell me, "Grandma hit me." They go to bed. They get washed up every day. When I was up there with my mom house for that eight days, I had to make sure they took a bath every day. They were in the bed at nine o'clock. Breakfast. They on a schedule, a routine. Breakfast at nine in the morning. Lunchtime. They take a nap. 'Cause they had to get broke out of all the shit that they was used to in the projects. If they took a nap it was only for like a hour or couple hours so that they wouldn't break that nine o'clock. They lay down at two, they wouldn't get back up till five. 'Cause you know I'm doing my thing. They don't go to bed till when the fuck they got ready. So it was all new to them.

But they doing good at it. Child, they're doing good at it. I brought them up Laurie's house the other day, and it was just dirty. I said, "Well, you've been living in this dirt. Who told you to say that?" "It stink in here. I'm not gonna sleep on that pissy mattress." I seen the hurt in Laurie. I said, "But, baby, it's been like this." "I don't care. There's doo-doo and that cat doo-doo there. I ain't . . . uh-uh. Uh-uh. It's filthy in here." I said, "Well, Laurie, they only telling the truth." But I said, "Damn, y'all."

I wasn't providing them with enough food when they were living with me. We manage something. Scrape up something. Give them grits. Grits would keep them sustained and filled. I would take them somewhere and somebody would feed them. 'Cause I tell you, I've been down there all my life, so they'll say, "We ain't gonna see your kids hungry." My mother, friends of ours, and shit. And they give me something to eat.

My kids know what Mommy do. I don't think they could say that's a bad thing to do or a good thing to do. They see me happy when I'm doing it so I don't know if they could differentiate whether that's the wrong thing to do or not. I don't know what is going through they mind right now. I wouldn't let them come back in my life. No way. I wouldn't subject them to this life. Not if I didn't have to.

The kids were just hanging out in the apartment. They were seeing everything. I'm guilty, very guilty about that. Very guilty. Like say if I'm calm, cool, and I have time to think, I just cry. Cry. Cry. Cry. I just go hold them or something like that, and I tell them that Mommy is very, very sick. She's sick. She has a disease and once she get herself together, she'll be there for them. I just constantly tell them that. It's outta my control.

I still wouldn't straighten up for them either. You know what I mean? I wouldn't do that either. It's nothing but just my mind and me. This baby can't do it, and that's fucked up to say. But we talking truth and we talking real. This baby can't do it. Them threatening to take my kids. I told them, "Take them then." Shit. 'Cause they getting on my fucking nerves anyway. I gotta pay somebody to watch them when I wanna go out on a date. Something like that. See, you know what I'm saying? It certainly ain't me dying. That won't do it. 'Cause a addict lives to die. It ain't that! If I knew I was dying, I would still crawl and get that fucking hit. Let me smoke this last cap if I gotta go. So it got to be you. You. You. I haven't reached my bottom yet and I don't know what thing will get me there. Only God knows.

That's right, my children can't do that for me. I said it's gonna be a reason. My mind or God. I have to find Jesus or something else 'cause, you see, pregnancy, children still ain't stopped me. Still going. So got to be something, and even though everybody says you have to want this in your heart, I do. It's in my heart and everything, but, shit, I still ain't stop. And actually

I don't know, if I really had to stop for their sake, if that would be it. 'Cause if I had it my way, I swear before God, I probably keep on going till the day I die. They say the only way out is in a institution, that or jail. And I'm starting to believe that.

That's the only way out for me. It's like I fell in love with the shit. You never know the feeling unless you been on it. It's a feeling inside of me. It's where you have to find like a replacement. What can replace that fucking feeling? God? Nothing.

The crack. The crack. The crack. The pipe destroyed my life. When I was with Clarence he controlled my heroin use somewhat. When I was on heroin I could buy a bag or two and that was it. I'd be satisfied for the whole day. That was it. I've been using crack for a year, and that's the last time I shot drugs. Before I went to the shelter I had just gotten started. I came up here in April, at Easter, and things just got completely out of control. When he—Clarence—left I knew he was out of my life, so I knew it wasn't no stopping me. Wasn't no stopping me. He didn't know where I was at or nothing like that, so it wasn't no stopping me.

When I lived with him, that was the one time when there was somebody who exercised some type of control 'cause my mother never did. He was the only one. The only one put some kind of stoppage on my uses and made sure that the house, you know, I took care of business first. Did shopping first. Took care of me first. Cleaned the kids up first. Yes. Definitely. But that's the reason . . . I think that's the reason why that I wanted to be away from him and everything because I couldn't go and get high the way I wanted to.

I came up to the projects here and moved in with Laurie. When I lived there I would get up about nine or ten, go find something for the kids to eat, and start getting on. Somebody would always come with something. There was a lot of sharing. You sort of have to. Sometime people don't have a place to smoke or they don't have they own equipment to smoke out of, you know. Sometime you have your off days and, you know, you give somebody some and they remember when they come down. They say, "Come on, let's get high."

Laurie has two children. So there were four children there and two adults when I was living with her. The children was a part of that, and that's why

I was like "I be glad when somebody come and get them" because people was always dropping by and the kids be there. As soon as we got high, they knew it. They would go haywires and just do what they wanted to do. Say what they wanted to say. And some people would leave 'cause the kids was there, and then, you know, I might have a date or something like that and Laurie might have been too on to deal with them. At that point, to me, they was just in the way. That's the way I felt. They're in the way.

If I had a date, I would give her money. Okay, depending on who the date was and how much he had. Like, say, a person come over and they got about fifty dollars in they pocket. We would give her ten dollars for like maybe a hour's time to be alone or something like that. That's how that was. So I had to pay the house and some of those payment were in crack. Now if she had a date, same thing.

My routine was hoping somebody knocked on the door. And that's how I would feel. I would start smoking as soon as somebody came. Or if I had money, you know, I would start as soon as possible. Sometimes eight in the morning, nine in the morning. And sometimes nobody would come till like in the evening. I would wake up wanting drugs. That's right—anxious, and I get so miserable-feeling, you know. My mind was always on where my hit was coming. When would I get a hit? And I really couldn't function until I got a hit.

Sometimes I would be out looking to make things happen. See, you know, when the kids was around I couldn't leave. Couldn't do the things I wanted to do. Couldn't really take them out. Sometime I would go to the markets and steal. Lotion or meat, you know, go sell that, or I can borrow some money. Like I said, some people would come in and they would need a house or they need a . . . you know, a straight to use, so I be the first one out there to catch them. They'll say, "You got a straight on you?" "Yeah." "Come on. Let's go." Like that.

After I got that first hit, I was more calm, you know. I wasn't as anxious, as evil. Without that hit it was like damn near unbearable. Laurie would like damn near make sure I had a hit and stuff like that 'cause I was very evil, you know, snap at the first little thing.

In the afternoon it was basically the same thing. You know, you get one hit, right, you want more. Just anticipation, waiting for more. If I had money, just constantly spending money. Most of my day was waiting to cop. That's what I do every day. But the kids got to be worked in there. I would have to take, you know, some time out for them. They still had to eat, still needed some of my attention and baths and stuff like that. So I had to learn how to curb, you know, to stop for a minute. Laurie sort of taught me that, how to just cool out. Take a hour's time and get them together, you know, then start doing your thing. I had to learn to do that.

At the end of the day, you know, after a while I finally realized, "Well, there's nothing out there to really get," and I just really had to say, "Well, fuck it, tomorrow's another day," and force myself to get a beer, a can of beer. Usually I would take pills, but I'm really kinda skeptical of taking Xanax. That would bring me down. So would beer, you know. Helps me sleep. So when I feel jittery and on edge, it's beer time. That come like about three, four o'clock in the morning. Ain't no more money out there to get.

So the house was a hit house, and, you know, we made a little money from anybody who . . . not anybody off the street, but anybody who needed to use a house for a date. Sometimes people come in and rent rooms. Five dollars for thirty minutes. Like that. It was a hit house before I got there, you know. So only the people we knew came there. If they wanted to use my straight, then the cost depend on how many. . . . Like it's either one dollar per cap or you give up a hit outta your cap. If they wanna use a room, it's five for a half an hour. Either a cap or five dollars. But every thirty minutes you got to be up. It's pretty busy. Sometimes we would make good money a day, maybe over a hundred dollars. We always shared. Shared everything.

Honey, it was one day I was so damn mad. I had caps and I ain't had no matches. I went the fuck crazy. I said, "It's a goddamn shame. You got a hit house and we smoking and ain't got a goddamn match in the house. . . ." Oh, I went off. So after that, man, I make sure I had some matches. I buy a box of goddamn matches. I sell matches. A quarter a book. I sold a book of matches once for a dollar. Depending on how bad the mother-fuckers want a hit. Especially late at night when the Chinese store is closed. Where you gonna go? Shit, I be right out there with my matches.

Matches are gold. Goddamn right. I'll never forget this guy come over from work like right around two o'clock. I had a few matches, right? We lighting up. That bitch had two more caps left. I said, "Please don't go nowhere. Please don't." 'Cause sometimes I'm greedy. He ain't want me to run to the store to get a book, right? Shit, I go find matches. Oh God, I went and I knocked everywhere. This time nobody would give me no matches. He left. I said, "Kiss my ass." After that I made sure I had some matches.

I got started using drugs because of peer pressure. Everybody was doing it. It was the thing to do. I was taking reds, red devils, Tuinals, black beauties, Nembutal, Valiums, pancakes and syrup. I had a period where I was hooked on every fucking drug that was out there. My mom would give me money. You can make money going to the store, doing chores, doing errands. As I said, I was a nice girl. Somebody always wanted me to go the store or clean they house and stuff like that or babysit. Shit like that.

Vanessa Taylor, a girlfriend of mine, was the first person to turn me on. Vanessa gave me my first pill. It was a red devil. That's a sleeping pill. Seconal. After that I stayed on Tuinal and stuff for a while. I think pancakes and syrup. By thirteen I was snorting heroin. A friend of mine was pushing heroin and, you know, he say, "You wanna try this out?" You know me. "Yeah." So I snorted that, liked it, and from then on I started snorting heroin. So from twelve until thirteen I was on pills periodically and everything like that, but my first choice was to buy me a bag of dope.

I stopped going to school completely in the sixth grade. That's the last time I got promoted. I got promoted from the sixth to the seventh, so I can say I finished sixth grade. That's it. My mother left that type of responsibility on my older sister. And like say, if I left out the house to go to school, they didn't know, you know. Whatever I said went. I was on my own. Do just exactly what I wanna do too.

When I was raped I was in the house. I think I was almost fourteen. These guys came up, right? I think I was in the house alone or I had company in the house and they made everybody leave. I knew what was up when they said everybody leave but me. But see, since the house was my house, they never bother me before, always left me alone. You know, they figured . . .

they said, "She ain't . . . she don't do too much fucking." But this particular day, this night, they come up to the house and when they started saying everybody leave and shit, put the . . . lock the doors and shit, I knew what was up when they asked me to come in the room. I said, "No, I don't wanna come in the room." So they say, "Get in the room!" So the guy, Ray Nay, put the gun to my head. I said, "Oh shit. Why me?" I was scared to death. Scared. So he came in, did what he wanted to do and finished, left out. "Tell your mother . . . you tell anybody, you gonna die." I'm . . . you know, I'm scared to death. Shit. He didn't knock me down or anything like that. Only thing he did was hold the gun to my head. That was it. Then when he left out, another guy come in. Same routine. Had the gun, scared me to death, threaten me. Then when he left out, another dude come in. And I went through that. After they finished, they left, and I was just fucked up. Miserable. I ain't know what to do, who to tell, who to turn to. Scared to tell my mother. Scared to tell the police, 'cause I figure they were, you know, bigger than my mother. They . . . you know, they had threaten the whole family, "Not only you gonna get it, the whole family gonna get it." So I kept that in till about a year ago. All that time. So I would really extra stay high to forget. I never had to remember. 'Cause if I was caught sober or something, I would remember and just cry and everything, you know. I look at my mom and wanted to tell her. So I got high and stayed away from that house for fear they would come back again. 'Cause I didn't tell nobody. I was too scared. Eventually my mother was the first person I told. She was very sad. Sorry and saying, you know, it was her fault. She should've been there. She didn't know.

I saw those boys every day! Every day! I had to look in they face every day of my life. They never said anything else about it, but every day I had to see them. Every day I wanted to tell somebody or tell they girlfriends what they did, but I just couldn't. Too scared to.

I think I started using drugs because I didn't have no supervision. I didn't have nobody say, "No, that was the wrong thing to do. Don't do that." You know, if you get in trouble, you get punished for it, you know. I didn't have no supervision whatsoever.

When I started snorting heroin I knew I was addicted then. It took maybe a week. Maybe less than that. My friend say . . . she said, "Damn." She said, "I did something with the needle." And she said, "When we snort it take a long time. When I do it with the needle, it's just like that." And I said, you know, "Come on." And that's how I started mainlining. I had this immediate rush. Immediate, immediate get high. It lasted longer too.

It took longer for me to hit myself. A real long time. I was scared. I was well into my twenties before I could hit myself. The girl I used to go with, she used to do all my hitting and stuff. Then I would get tired. She would always go first, and then I would have to wait for her to finish nodding or whatever and go to the bathroom and stuff.

When I started I never worried about becoming a dope fiend. I wasn't powerless. I was not powerless 'cause I still had money at the end of the day. I could have went and bought more dope, but I didn't. Like five dollars a day was enough for me. Pack of cigarettes. Something like that. I would share a half a bag. Plus I was babysitting for people who sold dope and I would steal out of they packages.

So in the beginning my habit wasn't big. I would get a five dollar bag, and a half a bag would sort of do me for the day. I did that for the longest fucking time. Then I did a bag, right? See, you can still get high and nod off a fucking bag for the longest time. They sell ten dollar bags now, but damn near the same thing. I never really got to that four-, five-bag stage like people was doing. When I stopped using, I was using a bag and a half a day, but it depends on how good the dope was.

I never went back to heroin 'cause that's how powerful this crack is. Wasn't my choice. Once you get it, you don't want nothing else but that. Shit, if I go buy me a can a beer, shit, I'm a need that same dollar to get me a cap, you know.

Now why I continue to use drugs is the question. That's the big one thousand dollar question. I have no idea, other than the fact that I like the feeling I get. Other than that, I have no idea. It keeps me broke. You know what I mean? I'm away from my children. Everything about it is negative but the high. So that's the only thing. It's the feeling I get.

Oh, my mother hate my drug use and wish I would stop. Wish she could make me stop. But like I told her, it's in my time. It's only in God's time. It's nothing that she can do. No kind of threats or nothing, you know. She just prays every damn day. She lets me stay in her house if I come in and that's my cool-out period. Follows me wherever the fuck I go though. Makes me take the kids wherever I go 'cause I don't have as much rein down her way as I do up here. She lives over Twenty-fourth and Ivers, North Jefferson. So I don't have as much access to drugs as I do up here. So whenever I'm down there, it's a cool-out period.

My sister was an addict too. She's in recovery now. We have a close relationship. I guess we see so much in each other. She really gets mad and upset when I say I have to have it. She's trying to recover and she sees me just walking out the house and going to get high.

In those days, when I was using heroin, heroin users were much more compassionate than crack users today. People shared their dope. Nobody would see another person sick. People would be physically sick if they didn't have a shot that day. Shoot, they bowels break on them, break out in chills. I never experienced that. You wouldn't see a person sick in no shape, no form. It wouldn't do. Even if you had to give a person a G shot. That's . . . you know how you got ten, twenty, thirty, forty, and fifty. A G shot, that's less than a tenth. Just to get them, you know, just to get the edgies off.

The amount of dope I used depended on how much money I had. Even when I was on dope, even if I had a whole lot of money, it still didn't, you know, make me go get more and more because I didn't need no more. Maybe later at twelve or one o'clock at night it wore off and the house was closed or something. 'Cause the heroin people didn't stay up all night long, twenty-four hours a day. They had time limits when they sold dope and stuff. If I was fortunate enough to catch somebody out or something like that at that time, I'm gonna get some more.

Everybody sold works. Diabetics sell works. I used a set for a long time. I used them for maybe four hits, four or five hits. I used to share my works, but I stopped when the AIDS came out. I don't worry about being HIV positive. It's too much other shit on my mind to worry about that. I'd be batty. So I put that shit on the back burner for real.

When I look back on my addiction, I wish I had never started. I wish I had never started and wished my mother was there a little bit more. I wish she was there to stop me, to tell me don't do that. I wouldn't give it to my worst enemy. That's how bad it can get. To my mother I wish I had never stole from her or cussed her out 'cause she be in my business—you know, telling me to calm down and don't do this and take care of the children and "you mean to tell me this drug mean more to you than your babies?" shit like that—and I would just cuss her out and steal from her. I wish I hadn't had done that. As for my children, I just wish . . . that goes back to wishing I had never started. 'Cause my mom told me one day she said she wish they were never born. "Wish you never birthed them." That was painful. Oh man!

I always go back to how much this thing has got me. It still don't make me stop. It ain't that painful enough to make me stop. I seek help after help after help, but in the long run I still go back to the drug, so it don't do enough. It just makes me sad. I got these scars on my arm from shooting drugs. Abscesses. They're great big pussy sores that drains blood and puss, and this scar here resulted 'cause I'm keloidal. The abscess turned into keloids. You go and you shoot some drug in and maybe the hit wasn't a good hit. The stuff goes into your arm instead of going to the vein, and it develops a sore, a pussy sore, and a hole, big hole, comes into your arm. Everybody don't heal.

I've seen people OD. They just go into a deep nod and start foaming at the mouth and at that point, all the ice, all the shooting them up with vinegar or anything . . . it's nothing you can do. I've seen them die. Every time I stuck that needle in my arm I thought I was going to die. That thought was there. Is this the bag? Is this the bag? There may be some battery acid or some shit in it. What the fuck is going in my arm? You never know. So the thought is there every time. But who the fuck cares? Not I.

When I thinking about getting high on crack, all of them was my best hit, best highs. I mean, it's. . . . Oh God! Oh God! My best high? Oh, Lord. It's so hard to describe and it's indescribable. Man, my God, I get that hit and I jump up. Bend over. I say, "That's it. Laurie. Laurie. That's it!" Goddamn drool. . . . Here come the spit coming out. Next thing I know, cigarette. Gotta . . . God, I got to have my cigarette next. I got to have my cigarette. Whoop, the scarf come off. Clothes come off. I'm walking 'round. She say,

"Girl, bend up!" I say, "I can't. I can't bend up. Oh, Laurie, this is too rich!" I gets on my knees. I say, "God. That was too good." I say, "Laurie, I don't need no more right now. Take it 'cause you know I'm greedy." I was crazy. "Laurie, just take it. I don't need no more like that." I said, "Whoo, it's still coming on." That's when you know . . . lips gets to moving . . . I can't talk. One time I say, "Look." She say, "What's going on?" All I can do was say, "Give me five fucking seconds," 'cause I was speechless. That's it . . . I couldn't describe it, God damn. I never thought about that shit, boy. I just thought . . . I'm still on my knees and that's how good it be. I just thought about that. I could not talk. You can't hear.

See, to us that's good. You can't hear. Lord knows I couldn't see a motherfucking thing. I couldn't see. Then when the bells ring, that's a hit. You hear the bells in your ears. Motherfuckers get to ringing. Goddamn! You know . . . mostly I got that. And it's been a while, a long motherfucking time, since I had a hit like where I said, "Laurie, that's it." Everything . . . you know what I say now . . . everything is bullshit. They ain't got no fucking cocaine up here. Ain't shit out here no more. Ain't no cocaine. Know what I do now? I just look for the best bullshit. It's all bullshit, but I try to find the best that's out there.

When you hear them motherfucking bells! Goddamn, that shit drive me . . . can't move, them bells is ringing. Goddamn it! And that's how it goes. It's so fucking good you can't have no more, but you don't even need to 'cause like ten, fifteen minutes later, you ain't at this point no more. Then you can get back up and smoke your cigarettes and talk and I be pacing. "Yeah, Laurie. God. Yeah, Laurie. Shit, that was a good thing. Where the kids at? Yeah. Where the kids?" And shit like that. That's when I get to schitzing. "Where Ethan and Nita? Get them a Popsicle." That's it. That's a goddamn hit!

When I start schitzing, I start worry about where my fucking kids is. "Where they at? Who put them in the room by theyself? Fucking socks in the room. They gonna play with them damn socks. Ah shit, the window. The window." 'Cause you got like a can propping up the window 'cause it don't have no spring. "Oh, shit. They gonna take the can out, snap they whole head off. Oh, shit. I can't go to the hospital looking like that. Did I drop something on the floor?" Shit, picking up fucking soap powder buds and cigarette ashes and shit like. "Damn, I drop something on the floor." And you looking and looking in your pocketbook. Then I was so high one fucking time, something was crawling. . . . "What the fuck is crawling on me, Laurie? Laurie. Something crawling, crawling on me." Shit like that. That's my schitz. Walking. Walking. Looking. Looking in everything. Water. "Where my water? Where my kids. I want them here. I want them here. I want them here." "Tracy?" "No, they ain't fine. No, they ain't fine. Ah shit. Where they at? Where they at?" Like that. That's my schitz. That's when I'm high. I ain't been like that in a long motherfucking time. I get high I wouldn't go outside. Not me. Now I take a blast, go right the fuck outside. It's just not that good no more. The last time I had a hit like that was in April.

The length of a schitz depends on how good the coke is. You might get schitz for a fucking year. Might not never come the fuck out of a schitz. You understand what I'm saying? Your brain, you know, your mind just might snap. It don't last that long. Five minutes, ten minutes. And when you finish schitzing you ready to go schitz again. You ready to re-up. You ready for another blast, man. You ready to go again.

In a hit house, the unusual thing was just basically people lip moving and them walking up and down your fucking house and hearing things and seeing shit, looking for people in your closet and shit. You're fucking my high up. You're really making me annoyed and shit. "Get the fuck outta here." I puts them out. They talking 'bout, "Let me get my. . . ." "You ain't getting nothing together. You just get your shit and get out." I don't fuck with nobody schitz. When you schitz worse than me, you gotta go.

Shooting galleries are more calm. More peaceful. It's a more relaxed atmosphere. You don't schitz or nothing like that. You just be cool, calm. Usually you're in somebody's house. A nice house. I ain't never been in no abandoned house. I been to somebody's house that had a gallery up in they room. They had families and cook dinners and shit, I mean, but it was still a gallery 'cause everybody came there to shoot. Another thing, a shooting gallery is not no all-night, twenty-four-hour type of thing. People take they little shots, and it ain't no schitzing. Don't have people arguing and all that kind of schitzing and selling bodies and all that stuff. It's just a more clean, more calmer atmosphere. Then we sit down and we rap, 'cause, you know, makes you rap and talk and all that. That's the difference. It's just a more peaceful atmosphere. You had your works there and your cookers and everything lined up for you. So you get your cooker, your beer cap or a spoon.

I prefer a beer cap myself. A spoon is too fucking big for me. I get a beer cap, Colt 45 beer cap. I take the plastic piece outta there, right? I rinse that out real good so no beer smell or nothing in it. I open my bag of dope. I drops my dope in the cooker. I add my water, depending on how much . . . how potent it is to make. Most of the time . . . majority of the time you put forty cc. in there. You put your water in your cooker. You holds your cooker, you heat it up till it sizzles . . . till it sizzles, not boiling. You put your cotton in there, so anything foreign would come in the cotton, right? You know, you may have a speck of this, a speck of dust or something. Anything foreign gets trapped in the cotton, so everything you draw from out the cotton just pure liquid and dope. Then you take your tie if you need to tie. Some people don't need a tie. Then you tie up and you hit yourself. Then you go clean your works out and that's it.

The nod kick in . . . oh, goddamn . . . I tell you now, immediately. I get my hit, and by time I'm taking the needle out I'm high. Before I can get that needle out I'm on. While I'm pushing that shit in, if it's good, that's how come people OD and die. See, I'm a greedy motherfucker. You don't push no whole thing in, 'cause you never know how good it is. You always just put like twenty cc. See what that do. And then if you, say if you get real fucked up, come the fuck out with the rest. Put the rest up, you know. That's how some people get fucked up. You shoot it all in.

Sometime the purer the dope is, the less the rush is. Now I have had people that had . . . they don't know, there ain't no pure cocaine. But it was purer than anything that was on the street. Supposed to been pure just . . . not cocaine, pure heroin. And they shot it in, not . . . you don't feel no rush. The rush don't come till maybe seconds after. It's almost like you snorting. Seconds after. And they didn't know. So instead of them checking at that twenty point, they went on ahead and pushed it all in. Motherfucker left here!

Thing going on the crack house are much more hectic. Hectic, hectic, hectic, hectic. At all times. Somebody coming, all the time coming. Somebody . . . half of them trying to beg you for another hit. "Please, can I have another hit? Can I give you a dollar for another hit?" And they done sat there and spent up all they fucking money. Then they want what you got and "Oh, can I . . . ?" and then they wanna, "Well, I got this to sell and all this to sell" and all kind of shit like that. I had a motherfucker that was going in my motherfucking pocket to take back what they had gave me. So it's hectic.

Hit house and shooting galleries . . . I tell you it's different as day and night. The people is different. Heroin users are more, you know . . . they more family-orientated. They don't want everybody to know they business and stuff like that. The people come in, they work and own things and stuff like that. Ain't got to worry about nobody stealing nothing from your house and shit like that. They, you know . . . it's just a more . . . they more caring. Motive is still the same high, but they don't, you know . . . they don't schitz, they don't steal from each other, you know. Like that. I mean, as strangers, you won't trust a motherfucking soul, but you can trust them more than the person that's on crack. Bet you give them your money, they come back with it. I don't give a fuck how high I am, you don't get my money. I don't give nobody my money to go do nothing for me, 'cause you might be like me. So, nope, I don't trust nobody. Not even Laurie. Man, you can't trust nobody.

My stealing didn't increase after I started using heroin regularly. 'Cause, see, I would steal from friends and people that trust me. I didn't go out. I just kept stealing and doing devious things to people whom I was in close contact with. But they never suspect me. I've done stealing, shoplifting, and prostitution. I started prostitution in my twenties. I just did it as favors for drugs, you know. Not that I went out on High Street and walked the streets for a pusher. A pusher, you know, he say, "You wanna get high?" And I say, "Yeah." "Well, you do me and I do you. One hand wash the other." And that's how that started.

Right now I just do prostitution. I wouldn't work with a pimp. I'm greedy. I want it all. So these are people who just come by. It's nothing. I tell you, I don't feel nothing. If I felt something, I wouldn't be doing it, and that's the truth. So it's nothing that I feel, but it's the dollar that you make. And the end results is money and/or caps. I would never work on the streets. I ain't trying to be killed. I don't go the fuck out there. No. I wouldn't work in bars either. I haven't got to that point yet where I have to work the bars and the streets.

The projects is a very good place to work. It's a very good place to be and that's how come I can't come from fucking up there. Can't stay from up there because it's just so easy to come in contact with a drug or get a drug. You don't even have to lay down. You might find a motherfucker that wanna have sex, but after he take a blast he just can't get it together, can't get hard, and you done smoked up all his money and all that, and like that. He schitzing or bugging too much to get, you know, get down. It's just very . . . for me, it's very easy to get a drug. Very easy.

I would rather do prostitution than go downtown and shoplift. Damn right. What fucking trouble can you get in for having sex? I go the fuck downtown and steal and get the fuck caught. I really be blast fiending then. I be sitting the fuck up in jail 'cause I done got caught. No caps, no nothing. I want something that's going to pay in the end. Plus, my shit be, "You gotta pay up front." Gotta pay first. I don't give a fuck whether you come or whatever. Then I go hide it somewhere. 'Cause I've had somebody want they shit back if they didn't get satisfied. So fuck all that.

You can't be addicted to drugs and work too, because you're not there. You be trying to steal from the boss. See who pocketbook you can snatch. What they got in they pocketbook. Or on every break you probably got a cap in your pocket or something and you gonna go and take a hit. And then you up all night long. How the fuck you gonna ever make it to work? So you can't do both. You can't earn a honest living and do drugs too. It's some people that do it, though. Some people work to support they habit. To me they one of the lucky ones. But I could never do both.

As for the people in the projects and what they do to make a living, I'm going by what they learned. I can only speak on what they know—pushing drugs, selling pussy, and shit like that. That's the only thing they know 'cause they never tried to come up out of this. This is all we know. You put us somewhere else I guess we'd fucking . . . I'm a survivor, I might would survive, but we would be dumbfounded. This is all we know.

I don't see any way of getting out. There's no way. Death, institution, or jail. And that's being honest. I see that for the black community. There's no way to save the kids. 'Cause the kids is just corrupt now. They're thirteen years old and selling drugs. On drugs. I know my girlfriend, not a girlfriend of mine, but a sister I just met, her son, he no more than fifteen, they get high together. His mother gave him his first hit. All day, every day, hustle together and all. No, it's getting worse. And I tell you, shit, I'm shocked. That's why my kids are away from me, 'cause I just might say, "Go ahead" and "It's all right. As long as you do it around me." Fuck that.

The kids in the project . . . like they're just terrible. No respect for adults, no respect for their peers, no respect for nobody. Fucking at ten and eleven and all that shit. Twelve-year, thirteen-year-old girls having babies. It's all that. Everybody in the projects is on assistance. They work, but they get assistance too. I'm a say 'bout thirty percent of them work.

Straight people don't understand drug use. No, they don't. How could they understand? They don't understand somebody selling they body, not feeding they kids, and hustling. No! How can they understand that? You gotta be there. Straight people wanna stay far the fuck away from me as they can. They don't want no part of me. That's the way I feel. And then again, it's a . . . I tell you, it's always a different thing. Some straight people don't want no part of me, don't want me near them, scared I'm a pick they pocket or some shit like that. Then there's some straight people who just reach out for me. Got to stay there. Fight and hold me. "I'm gonna help you." It's hope. It's help. I'm the fucked. . . . I ain't had to be into drugs. That's what my counselor said. I didn't have to live in and experience all that shit. Some straights say, "All I know is that I wanna be there for you. I'm gonna try my best, do all I can to help you." Or they would give me money so I could eat. My gang gave me five dollars to cop with to keep me from going off the street or something. To keep me from snapping out on my kids. So you know, some straight people genuinely wanna help.

I have a lot of contact with straight folks. A lot. My family is straight. My sister is a Witness. A lot. Hell, shit. A lot. I have a whole lot of friends, but I just don't go around them looking and being the way I am. But they will accept me warmly. Don't give a fuck. But I just don't go. . . . No, I don't wanna see them frequently because of my habit. The way I'm dressed and the way I am. I don't want anybody to see me like the way I am now. I'm not proud of where I'm . . . what I'm doing. It embarrasses me. But it's me right now. It's the way I am.

The city don't give a shit about the poor. They wanna keep you where you at. Why the fuck you think they still got welfare? They don't care. They just want them blacks right where the black and Puerto Ricans are at. They contented. Everybody's happy. That's how they feel about it.

I think the way most people in the city feel about people in the project is that that's where and what they wanna be. They are content. We gonna leave them right where they wanna be. They're happy. I know it's true. The people who live in the projects don't want to be noplace else but in the projects. They feel just the way I feel. That's where I wanna be right now. You scared to death to leave the projects. It's a world out there. It's a world. You have to take responsibility. It's a world out there without drugs. It's a world out there where you got to pay rent, you got to pay bills, you got to get up to maybe do work and support your own self. Not welfare! It's a scary thing. If you used to just having someone take care of you, someone feed you, you waiting on your welfare check, your food stamps, food referral, hustling, and selling dope. Man, that's a scary thing to do, to walk a straight line. You don't wanna do it. They're scared to death of taking responsibility. No. Lot of us is just not ready to do that. You have to tear this motherfucker down. Then we have noplace to go but up!

I think the government should tear the projects down. All the projects. Just tear them the fuck down. That's the only solution. It's just right there in them projects. That's where it all start. In that circle. You have your own fucking circle. Your own community. And tear them motherfuckers down, you might have a chance. I don't think they can get the drugs off the streets. No. Never. But you can minimize it and you can just, I guess . . . you can help some of these kids that's coming up. But, no, people my age and stuff, we done. It's some hope for young people. Not much. I would like to think there's hope. It's hope.

Welfare is a mistake. The biggest mistake Kennedy could ever had did. Yes. It's just made black people lazy and dependent on welfare. Just very lazy and dependent. And you got to keep on having babies and more babies 'cause somebody's welfare is gonna take care of them. You can tell welfare anything. They'll tell you they look for the father, but you gonna keep having babies to just make your check bigger. And you're lazy and you're dependent on them every two weeks. Now some people might not . . . you get this little welfare check and all you gotta do is stand in line for it. If you work hard for your fucking money, busting your ass, you ain't gonna just fuck it up every day. You just ain't gonna do it, 'cause you done worked hard for that money. This little money you ain't gotta work for, you don't give a fuck about it.

I don't see myself as being cut off from the rest of society. I'm only cut off 'cause I wanna be cut off. It's out there. It's out there. If you wanna take those steps you can do it. It's help. It's help.

Drug users ain't shit. They're not shit because there's only one thing on they mind at all times—drugs. We'll steal from you. Can't never trust them. Can't trust none of them. They're addicts and not to be trusted. That's all they wanna do. That's where they wanna be.

I like the feeling of being high. The warmth. I'll put it that way. Warmth and security. That can be the best. I'm secure as long as I'm high. Some people get high to forget, right? I get high to forget too sometimes. I do. But I just get high now 'cause my body don't know. . . . I believe if I was sober my body might crumble, 'cause that's all this body knows is a drug. If I stop getting high for a year, this bitch might just conk out. It's the way it ticks and function and all that old stuff. It's all made up from the drugs. Since I was twelve. To stop that, I believe this, you know, it ain't gonna know what to do, which way to tick. You know what I mean?

I have nothing to tell people about my life and how I feel about my life. Not a thing. 'Cause I wouldn't wanna lie. Nothing. Nothing. I have nothing good to say. But I have two beautiful children and thank God they're not with me. Ain't nothing else I can say. What I want and what I do is two different things. I wanna be drugs free. Believe it or not. That's what I want 'cause of my goddamn children. I wanna be drug free. I want that. I can taste it. But I can't see it in the near future. I can't see it. I can feel it. I cannot reach it—bad as I want this. As bad as I want it, I can't get it. I can't

. . . grasping at straws. It's there in the heart, but that's all. Don't go no further than that. I don't know what. I don't know what. Something . . . I even go as far as to say, you know how they say your life is written, you know, everything as you come up is already set up in the big book. I said this is it. I'm destined to be a addict.

"Shit! I was a survivor, baby."

Laquita

My mom's fifty-five and was born here in Jefferson. My father was born in North Carolina and came up from down South when he was about fifteen. My mother got up to about the fifth or sixth grade. I really couldn't tell you how much education my father had. I knew one thing. He was good, he was good at money. He was good at everything he did. He had to have a brain to be that good even if he didn't have any education. He was good and smart.

My father was 'bout forty-four or forty-five when he died. Drugs killed him. He used to come get me from school. You know, my mom was working part time, but she didn't get off until like five o'clock. I came home from school, went upstairs. He told me to do my homework. When I got upstairs I, you know, I undressed, had to take off my uniform. Did my homework, and I wanted some water or something. I was upstairs 'bout maybe half an hour. I came downstairs and he was on the couch with this thing tied around his arm, a needle, and he had something else, some cotton, and these little containers. Now I know what they were. One was for water and one was for cleaning out works, which they called bleach. And when I came downstairs I thought he was alive. His eyes was open, you know, but he had all this stuff around his mouth. So I went next door 'cause I couldn't get him to get up. Lady came over, and she was like "Call the paramedics," you know. She was like "Your father's dead, honey. Come stand out here with me." I was telling her, "How he's dead? His eyes is open." I was only ten.

They called the ambulance and they came and they closed his eyes and they took him out and they took me to my mother's sister's house, where I stayed until somebody contacted my mom. And she came and got me. My mother didn't react. She was kind of angry. Even though he was dead she was still kind of mad. Yeah, she was real pissed.

When my father moved out of there, I must have been about six. See, my little sister, my youngest sister, my father was already gone by the time she was around. When he died she couldn't have been . . . she was about four then. She didn't really get to know him. My mother had had her, and he wasn't around. Not that he was dead or nothing. I mean he left the house. So my little sister didn't really get to know him.

I was his favorite. You know what I mean? I had two older sisters, but I was his favorite. So wherever he went I went. At night I could hang out with him and everybody else was in bed. I could go into his pool hall and stuff. I think his death had a significant impact on me. As far as my schoolwork and stuff, you know, I didn't go to school for like two weeks. Usually the average kid might be a week. I didn't go for about two weeks. And I used to always tell my mother, "I wish my father was living. If my father was living I wouldn't never stayed with you," you know. She used to be like "I wish he was too so I could take you and send you right out there with him." We used to go through it.

They were separated and when he died he wasn't living there at the time. He was living with my grandmother on Eighteenth and Hubbard. He had been living with my grandmother for four or five years. See, I was his key through the door. He used to come, and she wouldn't let him in. She wouldn't let him and he would come and he would knock on the door and he would holler, and she would send us all outside. I saw my father every day. He was around every day. I went to school right across the street from my grandmother on Eighteenth and Hubbard. Faithfully, at lunchtime and after school. He was there all the time.

My mother couldn't control me when he was around. I am telling you, anything I wanted to do was all right. "Sure, you can have this. You can have that." She would say, "Don't give it to her. She can't have it" or "She can't go."

I was real close to my brother too. He was twenty-seven when he died. He got shot in the head. Two times. Right there on Eleventh Street. He worked for Crisis Intervention Services and somebody wanted some weight on some weed or something like that. He purchased the package for them, and what happened was he got in touch with the people that was working on his job and they didn't want it or they had already gotten it. So he wanted his money back, you know. And there was this girl name Gwendolyn and she set him up. She's not here anymore. She's down South with one of the Carters. But they said that Carter did not shoot him. Someone else had shot him. He was in the project building. The bitch lived in the project, on the seventh floor or eighth floor or something like that, and they found his hat, his glasses, his something else in her apartment in the project.

That was a big effect on my life. Because we were so close. He was like a substitute for my father. You know. His daughter, which is my first . . . that's my oldest niece, that's my first niece, her and my sister are the same age. We got a little tight. You know. I used to go and stay with him. My mother couldn't control me. I was in the ninth grade when he was killed. I was about fifteen.

Out of all my sisters I was his favorite. I tell you I've got two sisters and they don't look like nobody. But I look just like my brother. I mean me, him, and his daughter we pass for father and daughter, and me and her pass for twins. You know? He used to take me to jazz festivals. He used to take me to a lot of shows. He liked Grover Washington and Phyllis Hyman. Those were his favorites. I tried to think of this jazz player we went to see one night. He took me to this concert, and I had to go to school the next day. My mother laid him out. She say, "That's the same shit her father used to do. You come here, you get her, y'all take her out, y'all don't know when to bring her back. She got to go to school." I would say, "Don't pay her no mind." He would say, "Don't say that." He say, "Pay her some mind." He would chastise me, but he would chastise me in his own way. He knew he didn't have to beat me. She would say, "Fuck that, get the belt, and I'm gonna whup this ass." You know what I mean?

When my brother died, oh, my mother was out of it! My brother was her heart. I am telling you. They thought she was committing suicide. If it hadn't been for my other brother catch her just in time, she was taking a sho'nuf dive out the second floor. We were just at the hospital too, and my other brother came in the door crying. He just stood in the doorway. I was in the chair rocking, and she was like, "What's wrong, what's wrong?" She was crying, and he was crying, and he was saying, "Mom." And I guess she just figured. She could feel it, 'cause she was like, "No, they didn't." 'Cause what happened was they pulled the plug, you know.

I don't know. It all happened so fast. It seemed like her feet didn't even touch the floor. It was like she was laying there and she went from the head to the foot, and like whooo! straight to the window. You know what I mean? She was actually fighting to go out that bitch too. They were trying to hold her down. My mom, she's kind of heavy-like, you know. She's solid, but she's strong. So it like took all of them to grab ahold of her 'cause she freaked out. He was the second oldest.

She had to take tranquilizers, you know. Everybody was taking tranquilizers in our family. Everybody was on drugs. Everybody was prescribed with heavy-duty medication and that was like a real downer. That year, '80, was real fucked up for us. And then it took everybody couple years to even to start to even accept it. You know, that he wasn't there anymore.

So it destroyed my little world for a long time. My brains were all wacked up. I was like a zombie. I mean it was like I was brain dead. I wouldn't talk to nobody. I wouldn't eat. I wouldn't . . . you know, I had freaked out so bad. I started lagging in school. I got pregnant. My mother really couldn't control me then. I was just too grown. When he was around it was like, if she did something to me I'll be like, "I don't have to take this from you. I can go stay with my brother." It was part of her fault too that I sort of drawn more closer to him, looking at him like a father instead of more than a brother, because I'm saying she used to tell him, "Beat her." He would say, "Come on, Mom." Now he wouldn't beat me. He would do the same thing my father would do. He would sit me down and talk to me and say, "Look, you know I can't go against Mommy." You know, blasé, blasé. I would say, "Okay."

With her it was different, 'cause she want to knuck. She wanted me to fight her back and all that old bullshit. She want to kill me and beat the shit out of me, and I just wasn't with that with her. I used to tell her, "I'm not going to let you hurt me. You must be crazy. What's wrong with you?" It took a real big effect on my life. That was worse than when my father died. When my father died I was young. I was little.

When my brother got killed, my oldest brother and the third oldest, they were fighting. The hallway wasn't that big, but it was real long. And they were fighting. The next day after he had died, they were fighting. I don't know why they were fighting . . . . I came in on the spinning tail of it. I came in, my mom was standing on the step. Everybody was standing in the hallway. We watching them fight. We were like little kids outside, hanging around watch the fight. My mother was sitting on the steps, leaning on the banister, and my aunt was there, and she said, "Virgie, Virgie, oh, Virgie, please, please, break them up, don't let them fight." My mother said, "Ethel, I'm not getting in between that." She said, "They're brothers." Then my Mom said, "I'm not getting into that shit. I'll never get in none of them quarrels with them. If you want to go over there and break it up, be my guest, honey. Go right ahead." Ethel went step down off the step to break it up and caught a right. They stretch her ass out on that floor in that hallway. My mother went right over there and pick the bitch up, and said, "See, I told you not to get in that shit, now. You come over here. You stand and you watch like everybody else, and when they're finished they'll let you know."

I was ten when my father died, but I was so close to him. Him not being around anymore it was like, you know, it was real strange for me. 'Cause it was times when I get and it be like "Today, Mom, can I go over Grandmom's and see Dad?" And, she would say, "Your father not here." I would actually forget that he was dead. You know? And she used to say, "How are you going to see him, in the grave?" She used to make little sarcasm remarks and shit like that about it. You know. I used to say, "Why are you so mean? Why don't you like him?" She used to say, "I can't stand him." She used to tell me all this shit. I used to say, "You're just jealous." She used to tell me, "Jealous?" She said, "He never had a damn thing. Jealous, jealous of what?" I said, "He took care of us." Which my father did.

He always kept his job. Even though he didn't live with us, he always gave her money. He gave that lady money almost every single day of the week. 'Cause we were all going to Catholic school. You know what I'm saying? He's still pay for it, and then when he is dead and gone he was still paying for it. She received his Social Security insurance, you know, and I tell her, I say, "He didn't have to do nothing for you. He didn't do it for you. He did that for us." She used to tell us, "Shit, your father don't love y'all." I say, "Yes, my father do love me. I know he don't love you, but I know he loves me."

My father was a con man. My father was good. He had a legal job too. He could do construction, and I know he worked for the city, cleaned streets. But he was a con man. He used to con the motherfucking drawers off my mother. He used to swindle her into giving him everything. He used to do a lot of people in the streets too. Unfortunately, he got the wrong person because they gave him some bad shit.

Yeah, he was doing it all. Ritz and tees, you know. I never saw him get high in front of me. He would never do that. It was just an accident that I found him on the couch. I'm sure he was probably gonna do it before I came down, or whatever.

Yeah, my father did hustling and the nigger been to jail too. He went to jail and Grandma used to go and get him. I know he would boost. I know he would steal. I know he would flimflam. He would talk his way out of anything. Sometimes he used to swindle me. My mother told me he was a con man a year after he was dead. She said, "He's a con man." And then after I, you know, I got older, other people used to tell me, "Your father was good. Your father was one of the best." They say he used to con the pants off everybody.

My parents would fight. I remember one of the fights they had. Matter of fact that fight was in my room. Me and my sister shared a room at the top of the steps, and when you got to the top of the steps you would make a left and that was our room. We were in there. Oh, me and her were in there then, writing and drawing. We were coloring, me and my older sister, and they were arguing. They were argued from their room to the back. Then the next thing I knew, they said, "Come on. Y'all get out. Get out of the room." My mother said, "Get out of here." And we went out, and we were crying in the hall and stuff. And then we were looking through the keyhole in the door, and they were knucking. They were getting that shit on. I don't know what was going on. He probably swindled her some more or some shit. He probably conned her out of some more. She probably got mad, because she knew what he was into.

My mother and father didn't get along at all so I didn't know how they had eight kids together. They were knucking. I mean shit was breaking, the hinges was coming off the doors, the ceiling was dropping and all that shit. I was young but I remember and I used to get very highly upset. I would take my father's side. I would be screaming at her, "Don't hit my father. Don't you hit my father." She would say, "You and your father, get the hell out."

I used to say the fights started because of her. 'Cause she was always bitching about him being in the streets and him doing drugs. You know. He might come in and say, "Here some money." And she would accept it and then she would start talking shit. I used to ask her, "Why do always pick fights?" And she would always tell us when we were coming up not to fight in school, not to do this, not to fight the kids on the block, not to . . . you know, and here she was fighting her ass off.

Nobody ever jumped into any of those fights between my parents. They better not. Shit, my father was seven feet tall. Shit, I remember he had me one day. I don't know what I did. That was the first time. He didn't hit me, but he picked me up with one hand and held me up on the wall, and told me, "Don't you ever. . . ." I think I was fighting my mom back. Telling her how I hated her.

My brothers never jumped in there. My father beat they ass. Shit, my father was not no joke. That was a big fucking man. And all of us had to look up at him. When he was talking to us, he say, "Hold your head up and hold your eyes up and look at me." He was high up in the sky like he was a giant.

My mother and father didn't get along at all, so I didn't know how they had eight kids together. Altogether there're eight boys and three girls. They all was older than me. I'm the seventh. I have three half-brothers. I don't consider them half-brothers. I consider them my brothers. I had five original brothers and my mother.

So the only help my mother really got was from my father, the help that Larry gave her, and from my brother. When my father left the house and moved in with his mother, Louise. . . . There is this guy, Larry . . . . This girl, we call her Nicky, 'cause her name is Nicole. She lived next door to me all my life. Know what I mean? We lived at five-nineteen, she lived at five-seventeen. We were always next door neighbors. It was her uncle from down South. Lawrence Anderson. He used to come over. He was just a friend, though. He used to come over there. That was my mother's friend. Yeah, now he is my mother's boyfriend. They have been together since my father passed. He helped my mom with the bills.

Her relationship with Larry didn't affect the amount of time me and my mom spent together because we never spent no time together. Never! I mean, if you call spending time when she might take me shopping to get new clothes or something like that. You know what I say? We didn't spend time together like sit down and hold a conversation. Me and my mother never sat down. We never talked about nothing. We always argue.

And then as I got older, we still don't talk. I don't fuck with her. I hate to say it like that, but I don't, you know. I only go up there to see my child. You know, I go up there and I say, "How you doing, Mom?" I just steps the fuck off and goes on do my own little thing, you know, and be all wrapped up in my kid. I don't be having time, you know. Sometimes she might say things to me, and sometimes I look at her, and I say, "I didn't ask you. Why you bothering me?" You know. I tell her shit like that.

The relationship with Larry was the only one she had after my father moved out. They didn't fight. She curses Larry out. Larry lets her have her way. She starts talking that shit and "Fuck you" and "I don't owe you, shit. I was doing all right before I fucking met you, shit." She curse him out, and Larry just sit there. Never open his fucking mouth. Larry just sit there and take it. He don't feed into that shit with her. He just looks at her and say, "Oh, Virgie, come on now."

I hated Larry. At first I used to hate him. 'Cause one time me and my mom. . . . That was the first time I. . . . We had one real real serious fight with my mother and that was before I had my baby. And my best girlfriend told my mother that I was sitting on this guy's lap around the corner and my mother beat me. And she was like "You think you're grown." She closed the door. We had a big front room. The front room doors would open up. They were double doors. My father could walk right through those, but all the rest of the doors he had to stoop. And she beat me. She closed us up in the room, and she said, "Wench, I'm gonna whup your ass." And she grabbed me and I mean she sock the fuck out of me, and all I knew, I saw stars. We started fighting and the next thing I knew she was in the chair. It was all reversed. I had her in the chair, and I was beating the shit out of her. And Larry happened to walk in. 'Cause she was screaming. She was actually screaming. I had my mom screaming.

Larry walked in and grabbed me, and he held me down in the chair and she beat me with an inner tube off a bike. I was telling him, "Get the fuck off me. You ain't my father. You ain't got no right to have your fucking hands on me." This and that. She said, "He did more for you than your fucking father." I said, "He didn't do shit for me. He did it for you." And I left and I never came back home. I stayed with Gramp for about a month. She had my brothers and everybody hunting for me high and low and they could not find me.

My mother would fuck us up. Specially me. I got my ass beat. I'm telling you. In a week, trust me, I got my ass beat at least five to six days a week, every day, because I stayed in trouble.

Yeah, I hated Larry because I used to think he . . . 'cause he used to always try to tell me what to do. But then again, now that I've gotten older, you know, I can respect him a little more because I'm seeing, you know, he was a big help in her life and he is a real big part of my daughter's life now. You know. She calls him Grandpa. That's the only grandfather she knows of. Even though he's not her grandfather, you know. She looks up to him and . . . you know. I actually trusts him with my child, you know. I would never think that he would try to do any child molesting or anything like that to her, you know. And they hang out. They swings. They go everywhere together. You know. My daughter tells my mother, "I'm going with Larry." Larry grabs his coat and she grabs her coat and they just go in the car.

I think my mother was religious. Yeah, she's Catholic, I'm saying. You know. She used to go to church with us, and then she stop, and then she was just sending us to church. By the time she would get us dressed, she would be late for church herself. So she would stay home and watch stuff on television or listen to the radio. All that let me stay home shit, "You can't go to church, you can't go out." You know. You could be sick if you wanna, you better get healed by ten o'clock to go to church.

Was she strict? Oh, wow, was she ever! She was strict because she was so old fashion. She still is. I'm saying, she ain't came up out of the roaring thirties yet, the roaring forties. You know what I mean? She so stuck back there in time, and she always tell us about how she got to the sixth grade or why she don't got to the fifth grade in school. You know, she's smart for the little education that she has. She is very with it.

When I say strict, I mean she used to tell us shit like. . . . Okay, school would get out for the summer and all the little kids could hang out till maybe ten or eleven o'clock, you know. We were ten, twelve, shit like that, thirteen, and we couldn't hang out for a little while. She would still have us in bed at seven o'clock. The sun would be shining. It be daylight saving time. She be saying, "Come on, get washed up and go to bed." Like we had to get up and go to school the next day. I think she did that so she have more free fucking time with her selfish-ass self. She wasn't doing anything. It's not like she was going anywhere, and she was putting us to bed. She was putting us to bed probably 'cause she was tired from all . . . from when she got up in the morning or something, and she just wanted us out of her hair.

She used to tell us shit like "You better do your chores. If you don't do your chores, I'm not letting you go outside." You know what I mean? I used to scrub down from the third floor to the first. It was approximately about fifty steps. We had a three-story house. I'm not talking about the front door steps. You know, I was a cleaning ass. I am talking about steps, basing, banister pole. It's not like I took a rag and just wiped that shit up. It was like get the scrub brush, get the pan, get the soap powder, and get the rags, get the works. We had windows like . . . each floor that you came down at the top of the first floor would be a window there. "Get the Windex too, baby, 'cause all that's coming right down your alley." You know what I mean? "And get busy."

House was immaculate. House stayed immaculate. Even though she had eight kids, the house stayed immaculate. She would not allow us to tear up, fuck up, none of that. Yeah, 'cause she made us help her clean it, and if we

didn't do the job right, she would show us, and we would redo it. If we had to do it three or four times, we would redo it. My mother didn't collect welfare or anything like that. She worked every day, and he worked and he supported us. She did get medical assistance for the kids.

Some of her important rule when I was growing up was . . . she used to say to me . . . she used to tell me a lot, "You're grown, you want to be grown. If you want to be grown, be responsible. Go out find you a job. Take care of yourself. Feed yourself. Nobody owe you nothing. Don't look for nobody to give you anything because nobody has to give you nothing because you the only person has to take care of yourself. You the only person who has to do good by yourself." She used to tell me that a lot of time. Well, like "Grow up, be an adult. If you're gonna be grown, be grown." Her point of view of a man was if he ain't got a job, and if he can't take care of you, he ain't shit. She was like, "Nobody needs nobody underneath nobody who can't help nobody let alone help theyself."

She was always concerned about the way I dressed and how I looked when I left the house. She used to say, "Look at you." Sometimes we get dressed for school and my mom pull our collars out over the thing or something and put our ties on right to our uniforms. She would say, "Come here, look like a bum, disorderly dressed." Before we walked out the door she would have us ship shape.

I didn't skip a lot of school. Naw, 'cause in the Catholic school you skip school they call home. I went to school. I got in a plenty of fights too. I got in two or three fights. My mom was like "Kick her ass." You know what I mean? She wouldn't care whoever was standing there, and she would turn around, tell me, "Kick her ass! Beat the shit out of her!"

My mother only visit school when she had to, and she used to get mad and she used to say, "Why you got to be fighting all the time?" She used to tell the teachers, she say, "Hey, I ain't sending her here to have nobody beat her up. I want her to protect herself." You know. She be like "Don't fight all the time, girl." She like "Shit, I spend too much." My mom cursed. Boy, she used to get mad and she used to curse up a storm. Curse up a storm, and could read you, and write a book on Zorro, with a "Z."

She wasn't with bringing home bad grades either. I don't know 'cause I never brought home no bad grades. One time I brought home a D. She was like "I'm gonna accept this 'cause it was just one D," you know, and it was history. She was like "Next report, I better see a rise up to a B." Next report that bitch rose to an A.

If my teacher told her that I was acting up in school, she get in my shit. She be like "Don't make me have to do this and do that to you 'cause you know how I want you to act. You know you are supposed to behave in school." You know what I'm saying? I be like "Yes." My mother was never with that old "Yeah" and "Naw" shit. We never talked like that. It was, "Say 'yes.' Say 'no.'"

My mother really didn't allow me to hang out with anyone. I did have a friend in the neighborhood. The boy who I used to go to school with every morning, Steven Smith. I used to take my little sister, and he used to take his little brother, and we used to all go to school together every morning. And his cousin was my girlfriend. We would all come home from school together and stuff.

I really didn't start hanging out with folks until I was about fourteen. My mother was just too through. She was through 'cause I had really got beside myself. She was talking that old "I want you in the house at twelve o'clock," and the party still been running until 'bout three or four, and. . . . Shit! I started hanging out with my girlfriend, Gay. I really started getting my ass beat. I would stay at the party until three and four too, and she would be waiting for me at the window when I came in. As I gradually went on and on, you know, I started hanging even more, and I met this guy I liked and I got knocked up.

I didn't listen and do what she asked me to do. She used to beat me. To make me do what she wanted me to do. I've always been a little hard-head, stubborn bitch. She used to tell me, "You's an old evil black bitch." She used to tell me, "I can't stand you. You remind me of your father. I can't stand you." I used to say, "I don't know why, 'cause I ain't done nothing to you." She used to say, "Don't be smart."

I am in a way like my father 'cause my daughter she gets everything. She don't want for nothing. I don't give a fuck how much it cost. I'll go get it. Whatever extent it takes, 'cause I'm saying, when my father didn't have no money, he would go get me some money. He would take me with him, and we would go get some money from somewhere.

I would never want to be the kind of person my mother was. She's too strict. I am saying, new clothes come out, up to date shit, and she just not with it. She used to tell me, "You ain't gonna be no good. You gonna be a bum." She used to tell me that shit every day. Because I was like my father. She say, "You're not a dummy." She say, "You're smart and real intelligent," but she say, "You ain't gonna do shit with it. You gonna be a bum. You gonna be a bum with education." You know, shit like that.

She tried to ship my ass into Hanrahan and put me in business. She did the same shit to my sister too. She'd send us to school and ask us what we want to take up, blasé, blasé, and then she make us take up what she wants us to take up. Understand, who's going to school here? Her or us? She made me take business courses. Yeah, typing and all that shit. I can type ninety words per minute. I know she still loves me now. I might not be leading the kind of life she wants me to lead, but this is my life. This is the life that I've chosen, and I chose it, and until I'm ready to turn it around, nothing she can do about it but accept it. Accept it or fuck it. When I was growing up I used to think the bitch hated me. I thought she was too mean. She was! She was a mean-ass lady. All the people on the block used to say, "Why your mom act like that? Why your mom don't let y'all come out? Why your mom don't let y'all go nowhere? Why your mom. . . ." You know, I'm saying, she used to make a strict policy, "Well, if your sister can't go, you can't go." I used to be saying, "I don't want to go with her." You know what I mean? I wanted to go somewhere, I didn't want to go with her. So she would stay in the house, make me stay in the house.

If the neighbors on our block saw you doing something, they go tell your mother right away. You know? They would say something like "Well, don't do that 'cause I'm gonna tell your mother," or "Don't mess with that" or "Don't bother. . . ." We used to pick on other kids and stuff who used to come around the neighborhood, and they be like "If you do . . . if you hit them with that, I'm gonna tell your mother." You better not open your mouth to speak back. Oh, you open your mouth and speak back, uh! They take you to your mother, and my mother would chastise us. Tell you that you disrespectful, stay in a child's place, be seen not heard, not be too grown, speak when spoken to. You know? And she would say, "Don't say anything when they say something to you. Don't fat mouth."

Oh, when she learned the first time that I was doing crime, she beat the shit out of me. I was boosting. She found out because I had all these fucking new clothes. And then I got caught in the store. She came and got me. I wasn't in jail. I was up at Eighteenth and Lincoln at the police station. She came and picked me up and she let me go to sleep. And next morning she beat my ass in my sleep. It was before I had my baby. I was fourteen. She had a fit. I was ready to do a dive out the window, but I couldn't get away from her. I'm telling you. It just seem like I couldn't escape, to get away from all them fucking. . . .

She used to tell us that phrase about, uh . . . that's in the Bible . . . she used to say, "God say spoil the apple, rot the apple, beat the child," some shit like that. Uh-huh, which mean beat your ass. Chastise you, uh-huh. She would beat us with anything she get her fucking hands on. It might be a motherfucking belt. Might be a motherfucking extension cord or ironing cord or might be a shoe. She tear your ass up! Might be a brush. One time she beat my motherfucking hand so bad with that damn brush. . . .

The last beating I got was the time when the dude held me down with the inner tube. My mother's friend Larry. That was the last beating, and that was the last beating I was involved with her.

But I suppose the worst one was the time when she beat me with the extension cord and put me in a tub of cold water. There was this guy I was seeing and she was telling me how she didn't want me messing with no boys. I was thirteen. I had a lot of guys coming around and she . . . I was saying they're just friends, and she say, "What did I say?" I'd say, "I'm not doing anything with them. They're not doing anything to me." And she say, "If you were that smart with your books as you are with you mouth maybe you would get somewhere in life." And I would say, "I am smart in school." I say, "I get A's and B's every report card." And she say, "You just being real sassy, aren't you?" I tell her, "I'm not being sassy. You just try to call me a dummy." That's what I told her. "You try to call me a dummy." She said, "You far from being dumb, honey." And she told me to tell them not to come around there anymore. And I didn't tell them.

So she told them, and they still came around there. She say, "Every time they come around here I gonna beat you, 'cause I told you to tell them not to come to my house anymore." And these two guy came around here, and I was sitting on the steps, and I just laughing and playing with them. And she got mad and snatch me off the steps, and she said, "What did I tell you? Now, I'm gonna whup ass." She said, "You think I'm playing with you. I don't want them boys hanging around my house, 'cause I don't need no babies." That when she was telling me about the birds and the bees. She never would come and say "fucking" and that old bullshit. She say, "You know about the birds and the bees, and all that old shit?" I used to be like "What is the birds and the bees?" So then I never found out about the birds and the bees 'cause I already got my motherfucking baby. I'm out there on my own.

But I'm saying, she snatched me off the step, and she told me I had to stay in the house. So I stayed in the house. So she told me she was gonna beat me, and I said, "Why you gonna bet me?" She said, " 'Cause you defied me. I told you to tell them," she said, "and I'm sure they. . . ." I said, "They don't listen to me." I saying they're young like me. She say it's my fault that they around here, that's why they keep coming back, because I'm not telling them not to come to my house, you know. I think maybe if I might have told them that, they mightn't have came, but I didn't tell them, and she promised to beat me, and that night she did.

She beat me in my sleep. She put me to bed early. She beat me in my sleep, and after I woke up she beat me. She had some cold water with ice cubes in it. It was wintertime, about twenty fucking degrees outside, and she told me to get in the tub, and I better not close the windows, close the doors, close the bathroom door. I was cold. She made me stay in there maybe forty-five minutes. It was cruel. It was. It was really cruel.

I used to cry about that shit. None of my other brothers and sisters got treated like that. I was saying my older brother he used to catch flying mugs and flying shoes. I tell you her shoes were like . . . like darts. She could throw a shoe, boy, she wouldn't miss you. I saying, you could duck, you could jump, that bitch would hit you! Them fucking shoes had wings.

The child abuse, yeah, and people came there, and she thought I called the people over for child abuse, but I didn't. My teacher did. Yeah, I had welts all over. She beat me for two days straight 'cause she caught me doing the hoochie coochie. I was in Miss Joanne Robinson room. I was in the fourth or fifth grade. I wasn't having sex. He was just grinding. And she beat my ass for two days. The lady thought it was child abuse, 'cause I had all these fucking welts, I'm saying, with the extension cords. I'm lucky I still have my eyes 'cause I had welts on my face and everything. I was trying to duck her, trying get away from her, and she would hit me, and I couldn't tell where she was gonna hit me at.

Her little put-downs didn't come until I was like a little older, until I was eleven or twelve really. That when she used to start that. I'm saying, when I was younger coming up, you know, she used to embarrass me. She used to tell me a lot, "You not dumb. You're far from being dumb. Use your brain." That's when I was little, coming up. She used to tell me that. Then when I got about eleven or twelve she used to say, "So fucking grown. You're dumb. You're dumb." I used to say, "Before you told me I was a brain." She say, "Shit, that was a long time ago." I say, "Really." Because I'd always been a A-honor student. I always got honor roll in school clear until I graduate twelfth grade. All A's. Always made honor roll, you know? One year I didn't make honor roll, and she was hot. When I first started flirting and grinding with boys she used to say it was nothing wrong with it. At first! But then the boy was getting fresh. I don't know who she was trying to protect me from. From what I could see, she used to make me think that she was running a monastery of her own.

I had my period when I was twelve. I freaked out when I had my first period. I freaked right out in school. It came on when I was in school, and I was outside in the yard, and all this blood just started dripping from nowhere, and you couldn't tell me I wasn't gonna die. I'm saying, I went off! They took me to the nurse's office and everything, and the nurse was telling me to calm down. I was saying, "I'm dying. I'm losing all my blood. I'm bleeding. I'm bleeding." They had to call my mother up there and have her come and get me.

My mother started to change about then. It was like she had a dog on a leash. I mean, she would sniff me out anywhere I was. Come find me. I could be on the playground and she could. . . . When we were living on

Fifteenth Street, she had the second floor window open and she could see me in the playground, you know. And she thought that if it looked like I was getting out of hand or. . . . I used to do a lot of fight. I still do.

So it seems that when I got my period, the discipline got stronger. I started getting more beatings and stuff, but I was becoming more defiant. Yeah, I was. Because she was like "I don't want you with this person, I don't want you with that person, I don't want you with the guys." And I was like "Fuck this," you know. "You're not going to knock off my fucking fun. I'm gonna hang out with who I want to be with and I can talk to who I want to talk to and I wanna go where I wanna go. I can deal with all the consequences when I get the fuck back." That how I used to look at it. Like fuck her. You know what I mean? I see her when I see her. I started getting brave.

I don't know how she could have thought I wouldn't get pregnant. She never told me shit. She never told me nothing about birth control. She never told me nothing about taking no . . . taking no nothing. All she start saying was "Don't get your ass wet and whatever you do you better take care of it." Shit like that. That ain't telling me nothing.

My oldest brother was sent to prison. He done did time at Abingdon for robbery. For like a year, almost two years. We used to go see him. We used to have family day down there. We would take him money and stuff down there. But when he came home that was one of the best Christmases. He came home around Christmas holidays, and that when my second oldest brother was living, and they went down there and they got him, and picked him up and everything and brought him home. That was a real Christmas that year. I was still going to Saint Thomas. I must have been about in the sixth or seventh grade when he went to prison.

When he was in prison she used to tell us shit like "You see where he is, don't you, from being stupid. All y'all got education, none of y'all supposed to be, why don't you go to college, why don't you do something with you life, why don't you . . . ," you know, tell us shit like that. She used to make an example out of him. Everything we did wrong, he was the example for everybody else. You know, when they were young they used to gang war and shit. My brothers and shit, you know. Cops might have snatch they asses up and whatever, you know. All four of them were in gangs.

Nobody helped me get into crime and hustling. I did all that shit on my own. She didn't do nothing to keep me out of trouble, though. She used to try to keep me away from them. She would take me places with her. So, you know, certain days I wouldn't be hanging out with certain people and shit. Like you do shit that I would normally do, you know, she would say, "Come on, I'm taking you in town." You know, "Come on, I'm taking you to the movies." Shit like that.

I've got five brothers and two sisters, and three more half-brothers who are my father's kids. One brother works in a book factory. Two work for the city. And my oldest brother, they say he got a job now. The one that was in prison. One sister works in a supermarket, one works in a bank. My third oldest brother does drugs. Woody is about thirty-four. Everybody graduated, though. My second oldest brother went to college. My oldest brother went to college too. He got two years of college. The one that got killed, he got eight years of college.

Us kids used to knuck. We used to try to tear the house down. We used to keep the bitch shaking like it was a party in there, and, boy, she used to come from work and somebody be sitting there with a bruise, with a scar, and she would say. . . .

Outside the house—we turned into motherfucking Mafia on the outside. 'Cause then we'd be thick, you know, 'cause we all hung in the same area. My mom was real strict around us. She was like "'Cause I might leave and all y'all got is each other. Y'all stick together. I don't give a fuck what y'all go through. Y'all just stick together when it come to a bond on the outside against another motherfucker on the street."

From '70 clean up until almost 1980, the neighborhood was pretty cool. It was clean around that section. There wasn't any crime. It was pretty cool and calm around drugs too. See, drugs ain't really started getting to get hip and popular around this shit until the eighties. The eighties jumped through here and everybody just say, "Here I am."

In my neighborhood, having mannerly kids was the thing that was important. Mannerly kids, kids with respect, that were chastised and who listened. Clean the block, having meetings, block meetings. They would throw block parties just for the kids. I'm saying, this is just for our section of the neighborhood. We used to throw block parties, and they even let us have a clubhouse. It was the neighborhood clubhouse. Nobody, no other kids from outside neighborhood, could come there, you know. They strict on shit like that, you know.

When I was twelve, my best friends was Celeste, Lauren, and Gay. We stayed fucked up. We smoked plenty pot. I was stealing it from my fourth oldest brother. My brother was a big-time weed seller. I used to steal five or six bags at a time, and take my niece . . . I used take and pick her up every day from school. And I used to take her with me and, boy, I used to have her fucked up. I was twelve. She 'bout eight. I used to take her with me to school. "Puff on this." And she used to puff on it and choke to death, and next thing she say, "That's okay." Yeah, that's my heart, that's my niece.

Me and my girlfriends would go to the parties. Talk to the niggers. Went to house parties, you know. We would sneak in the house. They would let us in. Yeah, like on the weekend there would be friends of ours, and somebody we knew would be having a little house party, and we would go. And we used to go to the parties on the street, block parties, shit like that.

Celeste, Lauren, and Gay were almost like having three more sisters. Straight up! 'Cause I'm saying I give a fuck what was happening, what jump off, they might have been there, but that shit was dead and deceased. And when they were there it was like "What's up? Who the fuck is that? What y'all want, some static?" I knew they were real friends, you know. They never would let me down. If I had been in trouble or if I needed a favor and they had it, I got it. I could get anything they had.

I was fifteen when I had my first sexual relationship. I got pregnant the very first fucking time. First time I had sex I had got pregnant, but I lost the baby. But I didn't know I was pregnant, and the bitch fell out in the toilet. Like a clog of meat. And I put it in a plastic bag, and it just deteriorated away. I didn't know what it was. So I took it out of the toilet and put it in a bag. And I went to look in the bag again and it was gone. It was the same person that I got my daughter by.

That first time I was in pain. I met him 'cause I went to school with his cousins, and I used to see him a lot and I used to like him. Michael is older than me. Michael 'bout four years older than me. I used to like him, and I used to go the parties and shit, and he would be there. I don't know. This one particular time, I must been looking better than a little bit, 'cause this bitch was like "What's up, baby? How you doing? My name is Michael." And from there, it was like I liked him that much, I wanted to give him some. He asked me. I was all fucked up off weed. He asked me to his aunt's house. It was 'round the corner. I don't know what I was looking for, but I know when I got it I was sorry.

The shit was painful. I didn't enjoy it, but he did. Didn't use anything. I didn't know nothing about no fucking condom, no birth control. My mother ain't tell me shit. She didn't tell me nothing. I learned about having babies 'cause I kept trying to learn how to fuck. I learned about sex because what I used to do is, after him. . . . Alright, after a while it didn't bother you no more. It was like he used to get on me and jump up and down. . . . He used to get on me and jump up and down, but I didn't know what a climax was, you know. I hadn't experienced a climax. I had experienced that feeling of relief. But I never experienced with him.

And see he had a little dick, and my pussy was used to just that dick. I tried to go out and get dicks from somewhere else, and I ran into a horse, so. . . . Oh my God, that was painful! I cried. I told this nigger to get off me. He be saying, "Oh, baby, I just want to stick that head in there," and the head of his dick must have been about that big. I said, "No, baby, you got to go. You got to get off." Shit. And then I met this guy name Tyrone White, and that's who I experienced my climax with.

That was the first time I had a climax with a man. Back then it seem to be pretty more safe to just run out there and fuck somebody. Not now. I was pretty active. I was going through it. I was getting my fair share. I learned about babies by having one. Yeah, well, I'm saying that just about as much as I knew, but I'm saying as far as what to expect or how to know when you're pregnant, I didn't know nothing about that shit. When I was throwing up and shit . . . I'm saying, I had a girlfriend say . . . that's one thing I did learn, my girlfriend say, "When you are pregnant you get sick, you throw up a lot." So I started throwing up. That's how I knew. I wouldn't eat around nobody. I wouldn't eat around my mom and them. I get my morning sickness and shit, I be upstairs getting sick while they all downstairs eating breakfast and shit.

I learned about VD and all of that by the time I was in the ninth or tenth grade. Yeah, but I'm saying they didn't have herpes and AIDS and all that old killer shit running around out here. I said it was pretty cool then, you know what I mean? They could cure everything. Now, you can't find no cure for shit.

When I got pregnant I didn't know I was pregnant. So when I found out I was pregnant I kept it a secret to myself for five months. My mother found out because we got into an argument and I told her. She said, "Larry said you were pregnant two months ago." I said, "Larry's a damn liar, 'cause I was pregnant five months ago." They were always trying to pump me to find out if I was pregnant. See, I knew after my five months were up, I knew it was too late. She couldn't touch me. You know? And she couldn't do nothing to my baby. She had forced my sister to have an abortion when she was seventeen. She was graduating from high school.

I'm not with having no abortion. I ain't with it. 'Cause you know, I look at it like this. It's so many women that not able to have children, and I'm saying I'm not a fast breeder, and any kids that I got, I'm keeping them. You know, I don't really think I'm gonna have no big family. I might have another one, if God allows me to. I'm saying the thing is, if I have another one. I take no birth control, no nothing.

My mom was responsible for bringing up my child when the child was born. I went and stayed all the way down Twenty-third and Sajo, and then I moved from there down to Forty-seventh and Lafayette Avenue. I was staying with my niece when I ran away. Stayed there for a month. They drug me home. I didn't go back. They drug me home. It was the first time I really, really ran off. Yeah. I mean really ran off and stayed off. I mean I used to run off for a day or two, but I really ran the fuck off, and I wasn't trying to go back.

And I'm saying, I left. My mom moved up to Twenty-third and Beresford and I stayed there with her for 'bout, I say, October '81, when she moved up there. When I had my baby, we were still on Fifteenth Street. So we gonna say October '81 she had got the house, but I had my baby in June. 'Round October '82, a year later, we moved up there with them. I say around '83 or '84, I was out of there. It was history. I was like "I got to get the fuck out of here." I used to come home, though. I just didn't never stay there anymore. I never stayed overnight anymore. 'Cause I had my own place and was making a lot of money. I was seventeen when I finally got my own place. At seventeen I was smoking reefer, selling reefer. Hustling, making plenty of money.

So my mother got my daughter and is taking care of her. I'm saying I think that's her life. She treats her like it's her child. I don't know. I don't know. My little sister envies my daughter. See, they're the only two there. Oh, my oldest sister is there. She's getting a divorce. I fell out. She said, "That nigger hit me. I want out." She said, "He fucked up, he put his hands on me. He got one time, and he did and I'm out of there." She actually getting a fucking divorce because he hit her. She wants out. So my mother got three splits back in the house.

That's the youngest thing in the house. She goes everywhere with her. She's adorable. And a lot of them, my older brothers and sisters, they kind of envy that shit, because she spends every day with Quianna. See, all the rest of them, the grands, she hardly ever go to see them. She knows them all but, I'm saying, none of them get the attention that Quianna gets now. You know what I mean? That number one, uno. Quianna get 'fore any the rest of them will get.

I'm saying don't think she don't be on me for money. Basically, she leaves word, "When you see Laquita, tell her to get her ass up the house, and tell her I need to see her right away." You know, shit like that. And I know what that be meaning. It means something happened, or she needs some money. If Quianna is having problems adjusting or dealing or whatever, you know. Like I say, I always go see her at least two or three times a week.

I have no problem with my mother taking care of her because she is doing an excellent job. She's doing a good job. A great job. I'm proud of her. I'm proud of my little girl. Very smart, and she's not fresh. She'll be eight next week. The tenth. She'll be eight in six more days.

My relationship with my daughter is improving. I call her up consistently. I tried to make it up there at least four times out of the week to go see her. So I miss her. I miss the shit out of her. When I go see her, it makes my day even better. When I see her I hug her and all that shit. Every time I go up to see my daughter, I say, "Hi, Mom," and walk the fuck away. See, like I don't really talk to her. She's newsy. Mother is newsy.

Me and my oldest brother were the black sheep. The black sheep of the boys and the black sheep of the girls. She knows that I'm a lesbian. She knows about Zee. She can't accept it, but I don't give a fuck. 'Cause it's my life. You know what I'm saying? I'm happy. That's what count.

I've been with my girlfriend Zee for two years, but before I was with Zee I was with this girl name Tina. I don't know how that happened. I wanted to experience it. I say, I had been locked up and everything, and all that kind of shit, you know. I had been around a lot of bulldaggers and shit in jail. You know? I say, yeah, them bitches look like pit bulls. You know? I wasn't interested in none of them. They looked like mad dogs. Bitch, big Amazons! You know what I mean? I say, "Damn! Look at this ugly-ass bitch." So when I was down there, I had this bitch down there. Juanita Moore, that was her name. I had this bitch lap up on this pussy, but she didn't do the job right. It was like a new experience for me. I was sixteen when I was with Juanita Moore. They sent my ass there 'cause I would soon be turning seventeen. Then I met this girl name Tina.

I was getting high, and these people I knew, I grew up around them, I went around their house, and Tina was there and I could tell she was a stud. She was cute. I was smoking coke at the time. And she was into smoking coke too, but I'm saying . . . but I thought she was cute. She had the cutest little voice. I never fuck with no bitches with no deep voice. I hate it. They got to be cute. If they ain't cute, they can't fuck with me. They got to have some looks about them.

So I told her I want to try it, right? Yeah, she was talking all this good shit. I was like "Yeah. You gonna give me some head?" You know, like that. She was like "You can't have none of this." I was like "I can have anything I want," you know. "I don't have to take this shit from you, girl." She was like "Shhhiiit." We started playing around and shit, and then one thing led to another, and me and this bitch wound up at the Quality Inn for 'bout a week. We was living it. We were on the top floor. We had this bitch name Angela Owen's credit card and we were living well off it. That bitch had a bill out of this world. But, see, the thing about it is I wouldn't let her touch me. I likeded her, but after I . . . she had a nice body and everything, but I'm saying it just wasn't there like it was with Zee. I met Zee two years ago. It'll be two years on my daughter's birthday.

I met Zee 'cause I was at somebody's house on Johnson Street, and she pulled up in this cab. She knew my name, though. She said, "LaQuita, get me a couple of caps, 'cause they won't serve me." I said, "Yeah. I go get them for you." And then the bitch said, "Don't burn me, whatever you do." I'm saying to myself, "Bitch, I wasn't even into that shit." I wasn't even in that. I wasn't into burning motherfuckers yet. I learned that shit from her.

I got her the shit and I came back out, and then the bitch took me to her mother's house and left me there. I was like . . . uhhhh. Me and her mom stayed high all night long. Her mom slowed down a whole lot now. She still gets high but she don't . . . she done gained all the weight and everything. Zee's mother was getting high for two years. Getting high hard. So after that I really liked to go there and see her mom. I used to go there and see her mother a lot, and get high with her mom and Frances.

Then I went up to Virginia Beach, and Zee had got hold of my pictures and I couldn't find them anymore. So I came looking for my pictures one day. And then it used to be this old bulldagging bitch name Odessa. She's pretty, though. Dessa pretty, but no teeth. I know she suck a mean pussy. Anyway, Zee told her to tell me that she liked me, and one day I see her getting high, and Dessa came with that bullshit talking, "I got something to tell you that's important." I was sitting there, smoking my ass off, she say, "Zee likes you. She told me to tell you that she like you." She paid Odessa thirty dollars to make sure that she told me that shit. She wanted to talk to me. She wanted to take me out and all that shit. Dessa started that bulldagging talk shit and I told Odessa to get the fuck out. "Take this, get the fuck out. Lock the door!"

So then, I used to gag Zee. One day, Zee say, "Can I buy one cap from you?" I like "No shit." "Let me buy a rock for five dollars." I said, "Sure." I ran down the step and shit. She used to do shit that show me that she liked me. I wasn't with it, I didn't pick up on it. I was into making my own money.

Then one day Zee caught me around Johnson Street. She said, "Is this where we're gonna get high at?" I was like "Yeah." She was like "Where?" I said, "We go around Hamp's house. Hamp's at work." So we went around there, and she was like "Take that shit off." I say, "What?" She was like "I am tired of you fucking me around, bitch." "What's up?" Zee said, "You know we got it." I was like "Yeah, what's up?" She said, "Like, come on." She was like "Take that shit off." I was like dag, this bitch wants me to undress. I mean, I had fun with her, though. That shit like threw me off, but I likeded her. I thought she was cute. I really did like her, you know. Took that shit off.

So I define myself as a lezzie. I ain't had dick in so long. I don't think I'll go back and have a relationship with a man at this point. I like being a lezzie.

I see myself as a gay person. I take being gay as people in a world of their own. The kind of life that they want to lead just because they're not dealing with a sexual partner of the opposite sex. Doesn't make the next person no better. The gay lifestyle is different. Because you know what, I notice that a relationship between two guys usually is sometimes better than the relationship between a man and woman. Just like I say, me and Zee relationship, I think it's better than a whole lot of our friends around the way that's straight up. Shit, like I watch them bitches walking around with black eyes and, I am saying, it's also a little harder to get out of these kind of relationships also. It is. You don't just drop motherfucker like hot potatoes. You know what I mean? Especially when you really start to like them.

So being gay means being sexually involved in a relationship with someone of your own sex and being separated from the rest of the world. 'Cause we do lead a whole different life. Even though we are the same, we still lead a whole different life from them.

I think I'm gay because all my relationships with men is not what I expected. What I expect from a man is all the thing that she do. And it's not always about sex. You know what I mean? She spend a lot of time with me. And I'm saying, I actually want to be with her. I mean, I'm telling you, the relationship that I had with J.T. for five years, me and this pussy we didn't hardly do shit. I never wanted to go nowhere with him. I didn't want him to go nowhere with me. I mean, we go our own separate roads. Fuck that.

Some people look at gay people like dirt. You know what I mean? You might walk down the street, you might hear a person say something like "Ah, go 'head, you faggot," or "Go 'head, you dike." I mean, you be like "What the fuck that got to do with anything?" I never understood that, why people do shit like that. I am saying, when I was coming up, I never did that. Even when I was downtown. I am saying, I used to work around there with the drag queens and shit and I never would call them faggots and shit. If they wanted to be transformers or transvestites, fine with me. And I called them just what the fuck they want to be called. Soho, Diana, whatever. Ain't no sweat off my back.

Drug users say, "The hell with it." They don't care if you're gay. You can be whatever you want to be. They don't. They don't care. They want your money. They don't worry about that. As long as they bringing the money, they fine, they all right with them. They might actually speak to one of them faggots 'cause faggots spending a lot of money.

I didn't look up to anybody when I was younger. I didn't have any role models when I was a kid. The majority of my teachers I couldn't stand them. They were all nuns anyway. They were too strict, shit.

But when I was growing up I wanted to be an airplane stewardess when I grew up or either a lawyer or a doctor. I used to dream I lived in penthouses. I was rich. I owned a lot of cars. Had the best of everything. It's not too late for it now, though, but I'm saying. . . . When I was little I used to dream about getting away from my mother, getting out of her house. Dream that I struck it rich or found me somebody and they took care of me. That was my favorite dream. Shit, I have dreams now, me and Zee gonna be living in a penthouse. I even used to dream that one day I be one of them scientist. I used to have dreams like that. And I would discover something and become rich. I wanted to be a comfortable rich person and live a quiet life. I'd probably been a doctor or lawyer. I would finish school, finished college, and got my degrees and everything. I'd work for it. My mom tried to stick business on me and all that old bullshit. I had to work at it, baby. I know it takes a lot of work. I'm saying, in the dreams I didn't just become rich like snap my fingers. In the dream I became rich 'cause I was a drug dealer, or found some money, had money, and I came into money like that, you know, like the snap of my finger.

I got here by living the fast life. I got here 'cause my mother, by her being so strict, I never had a chance to really experience hardly anything, and it's like all the shit she talked and all the rules, regulations she was putting down, I was saying, I have to get the fuck away from here, and get away from her. I'm saying, once I got here I wanted to see what the fast life was, you know. I got all wrapped up in it. I'm unraveling myself.

Oh, I want to get out. I'm gonna get out. Trust me, I'm gonna get out. No one can understand, because all the people in my block only had one or two, three sisters, but I had a whole fucking heap mountain. We were like the old lady in the shoe. My mom had more kids than anybody on the block. The biggest house on the block. I grew up in a poor family. Very. But then again, in a way I didn't. 'Cause my brother and them had cars and all that shit. You know what I mean? I can't say we were really poor. I say we were all right. Comfortable. You know. It was a hard life growing up with all them fucking brothers and sisters and shit. My mother was too abusive. I handled it by running away. That's just what I did, ran right away from it.

I learned how to survive in the streets and what the fuck to expect sometimes. I learned a lot out here. It ain't like I just jumped out here and didn't take heed, and nothing going on, or paid no attention thing. I paid plenty attention. Plenty! I know a lot of my friends that tried to do this shit, come out in the fast world, won't make it.

My life was like two-hands, unbalanced, like a scale. Because I'm saying, you know, as I was coming up, I had dreams and expectations of myself, and things that I wanted to get together and put into perspective, but then I had this fast turn somewhere, and it was just like you got to experience things in life first to know anything about it. Being in the know. You know, nobody is just gonna tell me they go through life and never experience things. Everybody experiences shit every day in life, and it's about living, and how to deal and cope with certain things, you know. And I'm saying, I had to learn all that shit on my own. I learn all that on my own. 'Cause my mother was too busy working and too busy trying to watch the pussy and all that shit. And I just started giving it the fuck away. I ain't gonna never try to watch my daughter's pussy 'cause I'm gonna watch my own. Do what the fuck you want to do with it. You know what I mean? You want to give it away, give it away. It's yours.

But my life ain't all that great, but it's not all that devastating either. You know what I mean? 'Cause I done seen people in worse predicaments, you know. I see people who walk the streets. I say, you know, we live in an abandon house. "God forbid!" We don't have to be dirty. We got plenty of family to go and wash. We do this by choice, not by force. I hope, but I know, I'm gonna get this shit together.

I don't think Zee is gonna stay clean this time 'cause she done already relapsed three time. I was upset, you know, and I told her that. I was like "Shoot." We both had money one night. I was like "I'll be back. I got to go to the bathroom." I went to the bathroom and when I came back she done spent some money and got high. I was like "I'm not giving up my money this evening. Come on. You're going in the house. I'm going in the house." Fuck that! I'm saying I went in the house with my duds. I just don't want to get high no more.

The people I hung out with liked money, like me. They liked to get high. They liked to have fun. And in my term of fun, meaning like, you know, we go out and fuck with people. Yeah, I'm saying we rob somebody. You know what I mean? Me and my girlfriend snatch this lady's pocketbook, and she didn't have a dime in it. But she was screaming and hollering, so it was fun. Seeing this bitch get all hysterical. And girlfriend was freaking out too. You thought she had a million dollars in it.

Lauren was a friend of mines. We used to do the same. We used to go hang out, pick fights with people. I'm saying, I mean now, since I've gotten older, I think that wouldn't be too smart now. Nobody goes around just picking fights, but for a kid at the age of twelve and thirteen, it was something different. I guess it was part of a kid, just being bad.

So my mother pushed me out because she had all those fucking demands and stuff. Plus she beat me so much. I used to try to run away all the time. So when I used to run away I was on my own. And when you're in the street, you're on your own, you do what you want to do. You know, even if it's wrong or it's right, but as a child, you think you're doing what's good for your own benefit even though some kids don't know everything. You know, I got myself into a lot of trouble, 'cause I started stealing, but it was fun. You know, going into a store and seeing how much shit I could come out with. If I got caught, fuck it, you know, because she just have to come and get me.

I didn't pick the kinds of people who were in school, who were making good grades and who wanted to be doctors and lawyers, 'cause those weren't the kinds of people that lived in my neighborhood. I made friends where I lived at. The people I went to school with, they were long-distance . . . they were long-distance friends. I went to school all the way out at Eighth and Gregg Streets. I went to Immaculate Heart. You know what I mean? I'm living on Fifteenth Street. Wasn't time to go up Seventh Street and hang out with the dagoes. I mean, I went to school with all white people. So I'm saying, where I grew up at, everybody here is black. I'm right there with my own group of people, and they were the friends in the neighborhood that I met, and that's what they were into.

All the kids in the neighborhood was bad. Every kid on my block was bad, all the kids where I grew up was bad. We used to break people windows. You know, when kids hang out with kids like that, eventually they go with that flow. It was a lot of peer pressure.

I finally came to be on my own 'cause I got tired of my mother's shit. You know. That was when I was fifteen. I stayed with her until after I had my baby when I was sixteen. I had my baby when I was sixteen. Okay. I finished ninth grade, and they kick me out of Immaculate Heart, and then I went over to Hardwick for a year. So I went to Immaculate Heart, and I was an honor student there, good grades. I went to Hardwick.

I got kicked out for fighting. I tried to stab this girl. Somebody else was fighting, right, and then, when the fight was over, we all went to the principal's office, and the principal was trying to tell me. . . . The girl I was trying to stab wasn't the girl she was talking about, though. The girl that was fighting my girlfriend, Sharice, she wasn't the girl that I was fighting. The girl that my girlfriend was fighting, my girlfriend tried to stick her, but they were trying to say that we tried to jump her too. She's got a fingernail file in my locker, and she was telling me that's what I tried to puncture this girl with. So I told her, "Look, just give me my keys. Give me my fingernail file." She told me that I was out, I was expelled, and don't never come back. And my mother was too through. My mother was like "Shit, they might as well promote you to the next grade." My mom spent fifteen hundred dollars for me to go to school every year. So they kick my old ass out of there.

I went to public school for a year and was an A honor there. I had my baby when school was out in June. And after that I went back. I finished school. My mother still paid for my tuition. You can only go back to Catholic school . . . if they kick you out, you have to be out for a year, and then you can go back to another Catholic school or that one. And I went back to Immaculate Heart and I finished eleventh and twelfth and graduated, but I'm saying even though I didn't live at home with my mother I still went to school. I was living with friends, people I met.

I left my mother's after I had my baby. I stayed with my mother's sister down in South Jefferson for about seven months. I stayed with my Aunt Yvonne for seven months, and then I moved 'round the corner to my other cousin. I stayed with her for about six months. Oh, I used to leave every morning and go to school. I wore long uniform blouses, own socks, own shoes, own cap, school shoes, because I was hustling and making money.

I started hustling after I had my baby. I started prostituting. I would go up to High and Pendleton, Metro Center, the conventions at the hotels, to prostitute. I started making so much money I was able to save, and that when I got into the reefer thing. I started smoking reefer. I got me a package, make plenty of money. When I was up there, I sold so much weed, I made a profit of three thousand dollars. I'm saying that this was without fucking with my flip money. Like when I flipped what I had left over, I might take out a hundred and use it as far as my school dress. 'Cause I'm saying, you know, I would have to pay them to eat, 'cause, I mean, that's my family. I would still contribute.

I finally got me an apartment downtown, Metro Center. I was in Metro Center for about nine months until I got busted for selling drugs. I was seventeen by that time. And you know what? I ain't never had no gynecological problems. Oh, baby, please! My shit was. . . . I never need the fire department. My shit don't never be burning.

I've never went back home. I refused. It's my pride. I'm saying all my brother and sisters, they are all grown. My sister is getting a divorce now, and my brother is getting a divorce, and this one is fighting with his old lady, and they pack up they shit and come right back to Mom's. I refuse to go back and live with my mother. I couldn't stand it.

When I was living with my aunt and cousins down in South Jefferson I was my own boss. I was hanging out with my cousins and their friends. They were into smoking reefer. That was they thing. I made plenty of money off of them and they friends. I lived there for eleven months and they knew I was selling weed. Nobody made accusation 'cause my aunt used to ask me like "Where you go at night?" "Ah, I go stay with my girlfriend." I wouldn't get mad with her because she would ask me, but she wouldn't tell me shit like "Oh, it's ten or eleven o'clock, you can't go out."

So she wasn't as strict as my mother was. Know why? Because I always got up to go to school every morning. That's all she used to tell me. She say, "As long as you still at school and as long as you still get good grades in school, I have no problem with nothing that you do."

So I hung out with my cousins and sold weed to them and their friends. I really didn't know nobody down there and so what I used to do is sit outside on the step or sit over in the playground. And, you know, they be like telling their friends, "You know, my cousin got some nice drugs." My cousins would tell their friends that I got something nice. "Come try it out." 'Cause everybody used to be into that real big at one time, smoking a lot of weed. I didn't start selling drugs until I seen how much money was involved in it when I got down there.

I got into prostitution by being involved with my girlfriend, this girl name Camille. They call her Sweets, though. And one day I was downtown, and she was up there on High and Eleventh, Eleventh and Cook, no, between Eleventh and . . . High and Mill, that's Cook Street. And I seen her stand on the corner, and I'm like "Bitch, what you doing down here?" She said, "Shit, I'm making me some motherfucking money!" I like "Yeah?" This bitch had a pocket full of money. I like "It's that good down here?" Well, that's when Metro Center used to have money. I mean, it ain't shit down there now. Done clean that shit up, boy, but it used to be money down there galore! So I was like "Yeah, bitch, I'm gonna come out here with you. That shit look all right to me." So the next week I went out with her, and we pulled up! When I first started out I was making . . . pulling at least five hundred dollars a night! Yeah, on a good night I would make five hundred dollars, at least, or maybe more. The money was good, shit.

After that with Sweets, I met J.T. That's the guy I dealt with for five years, and he was into selling weed also. I met J.T. up on Eleventh and . . . up at the Eight Ball, 'cross from the Municipal Building. Yeah, it's a gay bar. He wasn't gay. I'm saying straight people and gay people used to go in there, and he used to sell weed in there.

Oh, I didn't have any weed. I was trying to get a package, and I went up on Southbourne, but I couldn't find any of my friends that I always buy my package from, right? And it just so happened that I knew somebody up there that knew him. I was like "Man, I need me a package. I can't make no money right now, 'cause I ain't got no more weed." "Hey, like my boy J.T. sell weed, maybe he can hook you up with who he be getting from." So I be like "Well, introduce me to this prick." So, you know, my friend introduce me to him and shit. . . . I mean he was like. . . . I think I had like two bags of my own shit left that I wouldn't sell. So you know, therefore, I had a little bit of my own personal that I could blow, but I always had my package money. And I didn't like sitting there in that bar, right?

So he was like "How much are you trying to spend?" I was getting kind of suspicious of him. I didn't want to tell this prick that I had fifteen hundred dollars in my pocket to blow on a package. He was a small-time seller, you know what I mean? He was spending like seven or eight hundred dollars. He was only getting a pound. I had moved up to about two pound and a quarter. I was safe. So he was like "Fifteen hundred dollars?" He said, "How much were you trying to get?" I said, "I was at least trying to get me two pounds of weed." He said, "My boy might charge you seven hundred dollars for each pound." I was like "Yo, I could cover it." I said, "Like I got the money. I can pay for it out of my own pocket." He was like "You kidding? You ain't got that kind of money." He said, "You're like a kid." I said, "Look, brother. I wouldn't have wasted your time. I ain't got to bullshit you. Right now I'm trying to get back to my books, and I ain't got no business up here. Can you help me?" He was like "Yeah. But you gonna have to wait for 'bout an hour. So I'll call for you." I said, "All right."

So I sat at the bar with him, and like I said he sold weed, so he was like "Care for a drink?" I said, "Naw, I got weed." He said, "Well, if you got weed, then why stand here and try to buy weed?" I was like " 'Cause I got my personal." I said, "I don't have no weed for sell." So I sat there and I smoke some of my weed, and he was like "Can I smoke some of this?" I was like "Yeah, all right, here." So we sat there and got high together and shit, right? Then it was time to take care of business. But, see, I never got so high where I couldn't conduct my business. If I got like that, I wouldn't sell no more. You know what I mean? So eventually we did go. His boy hooked me up. He got the two pounds for me. He charged me sixteen hundred dollars for it. I had to go into my own money and add another hundred to it. I got the weed and shit. I gave the brother forty dollars, and like I appreciated it. I stepped off, you know what I mean?

Yeah, I gave him forty dollars for being nice enough to take me. I'm saying, that's what really fucked him up. He was like "This old bitch. She's into the money." You know what I mean? He older than me, and that was his thing, selling weed.

I just got into a cab. I was so paranoid. I got in a cab. Had the cab take me all the way back down to Twenty-eighth and Lenape. I got out. Got me some reefer bags down there. Bagged up my shit, sold 'bout half of a pound, put some money back in my pocket. Got myself prepared for the night, laid my clothes out, and then I hit the books. You know what I mean? I stayed hitting the books so that I could stay on top of my grades and shit. 'Cause they see that I was lacking, then that would have made my aunt suspicious.

I wasn't sexually involved with J.T. right at the beginning. He likeded me. But then I think in the beginning he sort of likeded my money more 'cause I had a little more than him. And then, like I say, I was younger than him. I was seventeen. J.T. was about twenty-seven, about twenty-eight. J.T. 'bout like almost ten years older than me. I say about six months later I became sexually involved with him.

I didn't want his help financially in the beginning. 'Cause I had my own. I was like buying my way into everything, you know what I mean? 'Cause then if I wanted them to get the fuck away from me, I would be like "Here, take this. I'll be right back." And step off. That type of shit. Or I would tell them, "Here, take this and I see you later. Bye!" He said, "Yeah, you cold bitch. You come into money and you just act so snobbish, so stuck up, so conceited." It's not that. It's just that's a way to manipulate some mother-fucker that want to be manipulated. So I used to sort of buy, used to buy motherfuckers, you know what I mean? I used to even buy head from men and shit like that. Buy blow jobs from men. Blow job, baby, let them suck the pussy. 'Cause a lot of them would be like "Baby, I don't do that. I. . . ." "You like this money, baby? You do that now, don't you?" "Yeah, come on."

So six months after I met him I got sexually involved and by that time I had moved downtown. I'd say maybe about a month later I let him move in. I started to really like him. But he still didn't make more money than me, and I don't know why I was liking him because, as much as I like money, I ain't got no business liking nobody that ain't got no more than me. When I was living with J.T., I was just doing weed, and clothes shopping.

Yeah, I really did like the poppy-eyed bastard. My mother couldn't stand him, though. Didn't see much of my family after he moved in either. I stayed away from them motherfuckers. 'Cause then they knew I was making money, and they all been handling me. I was like "Shit," then my mother would have got curious. "Where you get all this money from?" I couldn't go up there and show my mom fifteen hundred dollars. She'd hit the ceiling.

How did she feel about me living on my own? She was mad at me. She was like "You want to be grown? You grown. You had a baby." I said, "Okay, fine, see you." But you know what I used to do? I used to get money, put it in an envelope, and sign her name on it and slide it under the door and leave. I wouldn't go up and visit face to face. No! But I sent her a brand new refrigerator. It cost me eight hundred and fifty dollars. Matter of fact, it's the same one she has in her house right now. There are a lot of things I do for my mother that I don't tell her. And I think sometimes she wants to know whether or not it really came from my heart, whether or not if I did it for her. But I won't tell her. I won't give her the satisfaction. Know what I mean?

I'm living in an abandon condominium, an abandominium, right now. I've been living there since the middle of April, something like that. I've been knowing the place was there. I lived around there all my life. That house been abandon for years, honey. Because we used to go in there and get high. It is a house, only room in there clean is our room. You got a back shack where the kitchen and stuff was at. Yeah, so it's only two rooms downstairs and two room upstairs. Just me and Zee and the dog in there. It's in good shape. All it needs is a little cleaning. The place is mines. It's mines.

At one time I wasn't too comfortable living there, but I'm saying I feel safe in there, and when Zee was gone, I stayed there for twenty-eight days while Zee was in the rehab.

My next door neighbor, he's from Third Street. He's a friend of Zee's. This guy's name is Russ. And he don't allow people to go in there, 'cause he don't want nobody to set his house on fire. He lives right next door to us. Or like he know when we're in there, because the wall are thin. You know, like you can hear. Know what I'm saying, somebody else can go in there, and he can hear voices and he know it's not me and Zee, he come out of his house and tell them to get the fuck out. He call the cops. We don't have a lock on the door or anything like that. We've thought about it, but don't nobody really come down there.

Before I moved there, I lived at five-sixty-three South Fourteenth Street in an apartment house. We were staying there with this guy, with Wesley, until Zee tried to steal his money. We stayed with him almost two months. Before then we had an apartment on . . . what is it? thirteen-thirty-four Hubbard Street. I been like homeless twice in the last two years. On those two occasions I was living at thirteen-thirty-four Hubbard. This guy we used to know, we used to go there and get high in his house, name Brother Man. He just packed up and left. He got in some kind of trouble and he left. Shit, I was homeless for a whole year when we stayed at Brother Man. But like I'm saying, his house was still kind of livable. And then the Jamaicans moved into his house and started selling out of it. And they tried to destroy it. But other than that, the house was fine. It was in good shape. They ripped all the pipe and shit out of it, but it was no problem of getting no water nowhere and wash our ass. It was no abandominium. It was somebody's house. They just left it, and we moved the fuck in it. So I stayed there for awhile and in the house across the street. And matter of fact it was a nice three-story house until that boy was killed in there.

In the place we're in now, we don't have no water or electricity. At night I got a flashlight and candles, baby. That's right. And my flashlight got Energizers in them to make sure they don't die. We cook at other people's houses. People that are real friends, that's willing to help us. You know. We wash and bathe at other people's houses. We take a wash. I keep my room clean. I don't take no food shit up in there. So we don't have no rats. I don't take no food up in there. I do all my eating outside. The only type of food I take up in there is cans. Can food.

We sleep on a bed. We been had a bed, 'cause I tell you we had an apartment once. We used to live on the third floor on Thirteenth and Hubbard. We got our own furniture and everything. Me, I'm not sleeping on no mother-fucking floor. Shit. There are chairs in there. Couch set, two-piece set, a table.

I've never lived in a shelter. Some people say some of them ain't shit. They put up with a lot of bullshit. You know what I mean? Then a lot of time some of the shelters don't feed them and all that old dumb shit. So I never took to consider that, because I look at it like this, if they treat you that fucking bad, I can do better than that on my own. You know what I mean? We eat well every day. I would rather go to an abandominium than go to a shelter 'cause I still get my money, I still make money, and not put up with they shit. I can't sleep in no room with no hundred people. All clammed up. Fuck that! I got to have my own bed, my own space, and live with who the fuck I want to live with, not who they tell me I'm stuck with. Naw.

So when I leave the place during the day I pack my shit up, and leave my shit in a nice pack, neat, clean clothes on one side, dirty clothes on. . . . I pull my door shut and I leaves it. I don't worry about people coming in there while we're gone. I better not catch somebody up in there, fucking with my bags. I am safe. Me and my blade and my screwdriver. I feel real safe.

In the winter, I got Zee to keep me warm. We got blankets. Shit, we got about eight blankets. During the daytime we come out of there and at night we gets in the bed. When we smoking the pipe sometime we didn't go to bed.

I think I found my ideal partner. Zee. 'Cause you know, with all the men that I've been involved with . . . I'm not saying that men don't know how to treat you. Some men don't know how to treat a woman, and really respect them. With Zee, Zee don't fight me. She give me money every week. We argue, but she don't fight me. If Zee fights me, trust me, I must have done, what I'm saying, as long as I've know her for the two years, Zee has only hit me two times in two years. I likes Zee. She gives me my way, but if she feel as though my way is just not right, she makes me listen to what she got to say. A lot of time, I be telling her, "I don't need that shit." She go, "But you gonna listen, now." You know, she gets very demanding, and she put her foot down at times, you know. And she's sweet, and she shows me all the affection that I like to be shown to. You know, she has no shame of being with me, and I have no shame with being with her, and I know she loves me. Most of all I know she loves me. And, trust me, I loves the ground she walks on. She's my baby.

I stopped prostituting when I met Zee. She wasn't with it. She wasn't with it. A lot of men, they meet girls like that, and they just want them to go out there and sell they ass. I mean that. . . . Or they want them to keep doing it, or whatever. I met Zee and Zee was like "You're gonna be my woman, baby, you can't do that shit. That shit got to stop."

So my ideal person is someone who can show a real man how to treat a woman. She's supportive, affectionate, and very understanding. Caring, and all that good shit. I'm the femme, honey. I am the woman. That I'm the lesbian. And I cook and I do the deal. You got it! I do all the things that a woman's supposed to do to take care of a man. I feeds her. I pampers her. I shows her affection at times, and we do things together. We actually go places and do things. Even crime! Yeah, we do everything together. And I'm saying, you know, she'll stay home, like when we're living on Fourteenth and Roberts, I used to get up and go shopping. I go shopping for her wardrobe. I go buy me new stuff. I buy her new stuff. I pick out her clothes.

I was with J.T. for five years, and I didn't cook for the bitch. Not one time. I don't know why. I just wasn't with it with him. I would do laundry 'cause I needed clean clothes. You know what I mean? But I was making all the fucking money. I don't know what role I would play if I was in a heterosexual relationship. You know why? Because I'm saying I've dealt with a man, and I just can't take that bullshit. All that fighting and shit. Because I'm very aggressive. I'm very bossy. I'm very stubborn, but I'm unique. "Fuck what you heard." Shit. I like having my motherfucking way a lot of time, and Zee gives it to me. Zee lets me have just the way the fuck I want it. I have no real complaints. If I was in a relationship with a man, then it would be too confrontational. We would be fighting all the time for power and control. That's what J.T. used to tell me.

This pussy used to try to catch me doing shit, and I'm saying, eventually he did catch me on the stroll, on the whore stroll, downtown. We were at that bookstore on Eleventh and Cook, the Taurus. And I was in there. I was in this booth with this guy, but we were just getting high. We were smoking reefer and I wasn't ready to go to work. I was getting ready to get out there and I asked him to pick up a hundred dollars for my boss. Well, let me tell you. This bitch, I don't know how long he must have been watching me or whatever, but he came in the bookstore and he said, "Have you seen. . . ." And the guy who was working name Farmer, he was like "Is Laquita in there?" I'm saying to myself, "Well, who wants her?" So Glenn say, "Naw, she ain't here." He say, "You better come out of that booth," blasé, blasé, right? So we didn't come right out, but we sitting there eating and watching dirty porno flick, and shit, right? When we did come out, all this smoke came out. It was kind of dark out, and I said, "Oh, my God." I mean, I was fucked up too from smoking weed. I was fucked up, but when I seen this pussy it sort of like blew the whole high. I went outside and like I talked to him. I had a pocketbook full of rubbers. I was getting ready to make a killing. It was Friday night.

So I got outside, pussy was like "Got some money?" That's the first time he ever took. . . . See, Zee won't take nothing from me, 'cause I give it to her. She can have anything I've got. Let me tell you, baby. We got outside, this pussy was like "Oh, bitch, you wasn't gonna come and see me. You just gonna go on by your business, and you right downtown?" Blasé, blasé. I was like I was speechless. I was all fucked up anyway. This pussy . . . I went to break from him, and he was dead on my ass. He was like "You got any money? Is that the way you want to be treated, like a 'ho bitch." He said, "You got any money, bitch?" I was like "Yeah, I got money." I started getting smart. I like "Shit, I take care of my motherfucking self. You don't do nothing for me. I don't owe you shit." But then I forgot, he really assumed that I became his woman. I mean, we had been dealing for awhile now. So this pussy hit me. I started crying.

He bought a new piece for his bike with my money. I was . . . I ain't give a fuck, 'cause I still had money. That was just extra money I was making. You know what I'm saying? It wasn't all the money I was making. It was making me look bigger than him 'cause I still had more money than him. I had money home. So after that he took me home, and he was like "Why do you always be trying to outslick me, be trying to outthink me?" See, that's a part of that power game, 'cause he's a Leo.

He was always trying to sneak around and catch me doing shit. Until one day I had the upper hand on this bitch. 'Cause, like I'm telling you, he would know shit about me. Shit that I done done, and I wouldn't know he knew it, but he would question me and try to pump me. I be like "Yeah," blasé, blasé, but he would know already. And this one particular time when I was smoking a pipe, pussy came up Thirteenth Street. I used to be around Hurricane's getting high, and he used to come up there and look for me, and at first he would see me, and I wouldn't see him. But then I got my friends and introduced them to him, so if they seen him they come back and say "Quita, J.T. outside, he's around the corner." So then he couldn't find me no more, 'cause then I would know when he was outside.

Oh, I learned a lot from him. Yeah, he was twenty-seven. Old-ass motherfucker. I'm saying, he got me when I was seventeen. So I'm saying, he started dealing with me, he was like molding me. But he couldn't mold me. That was the thing that was all fucked up about it. 'Cause I was doing everything opposite. But I learned how to take a person, another person's mind and reverse it. He would sit down and talk to me, and tell me things about myself that he just sit back and watched me. I might be two blocks away from him or something and he sitting and he just watching me. Nigger told me, "Yeah, I saw you talking to so and so" or "I heard a conversation you were having." It was like that day when I was at that bookstore. See, he heard me, but I didn't know he was out there. He didn't let hisself be known right away. Instead, he stand around, he hung around, he listened. He was just paying attention.

And I learned about fast money from him too. But I'm saying, I hustled, because a lot of his people he was dealing and selling weed to, I took all his customers. I took his customers when I first started coming up here 'cause my shit was better than his. 'Cause, see, I only got that weed from his people that one time, but then I started just buying from people who I usually buy. But I'm saying, what he got me wasn't bad, but it wasn't as good as the shit I had in my purse, in my pocket.

He was the first person I had a relationship with. A real man. I was kind of young and dumb and all wet behind the ear and didn't know no better. I was attracted to his voice. He had a sexy deep voice. He's a ugly motherfucker, though. No, he ain't ugly, he just got big eyes. He was charming and he was sweet. But that's a little fucking front. The first time that bitch put his motherfucking hand on me, boy, he showing the real truth, black ass.

Let me tell you about this pussy. It be times when I might get mad with this motherfucker and he be trying to fuck me. It was one time when I didn't want to fuck this bitch, but he made me fuck him. I was highly upset. He forced me to have sex. Yeah, he was like "Oh, you're not gonna give me no pussy, bitch?" He said, "I'm your man. You live here with me, I live here with you, and you gonna tell me that you ain't gonna fuck with me when I want to be fucked?" I said, "I ain't giving you shit." I was laying in the bed. Pussy rolled me over and cocked my legs open. I was saying, we were wrestling and everything, but he got the pussy. He got the pussy. He was strong enough to get it. I was madder than a motherfucker, though. I cried. I cried.

I remember the bitch ran my head into the fucking door before we had moved from downtown. I'm telling you. I hit this bitch with a board, with a stick, with a board. I don't know how it all happened. We're talking 'bout some old, ancient history shit, and he was trying to make me sit down and tell about it and all this shit. Yeah, I say, "I don't have time to talk about that shit," blasé, blasé, this and that. And he was like "See, that's what wrong with our relationship." 'Cause he say, it's a lack of communication, and this and that, and all this other shit. So I said, "A lack of communication. It's a lack of everything, a lack of trust, a lack of love, a lack of you, a lack of me too." So he said, "What is all that supposed to mean?" I said, "Just like you said, a lack of communication. I don't want to tell you shit. I don't want to know shit about you." So we got to arguing, and then the pussy slap me, and that was it. I hauled off, and I slap the fuck out of him. And we just start going at it.

I lived with him for three years. So I had a relationship with a man for three years and all that bullshit. He got locked up for drugs. I'm saying, I could have kept the apartment, but I didn't want it. I told his sister, "Come and get this shit." I'm saying I paid seven hundred and fifty dollars for a pecan bed. You know what I mean? Like I bought the color television, the VCR, the stereo. I didn't want any of that shit. I had so much money I didn't want it. He didn't stay in prison. They kept him for about a month. He went and stayed with his sister. I'm saying, I used to go and see him. Then he started staying at the shelter on Winter, right, and then his business went down and everything, and I was still making money, so . . . uh. Yeah, we were still friends. That was it. And then this pussy wrote me this letter. Fifteen pages long, talking about how he loved me and how he needed me, and I don't leave him, and this and that. And I just wasn't with it.

When he was in jail for that month I stayed at the apartment until his sister moved all that shit out there. I was still prostituting and selling weed. Yeah. Shit! I was a survivor, baby.

There was a lack of communication in the relationship. If you don't sit down and talk and discuss your problems, it won't work. You have to communicate. That what love is. I think love is based on trust and communication. Without that you ain't got shit. You know what I mean? Everybody has problems in a relationship. If you can't sit down and talk about them instead of gonna fist fight. . . .

With Zee, I'm what's wrong with our relationship. Me! I guess by being so bossy. I mean she just let me have my little way just to keep the fuss down. I whine a lot. She say, "Ah, Laquita, baby, please." "Bitch, I don't want to hear that shit." But we share everything. Everything. Communication. Love.

I don't have no friends, but I don't like her be around nobody but me. The friends that I know in the street, I say, "How y'all doing" and I keep stepping. No real friends. I say, she got some bulldagging butch friends. She sees bulldagging-ass Bev every day. Bev come round there, "Zee, Zee." But the bitch, she get so upset. I think a lot of them motherfuckers she be with, they be egging her, to get her high. 'Cause I'm saying, Zee went away and got herself together a little bit and everything. Even though she is still into crime and stuff and shit. We both are. That bitch Bev, we fed her all day yesterday, the day before. I'm saying, these motherfuckers ain't got no job, and Zee wants to get a job.

We argue about who's gonna pick out the clean clothes for today and who's gonna go to the store, and shit like that. I be telling her, "I'm not going to the store." She be saying, "Yes, you are." I be like "I don't wanna go to the store." She like "You going." Little dumb shit.

When we were smoking the pipe we used to argue hard. That bitch used take a hit. One time she took a hit, and blew all this smoke. Then she looked around the room, and she made the fucking room so smoky. All the smoke she blew at one time. Bitch looked around and threw our shit out the window. Threw our clothes and shit out the window. She thought she was on fire. Geeking. That bitch flaked out on me. Boy, I was mad as a motherfucker.

We've gotten into physical fights. She got two gashes over her eye, and a split in her fucking face from thirteen stitches, and gash on her knee. We were getting high . . . that time we were living in that house that boy got kilt in, and the bitch stepped off for a long time. I didn't know where the fuck she was at and I was getting worried and I was scared. Yeah, I was scared and I was all by myself. I thought something had happened. Bitch came back. When she came in the door, and I touch that bitch in the face like this and just punched her in the eye. I mean, I had turned her face around just so I could sock this bitch. Bitch eye split open and I took her to the hospital.

That wasn't the most serious. The most serious one was when I cracked her with the bottle 'cause the bitch came out of a abandon house with this guy. I don't know what the fuck she was doing. Whatever she was doing, she ain't have no business over there.

The bitch has hit me too. Hit me for whopping her ass. I caught her in this other abandon house waiting for Meatball and them to come back. Meatball. At least that's what we called him, anyway. I went right upstairs and seen that bitch sitting there. She . . . I said, "You bitch!" I tried to put her through they floor. They were living in a abandon house too, so that shit was weak. I beat the shit out of Zee.

Most of our fights centered around drugs. We fought about how we act after the drugs was gone. Or what kind of thoughts might be in each other head after that shit was gone.

We'd make up after the fight. She usually makes up. She'll say, "Can I talk to you?" I be like "No!" She be like "Why?" "'Cause I don't want to talk with you no more, Zee." She say, "Come on, baby. Please. Walk me in here and let's talk about it." I say, "Bitch, I don't want no more to do with you. Get away from me before I beat you up." I used to tell her shit like that. She used to say, "But I love you." I say, "Bitch, you don't love me. You love the pipe." She say, "No, baby, I love you. I might like the pipe, but I do love you."

We hardly argue no more. Since we both don't get high, we don't argue. When we get high, boy, we go through stages. Zee picks the fight, but I'll finish it. She makes me mad and I hit her. 'Cause she start that old geeking. She really geeks hard. She be looking all around and shit. I can't stand that when I get high. She get all spooked.

We both earn about the same amount of money. Yeah, 'cause we both be out to gag everybody. See, Zee don't con motherfuckers. See, I'm into conning. Zee don't know that. All Zee know how to do is just take a motherfucker's money. She just go straight up and get a robbery case.

I learned the con stuff from old heads. From old, old timers when I was between sixteen and seventeen. I met this old guy name Puddinghead. Him and his old lady, they were into con shit. And she used to go out and play the drag and stuff. The money bankroll shit. Motherfucker come on off the boat and all that kind shit. Yeah, and I learned to talk it, how to swindle, and tell motherfuckers shit that they want to hear. Like they tell you on the con game . . . "Excuse me, miss, could you tell me where this address is? I'm lost. I just came here from blasé, blasé and I don't know my way around too well."

Greed is what makes a motherfucker get suckered. They think they're working you and they so greedy out to get your money 'cause then you show them what they call a paper roll, which is nothing but a roll of stuffed paper with stuffed phony money, but real money over it. And then you do like this, and all they see is a knot. They don't know what's in between, but they see a knot. And you say, "Okay, I'm going to put my money in with your money," and they switch, and you get the dummy roll 'cause they done pull their money off the top. But, see, the thing about it is that there are two dummy rolls. They have two rolls, in the same kind of handkerchiefs. See, you'll put your money with they money in a dummy roll and they'll take the dummy, and they'll say you keep it close to your heart and then come out with the other one and say, "Here." And then you think you got your money and they money, and you go running down the street and you open it up and you ain't got nothing but paper.

I learned how to grab, how to pick pocket with a bell. You start out with a bell, baby shoe bell. If it rings you fucked up. You tie the bell to your finger and keep it steady, and you make the wrong kind of move the bell'll move— you'll hear it move—and it make that little ring.

I learned how to cheat at cards under the table from the old heads. All that type of shit. That's about it. But I'm telling you, I'm saying, the shit they used to tell me, boy, I was amazed how it used to work. And then I used to watch them do it. 'Cause one time I was sitting down playing with the old heads and we was playing tunk, and this motherfucker he won ten hands straight. And then I got onto the game, 'cause there were more cards to the deck than there should have been. You know what I saying? There's two and three aces popping up of the same colors. Then I was ready to knuck. I pulled out my knife. I told the pussy, "I'm gonna punch you in your motherfucking head." He said, "Look, sit down, bitch. This is part of your lessons." I said, "Okay."

They were teaching me. They were conning me, but they were teaching me and I learnt. I didn't punch that old head. He was like "These are lesson to be taught, young buck. Sit down. You want to still play?" I was like "Yeah, I want to still play." Then I started spiking cards out the deck. I won all four or five hands straight in a row. They say, "You learn well." I says, "Yeah. Give me my motherfucking money," 'cause we were playing tunk for ten dollars a hand.

Drugs bring out the cold bloody freak in me. Cocaine. Weed used to do it to me too, but that fucking crack . . . boy. After I smoke this shit I want to have sex. It makes my hormones, makes my organism get furious. I don't what the fuck be going on. Boy, that shit does a job on me and Zee. I don't know. I guess it's being high makes that shit pleasurable anyway by itself, but I don't know . . . it has a reaction on a lot of motherfucker who smoke that shit. Boy, they do shit they ain't never done before. It's guys that me and Zee done bought. You know, like "We both want some head. What's up?" It's guys that me and

Zee might ran into and be like they don't suck pussy. We be like "Shit, we got some money. What's up? We got some coke too, you can give us a blow job, brother." He be like "Okay." We give them some crack, and they do the job. You dig it. I give them a hit of real coke, and then I give them about three, four dummies. They think they got three, four caps of real coke, and then they'll do anything I want them to do. I was doing that shit when I first started smoking that shit. I just been smoking this shit for now about two years now.

Some women are very sexy, I think, but men are usually more sexually active. 'Cause if the wind blow, they dicks get hard. See, the wind ain't got nothing to blow on down there. See, we ain't got nothing. I saying, you just rub it and watch that bitch rise, you know what I mean. See, we don't get in heat like that. It take a little more 'motion than just a stroke on the head. You know what I mean?

I don't think men should have sex anytime they want it. Hell, no. No! No! Because if the other partner don't want to have it right then and there, I'm saying it not no fun. If you both don't want to do it, it ain't no good. You have to both want it. If it just one-sided, then the bitch don't want to give it to you or the nigger ain't trying to stroke you the right way, then fuck it. Leave that shit alone.

I think some kinds of sexual activities is perverted or unnatural. Like S and M, getting tied up and beaten, that's unnatural. Yeah. That shit is weird. I had a motherfucker make his girlfriend do that bookstore at Eleventh and Cook. They paid me one hundred and thirty dollars. He paid me sixty-five dollars to beat him with my shoe and she wanted to suck my pussy for about five or ten minute. I was like "That's all." She said, "I just want to see how tasty you are." I was like "Yeah." I had a pump shoe, and I took my shoe and I beat the shit out of that bitch, and Glenn closed the door, my friend that work there. Wasn't nobody in there then, and it was fortunate, and he let me use it. I beat the shit out of him with that shoe.

There have been sexual situations that have frightened me. We were in a car and I didn't know he had a gun. Then we got in the hotel and this pussy pulled this bitch out. I thought the pussy was going to shoot me and leave me there. Yeah, he got into the hotel, pussy came out the side of his motherfucking sweater. I was like "Oh, shit." He was like "Like, baby, don't worry about it." He was like "This is just protection for me." I was like "Yeah, you right about that." I'm saying, I bet he let me see it 'cause I might have been trying to rob him. You know what I mean? I might have robbed this bitch and he might have shot me for real.

My morning routine was like get up, stand on the corner seven, eight o'clock in the morning, burn somebody, get high all day long, all night long, stay up for days, until my body would actually tell me it's tired. Then I would go to sleep. When I got up, I still would be tired and my mouth would be like cotton. That fucked up ass taste. Morning breath. I don't know what the fuck it taste like. A mixture of everything between the cigarettes I done smoked and all the shit I done ate, and whee! I used to wake up wanting drugs. I used to. I used to wake up and need a hit. But I used to go to bed with shit. I would be so tired, I couldn't smoke all the drugs. So I would have drugs left over from the day before when I went to sleep. We would wake up and smoke it, and start my day all over.

Our afternoons would be excellent. We gag, burn motherfuckers all day long, all the suckers on lunch break. They come through trying to sneak and smoke 'fore they got to go back to work. And some of them would come out sneak and never get back to work. And have all they money. We sell dummies all afternoon. All night. On that same corner. I tell you they would come up and be like "I got them caps, brother." A lot of them would just come up, "You know where I can get them cap at?" "Right here, brother. How many you want?" Pull out my little pouch. When you gagging a motherfucker and they see that you got a big bag of that shit that makes them think you're legit'. They don't be too skeptical of you. "Oh, my God," they might say. "Give me six, seven, eight of them babies." "Yeah, I got that many. Yeah!"

In the afternoons, oh, I wouldn't have to try to gag them, they would come. They were sucker. They just come to the street and ask. If they come back, I say, "Sweetheart." A lot of them would come back and wouldn't even have the shit. Be like "Well, where's the caps at?" "I threw that shit away, 'cause that shit." "Threw them away? Man, you better go get them motherfuckers 'cause I got to show them to my boss. Shit, I can't give you no money back. Maybe somebody switched them on him. Maybe gave somebody a package and they took them back and they put the wack on him. I don't know, but I can't give you back no money 'cause that's somebody else's money. I don't give a fuck how you feel."

I lied to my family to get drugs. Told them shit like "I got cleaning. I'm hungry. Give me some money." Well, sometimes I don't lie to them. Sometimes I say, "I'm broke, I need some money." They be like "How much money you want?" "Give me twenty dollars." They say, "What?" "Ah, just give me ten dollars, shit."

Since I've been using drugs I drew myself even further away from them. It used to be one time when I see them motherfuckers on the street, and they were asking me for money, they be like "I ain't hardly got no money. Can I get a few dollars?" I be like "Here." Now, I don't ask them for shit. I don't ask them for nothing, and when I see them on the street, especially when I was looking real bad, half the time I didn't want to even speak to them. I would still wave. I be like "How y'all doing?" and keep 'bout my business.

My mother would be like "You're on that shit." I be like, I be denying it, "I ain't on that shit. You can't be listening to those people up there. They're lying. Them people don't know nothing about me." She be saying, "Motherfuckers see you." I mean, I don't give a fuck what they see. I tell her, "Who do you believe, them or me?" She said, "I know you, you're my child, and I know they ain't lying." I've never conned or scammed her out of any money, though. If anything, I was giving her money.

Our relationship got worse because I'm saying she was . . . she got that feeling, I guess within inside herself, like "Bitch just gonna turn out to be a bum." 'Cause I tell you she used to tell me that shit a lot. "Ain't gonna be no good. You gonna be nothing but a bum." All this old bullshit. And then when she found out that I was had gotten deeper into drugs, she was like "Look at you. I told you wasn't gonna be shit. I don't want to bother with you. Get away from me. Leave me alone." I wouldn't even sit in her room. She be like "If you come in here with your shit, I don't want to hear. I heard about you." I be like "I don't want to hear that shit neither." We used to get into a lot of fights.

She'll let me stay over at the house though. Feed me and everything. I just don't. . . . I tell her shit like "I be back for dinner." Quianna say, "You always say that, Mom, but you don't never come back to eat dinner with me." 'Cause, see, I always took Quianna out to eat too. I had money. I be like "Did you eat dinner yet?" My mom and them might be saying, "No, I'm getting ready to feed her." I say, "Okay, we going to dinner right now. Get your stuff, let's get dressed. Let's get your book. Let's roll."

I copped at Fourteenth Street, Eleventh and Binnell, and the project, Saigon, at Eleventh and Herbert. When I'm copping, I go up to him, I be like "You got something?" They be like "Yeah, you got it." "What you got, dimes or nicks?" Then they say, "Nicks." Some people are just selling dimes now, you know. You say, "Let me see them." They show you what they got. Look at it. If you know anything about drugs, you know what you're looking at, what you buying. You purchase and you leave. No negotiation 'cause each cap is five or ten dollars a whop.

It all depends on how bad the coke is. Like when there is a drought, you couldn't get no nice caps. Everything was like comeback, with cut. Everybody was selling a whole lot of that horseshit. So then people were saving their money, people wouldn't even get high. There was nothing worth buying.

But I ain't never gotten no dummies though. Naw, ain't nobody gag me. I know who to buy from. Fuck that! Fuck no! Motherfucker ain't gonna burn me. I wouldn't know how to accept it. Fuck no. Taking all the money that I take, let a motherfucker take something from me, I wouldn't know how to accept it.

How did I begin using drugs? Because I ran with somebody that was smoking a pipe and they was like "You want to try it?" I was like "Yeah." The first time I hit I smoked five hundred dollars' worth of shit by myself. I was sick as a dog. I got this thing for five hundred by this Spanish guy, Alfredo Cruz or some shit, on High and Monticello. He was all drunk. He was lucky I didn't take his car. Didn't know how to drive then. We went to the Waverly Hotel. He wanted to fuck and eat pussy. Pussy told me he would give me a hundred dollars. But he had more than five hundred 'cause he paid for the room and everything. I went in his pockets and that's what was there, was five hundred, exact. Yeah, went in pussy's pocket and came right out the Waverly. Left the door open, left him laying in the bed naked, ran a whole block and a half, all past Broadway. "Taxi!" Taxi stopped, I tipped the cab driver ten dollars to take me downtown, Twentieth and Herbert. Went to my girlfriend's Wanda's house and she had a pipe, and I bought a brand new pipe and everything. I bought the works.

So that bitch name Wanda introduced me, who house I went to. Before then I had took a couple of hits before, and then I wanted to try it out myself. They were sitting there getting high. A couple of my girlfriends. And they was like "You smoking?" I was like "No, but I want to try it." Then they let me try it, and I'm saying, I like to see that cloud in the bowl. But I'm saying it something different, it was a new high for me.

When I started using crack, it took me about six months to really get into it hard. Yeah, it took me about that long—yeah—before you have to start smoking that shit every day, hard. I never thought I would become a dope fiend. You know, you say people use the expression, talking about "that bitch coming in here with that dope fiend and the game" and all that shit. Thought I could control it in the beginning. Thought that for a long time. I knew I was out of control at the beginning of this year and I faced it. I was sitting down and me and Zee were crying. I was like "Shit, we can't control this shit." I had been smoking almost two years then.

I couldn't really tell you what it's like smoking. I guess my sensation, my enjoyment is after I finish hitting, arguing with Zee. Because it would never fail. As soon as I get to enjoying it, me and this bitch get into an argument immediately. Smoke enough of that shit, you get . . . makes you paranoid. She would start geeking all over the place, feeling and searching, and I would get mad.

I don't geek. I don't feel the cocaine bugs running up and down my legs. I'll be cool. It's time I took a hit of that shit, and I was like "Whoo! Man!" and just sat still for a minute or so. I might have dumped two caps in the pipe. I'll be just feeling it. Just tripping. When I trip on cocaine. . . . Like I say, if I were to hit it and I got me a nice hit, I would sit there, and be like "Shooooh! Man, that was safe." You know, just sit there and enjoy it, a few minute of feeling good. Knowing that I got a good hit in peace.

In the beginning my habit wasn't that big. I spent about maybe twenty dollars, thirty dollars a day. Now it's about one hundred dollars a day or more. Shit started getting ridiculous, and then it started boosting, and it would be time for me, and this bitch might stay and smoke three hundred and four hundred dollars' worth of shit in one day.

I've never stopped for more than a month. The longest time I have ever stopped was twenty-eight days, and that was last year. Soon as them motherfucker let me out the door of that program I went straight to Zee's house. But it just seem like this time . . . seems to be working out a little better.

I kept using that time because . . . see, Zee's not as strong as me. Okay, like I say, there used to be time when we used to come in and we might not have did nothing for a couple of day. With Zee, she could smoke every day of the week. She don't give a fuck. I used to tell her shit like "Come on, let's chill out today. Let's do something different today."

Using drugs is like a person with an alcohol problem, and when they get drunk they can tell all the things they're not able to tell you when they sober. You know? But it never takes care of the problem. Just for a little while. 'Cause you still have the same problem after you come down. You be like "I have to deal with this and deal with that." What kinds of problems? The kinds of problems I usually have is my daughter used to be on my mind a lot, getting a place of my own. All the good positive thing that I think, that used to be my problem, but I was just never together enough to do them. ·

Drugs don't allow you to cope. No, what it do is it help a motherfucker hide from they problems. It don't help you cope with shit. 'Cause they still there, and as soon as you cope with whatever your problem is or whatever your addiction is you start to feel a little better if you can accept and know that it's the truth about yourself. Don't nobody know you better than you know yourself. Motherfuckers tell you that they know you, they don't know you. Not as good as you know yourself.

I don't like the way drugs make you act. How it make you treat yourself. To treat other people. Yeah. It manipulates you and it makes you manipulate others. That's what I don't like. Makes you scheme, makes you do shit that make you feel sorry for later.

I'm trying to control my habit now. Go to movies, go to arcades, take pictures, go the parks, take walks, read books, make meetings. It is fun. It really is. It's a change. It's an improvement in life, because all I saw from smoking a pipe was downfalls. The way I could see myself hurt.

When I was doing a lot of crack, it seemed like it was fun. Matter of fact it was. Fuck, you know what I'm saying, it was. It was real fun. See, them motherfucker come back with the looks on their face. It be like "What about my money?" "What about it? What the fuck do you want me to do?" I would return nothing. I mean me and Zee used to trip off that shit. Motherfucker used . . . look at the expression, how they act when they come back for their shit. They used to be like "Y'all bitches is stupid. Y'all hang around 'til a motherfucker come back." "What we running for? We ain't did nothing wrong."

I wish I hadn't fought with my mother. That the only thing. Everything else I don't regret. As for friends, what friends? I don't have no friends. Shit.

I wish I hadn't never found out about cocaine. That why I wish I had stayed in the fast lane and making money the way I was making it. Not that I still can't, but I'm saying, I'm just not ready for it. I would prefer to be into the cocaine business right around now, making it, striking it rich.

I wish I had not hurt a lot of people because I was using crack. I've gagged my sister-in-law. Bitch gave me thirty-some dollars to go to the store or some shit, and "See you!" and I kept right on going. We still talk and shit. I was round her house the other day, she was telling me beat this bitch name Jolene up. She say, "I told that bitch, I get my sister."

Then there were a couple of girlfriends. But I'm saying they weren't really friends. They mostly smoked the pipe with me. I'm saying, you know, this bitch name Paula . . . I used to get high with her a lot, but I'm saying she used to steal from me. I used to say, "Bitch, you ain't got to steal from me. A big fucking pile of coke on the table, help yourself. You ain't got to steal. All you got to do is to ask me. I would give it the same way I'm offering it to you now." Shit like that. I bust that bitch in the head with a pipe.

I wouldn't have been as sexually involved either. But I wouldn't change my relationship with Zee. I love Zee. But fuck them other assholes. The only relation that I really had was with Zee. As for strangers, fuck them. I ain't never feel bad about hurting no stranger.

Yeah, I never should have fought with my mother. They say you don't have no luck when you do shit like that. Like my grandmother. I don't give a fuck what she say, she can be talking out the side of her face or what, I don't never say shit. I don't give her arguments or nothing. She's always right even when she's wrong with me. I don't evil her. I refuse.

Crack. That shit don't make you want to eat. That shit don't make you want to do nothing but smoke. It takes your appetite. That shit keep you woke, don't make you even want to sleep. Your body's die out until your body get so where it can't stay up, can't function. I still used to do that douche shit faithful. Believe me. I don't give a fuck how much of that shit I smoke, I douching this bitch like mad.

I smoke crack and listen to music and fuck the shit out of Zee. I might even go to the store. But it doesn't make me all that active far as running around. I used to like to just see the smoke. I think the smoke excited me. Seeing how much smoke I could blow out. Especially if it's a new bowl, clear bowl, you can see it build. It look like a cloud in the bowl. The aftereffect and I blow it out. I say, "Damn, how much of that shit did I suck in?"

I don't have sex with nobody but Zee. I don't fuck with nobody. That's straight up. Don't fuck with nobody. Nigger come up to me and be talking that old "Let me run up into you." I be saying, "Run up? Please! You better back the fuck up." I'm not concerned about AIDS, because I don't have sex. That's right, I'm not concerned about getting nothing but the crabs. That's all that bitch can give me is the crabs. You understand that? She can't give me herpes, can't give me gonorrhea, she can't give me shit. Catching no disease, that's right. Motherfucking right!

I don't like to smoke in crack houses. I used to go in them and buy drug out of them, but I never liked smoking in them. I get the fuck out. I don't go to piper houses. Yeah, some motherfucker get in there and they want to fight. All that old dumb shit. And then you got motherfuckers, you open the door and it's so-and-so and they want to rob you.

In Zee and them house at six-oh-nine when Jerry and them kicked the Jamaican's door in on the third floor and robbed him, I was upstairs, and then they came in and they went upstairs. When they were upstairs they robbed the Jamaican. There was only one Jamaican at the time, and when I looked up it was caps and powder falling from the third floor all the way downstairs to the first floor, and bitches like me started picking them up, pocketing them, all the way up the steps. I mean caps were coming all down the steps. I mean like a trail. I trailed after them. I went all the way to the third floor, and picked up all the caps and powder I found. I went right outside and chilled. I sold some of them caps going down Hubbard Street. Shit, I went back, I told Zee. I said, "Zee, look!" We smoked all that shit.

Being in a crack house is wild. It's wild! It's wild! It's wild! In a piper house, they mainly just sell. You see it all. You see dick sucking. You see fucking. You see trick coming in and out all day and all night long. I seen a bitch get beat the fuck up for smoking dudes' . . . spending all of dude's money and not wanting to give him the job. Beat the shit out of her. Ain't that ugly?

I was in a crack piper house one day when this guy name Daryl was in there and stuck them the fuck up. He's dead now. He stuck them up with a pistol, though. I went to the store. When I came back there they were in there! Came back, I stashed five dollars in my pocket, and I had two dollars left in hand. That was Pooky's money. He said, "Whose money is that?" I said, "That's his money." He said, "Give it to me." I gave it right to him. That frighten me 'cause the pussy . . . what happened was, the pussy said, "Come here, baby girl, let me talk to you for a minute." We were standing there and he said, "Who got all that money?" I said, "You get that shit out of my face." I told him, "I don't know who got nothing." I say, "I just came here to go to the store. I don't know shit." I was already high. This pussy turn around, and all I could see was this black gun, and I was looking down this fucking hole, the barrel. I said, "Pussy, get that shit out my face."

A crack house is usually clean, but the piper houses be fucked up. I mean, I'm telling you I more scared to go in them than to go in an abandon house. Now, that straight up! 'Cause you see all the crack house they wind up they ain't got no gas, no electric, no hot water, no nothing, you know what I mean, all the pipe . . . they sold their pipes and shit out their house. They shit look like a abandon condominium, and they shit be looking fucked up, raggedy. That shit be looking just like abandon house.

Yeah, crack makes people do things they would not have done if they were not on crack. Like I told you. How I burned my sister-in-law. Shit, Zee done burned her mom, shit like that, you know. Thing that you wouldn't normally do to people. That shit make you do some stuff. Yeah.

I got a hundred and seventy dollars once for this bitch to eat my pussy at this guy's house. I told Zee about it too. This young girl name Bootsy. He said, "I pay y'all hundred and seventy dollars. I'll pay you to let me watch y'all freak out." I was like "I'm not eating you, bitch. You gonna eat me." I put the bitch in the car. I gave that bitch ten dollars. No, he gave her ten dollars, and then I gave her ten dollars, and I gave her a bag of coke and told her she had to split it with the dude. I kept all the rest of it, one hundred and sixty dollars. That was the most unusual thing. 'Cause I never fuck with no other women beside Zee. You know what I'm saying? I ain't going down on nobody. I'm saying, nothing wrong with me getting buffed now. Don't misunderstand it. I'm not eating nobody out.

The most unusual thing I've seen somebody else do in order to get crack was take it up their ass. I fell out! We were in this abandon house, and dude was like "Baby, look, let me stick it up from the back." She was like "All right." He was like "I'm talking about the back door!" She said, "What!" He said, "Baby, I give you forty-five dollars right now." Girlfriend was like "Baby, ain't. . . ." But at first before he said forty-five dollars, she was like "Baby, ain't with that shit. Fuck that." He said, "Forty-five dollars," that bitch said, "All right, give it here." And she let him stick his dick in her asshole. I was like bitch ain't never been fucked in the ass before and she gonna be in pain like a motherfucker. You know what I mean? She ain't got no grease, no nothing. I'm saying, "Lord!" I know she was in pain. But you know, I'm saying, I don't knock nobody thing, but that's why I get high by myself, because I might not be into everything that everybody is, like popping pills and shooting needles.

It's an old bitch name Courtney that I saw have a cocaine seizure once when I hustled on Twenty-first Street. Her name was Curtis—old bitch, old bulldagging bitch—and we is in that bitch's kitchen, we is getting high, and that bitch greedy. She got actually asthma. Bitch, she been smoking her ass off. Taxing everybody that came in the door. Bitch was, "Naw, give me mine. Give me mine." And she would get it, and we is sitting in there smoking. The whole table full of us. Everybody had all their own shit. Next thing we knew, we all sitting there smoking and talking and taking a hit, and I heard this bitch, "Give me a match. Give me a match." I say, "Yeah, give this bitch the matches over here so she can leave us alone." That bitch stood there and took that hit and said, "Boom!" And her fucking eye roll on back in her head. All of us grab our shit and went the fuck outside, called nine-one-one. We left that bitch right there. She didn't die. They made it just in time. Somebody stuck a spoon in her mouth. Gave her some salt. I don't know what the salt is supposed to do. I really don't know. They put the salt in her mouth and the spoon. And we left that bitch on the floor, just like that, with the salt and spoon. They got there just in time to take her to the hospital.

I don't trust other drug users. I feel like killing them. You can't trust them 'cause they probably just as rotten as me. Fuck that! Shit, I know what it is to be on it, to be real addicted and all that shit. It makes you conniving. It makes you scheme. Yeah. Makes you do shit that you wouldn't do if you wasn't all fucked up on that shit.

Money force you into hustling. I like money. There was no black slavery shit. Fuck that! None of that bullshit. Tell me to sell my ass and all that old motherfucking. Fuck them! No! I stayed a renegade whore as long as I sold my ass. I never gave no money to no nigger. I was always a renegade. You motherfucking right. Which mean I ain't got to pay nobody but my motherfucking self. Every dime is mine.

It doesn't bother me that I'm doing crime. Selling drugs was fast money. Wouldn't sell to kids, though. I never bought no drugs off no kids neither. Like little kids I know who maybe thirteen and shit, I won't buy no drugs off them. They be like "I got that, man, what's up?" "But, baby, I ain't buying nothing off you. I'm sorry. I can't."

Yeah, I've been sentenced to jail. I had all those open cases for prostitution and shit. Obstructing the highway. And then I got that case for drugs. They were just like "All right, we had enough of your shit." They sent me to the Falk Corrections Center for six months. Plenty fucking was going on in there. It was wild. With the women, with the men. Women were screwing each other too. Some was the young ones taking the young ones, and some of them was molding some of them, and some of them was just into getting the rhythm. Just getting their working and throwing them away like douche bags and shit. Just using motherfuckers and throwing them away like they was douche bags. The guards were fucking inmates. Them bitches were bulldaggers too. Female guards too.

I can't remember his name. He was so stupid. Used to be this black guy out there—he was a sergeant at Falk—and this pussy used to watch us. He was some kind of perverse. I don't know what the fuck his problem was. If the curtain were open, he supposed to knock and tell us to keep our curtain closed. But he's in a bubble. This pussy would sit there, at the bubble, and he would come outside the bubble and just stand there and watch the bitches walking around with no clothes and shit, going to take showers, and shit like that, you know what I mean?

Very first crime I did was prostitution, soliciting, obstructing the highway. Then I started. I went into stealing and all that shit. You know, just started increasing. It was the money and the night life. It was exciting. I started robbing motherfuckers unreal. I started going into motherfuckers' cars and shit. I did dates. I would take them in the hotel and shit and tell them to stay right here, and I break into their cars. I know where they put their money and shit at. I would even do a burglary job with somebody. Go into somebody's house, shit like that. I started getting fascinated with jewelry.

What I want to do with my life is what I'm doing now. All I got to do now is just find me a job, keep going to meeting, stay away from the assholes I know that get high, and chill and try to get my shit together a little bit, 'cause I didn't like where I was at. I'm gonna try to earn money some other way. The honest way. I'll see how good I can cope with it. I'm not good at taking orders. That's why I never had a job. I ain't have nobody telling me what to do and all that old bullshit. I want to be boss. I want to be boss of me. I've been without crack for three weeks. I'm proud of myself.